Armed Forces Guide to Personal Financial Planning

Strategies for Securing Your Finances
at Home While Serving Our Nation Abroad

6th Edition

Colonel Margaret H. Belknap, Ph.D.
Major F. Michael Marty, MBA

Contributing Associates, Department of Social Sciences,
U.S. Military Academy, West Point, New York:

Major Jonathan Byrom
Major Joe Clark
Major Spencer Clouatre
Major John Cogbill
Major Kris Colwell
Professor Dean Dudley
Professor Rozlyn Engel
Lieutenant Colonel Dan Evans

Major Michael Kuzara
Ms. Margaret Moten
Lieutenant Colonel Gary Pieringer
Captain Chris Springer
Major Roger Stanley
Major Thaddeus Underwood
Major James Walker
Major Michael Yankovich

STACKPOLE
BOOKS

To the members of the armed forces and their families
who serve in support of the Global War on Terror

Library of Congress Cataloging-in-Publication Data

Belknap, Margaret H.
    Armed forces guide to personal financial planning : strategies for securing your finances at home while serving our nation abroad. — 6th ed. / Margaret H. Belknap; F. Michael Marty; contributing associates ... Jonathan Byrom ... [et al.].
        p. cm.
    Rev. ed. of: Armed Forces guide to personal financial planning : strategies for managing your budget, savings, insurance, taxes, and investments / David C. Trybula, Richard A. Hewitt ; contributing associates ... Dean Dudley ... [et al.]. 5th ed. c2002
    Includes index.
    ISBN-13: 978-0-8117-3310-6
    ISBN-10: 0-8117-3310-6
    1. Finance, Personal. 2. Soldiers—United States—Finance, Personal. I. Marty, F. Michael. II. Byrom, Jonathan. III. Trybula, David C., 1967– . Armed Forces guide to personal financial planning / David C. Trybula, Richard A. Hewitt ; contributing associates ... Dean Dudley ... [et al.]. IV. Title.

    HG179.P55 2007
    332.0240088'35500973—dc22

                                                        2006031487

Contents

Introduction

This is a post-9/11 book on personal finance for servicemembers. This edition of *Armed Forces Guide to Personal Financial Planning* is not the usual evolutionary revision of a book. There are two fundamental reasons for this: First, our audience is a new generation that is planning, working, and saving in the information age; and second, many of our audience are deployed or are family members of deployed servicemembers. We completely revised this edition in response to the changes in technology that have revolutionized how Americans—military or civilian—plan, save, spend, and invest their income.

Previous editions of this book were written when we were a "garrisoned force." Today, we are deployed in or supporting the Global War on Terror. Many of our contributors have been deployed or are deployed as we write this edition. Thus, as our team of professionals created this edition of the book, we made a concerted effort to research information and to provide guidance that servicemembers could not find elsewhere in a single book.

We fully recognize that no book can keep up with the constant changes in policy that impact pay, benefits, and opportunities. As of this writing, there are proposals to change the compensation, retirement, and educational benefits of our servicemembers. In addition, there will continue to be changes in the structure of financial instruments and how they are marketed, selected, delivered, and consumed. Thus, we have provided suggested Internet resources that have the capability to provide rapid updates to changes in the law and to changes in financial products and services.

All of us who contributed to this book are devoted to our community of military members and their families' financial well-being. Thank you for your service.

Margaret H. Belknap, Ph.D.   F. Michael Marty, MBA
Colonel, U.S. Army   Major, U.S. Army

PART I

FINANCIAL
BASIC TRAINING

1

Realizing Your
Financial Goals

While most of us daydream about a particular standard of living, only a few of us make the effort to develop a realistic and detailed financial plan for achieving it. We are passive in the face of our financial future, making it easy to get sidetracked and later to feel disappointed in ourselves that we did not prepare better.

Financial planning and budgeting is the process of setting personal goals, determining how much money is needed to achieve them, and developing a feasible strategy to accomplish them. Financial planning and budgeting require self-discipline, but they also give you control over your destiny, foster important communication within your households about shared values and goals, protect you against accumulating unmanageable debt, and allow you to take full responsibility for your financial future.

BIG RETURNS TO SOUND FINANCIAL PLANNING

Becoming educated about sound financial planning has several positive aspects. First and foremost, your money can work for you. Patience, aside from being a personal virtue, also carries a financial reward. A useful rule of thumb is that at an annual interest rate of 7%, your savings will double every ten years.

For example, if a twenty-five-year-old corporal put $1,000 into a savings account today, the account would hold nearly $2,000 in ten years, nearly $4,000 in twenty years, and nearly $15,000 in forty years. Table 1-1 shows how a $1,000 investment grows over time.

The corporal's ultimate reward depends on the rate of return he expects to earn—which varies by the type of investment—and on the length of time he expects to hold the investment. The compounding factor reflects the multiple by which your money will increase, given a

TABLE 1-1
REWARD OF COMPOUNDING INTEREST

	10-YEAR HORIZON		20-YEAR HORIZON		40-YEAR HORIZON	
Annual Rate of Return	Compounding Factor	In 10 years, $1,000 becomes ...	Compounding Factor	In 20 years, $1,000 becomes ...	Compounding Factor	In 40 years, $1,000 becomes ...
4%	1.48	$1,480	2.19	$2,191	4.80	$4,801
5%	1.63	$1,629	2.65	$2,653	7.04	$7,040
6%	1.79	$1,791	3.21	$3,207	10.29	$10,286
7%	1.97	$1,967	3.87	$3,870	14.97	$14,974
8%	2.16	$2,159	4.66	$4,661	21.72	$21,725
9%	2.37	$2,367	5.60	$5,604	31.41	$31,409
10%	2.59	$2,594	6.73	$6,727	45.26	$45,259

Note: You can develop your own estimate of how your savings will accumulate. The formula for the compounding factor is compounding factor = $[1 + (\text{interest rate}/100)]^{\text{Number of years}}$. For example, at 6% over twenty years, we have $(1 + 0.06)^{20}$, which equals $3,207 in this example.

particular rate of return and time period. Compounding is simply a process in which an effect builds on itself.

Of course, prices are likely to rise during the time the corporal is waiting for his money to grow. The pace at which prices rise in a particular period is called the inflation rate. Recently, the U.S. inflation rate has averaged a little less than 3% each year. For example, if prices rose at 3% each year, then an item that costs $1,000 today would cost $1,344 in ten years, $1,806 in twenty years, and $3,262 in forty years. Table 1-2 shows how prices are subject to the same process of compounding as savings. The cumulative effect of prices is called the inflation factor.

It is not hard to appreciate the fact that inflation erodes the real value of the corporal's savings. It is a major reason why high inflation is politically unpopular; in some countries and some periods, severe inflations have wiped out the savings of many individuals. Our corporal's savings, for example, are worth $1,967 in ten years (when using an interest rate of 7%), but that money cannot buy as much in the future because prices have also risen during that time.

The growth in true purchasing power is the difference between the future value of savings and the future cost of living. This is called the *real* rate of return on the original investment, and it yields the total *real*

TABLE 1-2
REALITY OF INFLATION

	10-YEAR HORIZON		20-YEAR HORIZON		40-YEAR HORIZON	
Annual Rate of Inflation	Inflation Factor	In 10 years, an item that costs $1,000 today will cost ...	Inflation Factor	In 20 years, an item that costs $1,000 today will cost ...	Inflation Factor	In 40 years, an item that costs $1,000 today will cost ...
1%	1.10	$1,105	1.22	$1,220	1.49	$1,489
2%	1.22	$1,219	1.49	$1,486	2.21	$2,208
3%	1.34	$1,344	1.81	$1,806	3.26	$3,262
4%	1.48	$1,480	2.19	$2,191	4.80	$4,801
5%	1.63	$1,629	2.65	$2,653	7.04	$7,040

dollars (adjusted for expected inflation) available at the end of the period. The real *rate* of return is the difference between the stated (or nominal) rate of return on his savings and the rate of inflation:

$$7\% \text{ (nominal rate of return)} - 3\% \text{ (rate of inflation)} = 4\% \text{ (real rate of return)}$$

Using the real rate of return yields a better measure of an individual's future financial well-being. Table 1-3 shows how the real value of savings grows more slowly when we account for inflation.

Historically, investors in the United States have earned real rates of return between 1% and 5% annually. The specific rate depends upon the amount of risk the investor is willing to accept, as well as the prevailing interest rate set by the U.S. Federal Reserve. Riskier assets offer higher expected returns as compensation for that risk. When analyzing the intermediate value of 3% in Table 1-3, it is apparent that the corporal's original savings of $1,000 grows in real purchasing power to become $3,260 in forty years (much less than the $15,000 we saw at the outset). Although that return may seem disappointing, it should not. Our wise corporal has still more than tripled the real purchasing power of his savings. A dollar saved today becomes more than three inflation-adjusted dollars in forty years. A future retirement will be three times more luxurious than a current corporal's life. Such returns are available to everyone, including you. You just need the desire and the tools to save.

TABLE 1-3
REAL VALUE OF SAVINGS ALSO GROWS
(JUST MORE SLOWLY)

Annual nominal rate of return	Annual expected rate of inflation	Annual real rate of return	REAL COMPOUNDING FACTOR		
			Factor by which real savings rises in 10 years	Factor by which real savings rises in 20 years	Factor by which real savings rises in 40 years
4%	1%	3%	1.34	1.81	3.26
4%	3%	1%	1.10	1.22	1.49
4%	5%	−1%	0.90	0.82	0.67
6%	1%	5%	1.63	2.65	7.04
6%	3%	3%	1.34	1.81	3.26
6%	5%	1%	1.10	1.22	1.49
8%	1%	7%	1.97	3.87	14.97
8%	3%	5%	1.63	2.65	7.04
8%	5%	3%	1.34	1.81	3.26

Note: A negative real rate of return is possible when the rate of inflation exceeds the nominal rate of return. Such episodes are rare but not impossible. Not surprisingly, negative real rates of return discourage savings.

STEPS IN FINANCIAL PLANNING
Only you and your family can determine the ultimate financial priorities for your household. Everyone knows that middle class life in America is expensive, but the good news is that military personnel, especially those with longer careers, do earn sufficient income to achieve many of their goals. However, it requires careful financial planning and budgeting. The steps below offer a general outline of the process of setting financial goals. This phase takes time to complete successfully and should involve everyone in your household. Your goals should be reviewed at any major life change, such as a marriage, divorce, birth of a child, a relocation, and a retirement.

Step 1: Brainstorm
As a first step, you should develop a list of your and your family's life objectives. Consider the necessity of each item, as well as your willingness to wait for it. If you find it helpful, you can place each item into a matrix like the one displayed in Table 1-4A below. For example, a one-week vacation in Florida might be in the "Next Year" or "Nice to Have" column on the matrix. Another example is an emergency fund to cover

unexpected expenses. (Most financial planners recommend that you save three to six months of after-tax income for such a fund.) Another example is the desire by many retirees to have a manageable home mortgage payment by the time they retire.

This phase of the planning process could take some time, depending on the complexity of your household and how long it takes to achieve reasonable consensus. In addition, the matrix might be quite large, with each block containing multiple entries. You may also decide to add blocks. In the end, the matrix should accurately reflect your current needs and future dreams; it should serve as a useful roadmap for your financial planning.

TABLE 1-4A
MATRIX OF PERSONAL AND HOUSEHOLD GOALS

Goals	Now	Next Year	Three Years	Five Years	Ten Years	By Age 45	By Age 65
Must Have	emergency fund of three months' after-tax income; essential furniture; engagement ring (next six months)	small wedding; car repairs (if not done in previous year)	new roof on house				
Should Have			new car; college degree for your spouse	desired home renovations —new kitchen	two years of tuition at state university for your first child		reach a manageable payment on home mortgage for primary residence
Nice to Have— we will definitely use		one-week vacation in Florida; big wedding	new furniture		small lakefront cottage		
Nice to Have— unsure whether we will really use		fancy honeymoon					

Step 2: Determine Cost of Your Goals (in Today's Dollars)

We live in a society in which consumption has been raised to an art form. The median price of an existing home in the United States was $218,000 in March of 2006, and the average price of a new vehicle hovered around $30,000. In 2005, the average American wedding was reported to cost over $25,000. After the wedding, the U.S. Department of Agriculture has estimated that it costs between $125,000 and $250,000 to raise a child through the age of eighteen. The College Board rubs salt in the wound by estimating that it costs between $40,000 to $120,000 to send a child to college for four years.[1]

Of course, in America, every conceivable product and service is available—for a price. The cost of a particular item can vary markedly depending on its size and quality. The cost can also vary widely by region of the country; this geographical variation is particularly important for goods that cannot be easily traded across state borders, such as housing, personal services, and educational services. Fortunately, the Internet provides a powerful tool for researching the prices of different items in your financial plan. A useful starting point is *Consumer Reports* (*www.consumerreports.org*), which evaluates the quality of various products relative to their prices.

Once you have assigned prices for each item, you can expand your matrix. In Table 1-4B, prices are included for a few selected items, and there is also an estimate of the total funds needed at each stage of the financial plan. Although the importance of inflation has been mentioned, today's prices can be used for future expenses, as long as you use the real rate of return to estimate the needed savings. The *real* rate of return ensures that you are dealing in true purchasing power, that you are comparing apples with apples—today's dollars with *inflation-adjusted* future dollars.

To estimate a monetary goal for each period (i.e., a price tag for your financial plan), you must add all of the subtotals in the bottom row. The grand totals in the very modest example in Table 1-4B vary

---

[1] The median home price is from the National Association of Realtors (*www.realtor.org/research/index.html*). The average price of a new vehicle the National Automotive Dealers' Association (*www.nada.org/Content/NavigationMenu/Newsroom/NADAData/20052/NADA_Data_2005_newvehicle.pdf*), which reported the price to be $28,050. The price of a wedding is from CNN Money (*money.cnn.com/2005/05/20/pf/weddings/*). Expenses of raising children are from the MSN website (*moneycentral.msn.com/articles/family/kids/tlkidscost.asp*).

TABLE 1-4B
MATRIX OF PERSONAL AND HOUSEHOLD GOALS WITH "PRICE TAGS"

Goals	Now	Next Year	Three Years	Five Years	Ten Years	By Age 45	By Age 65
Must Have	emergency fund of three months' after-tax income		new roof on house				
Subtotals	$9,000		$3,500				
Should Have					two years of tuition at state university for your first child		reach a manageable payment on home mortgage for primary residence
Subtotals					$36,000		$75,000 mortgage, with $325,000 of original mortgage paid off
Nice to Have— we would definitely use		one-week vacation in Florida					
Subtotals		$2,800					
Nice to Have— we might use							
Subtotals							
GRAND TOTALS (in today's dollars)	$9,000	$2,800	$3,500		$36,000		$325,000

by subperiod, from $9,000 this year to $325,000 by retirement age. In principle, the grand totals could be much higher since we included *very* few items here. Your "magic number" may strike you as daunting, even unachievable. Before you despair, however, remember that you have "time." You may be able to achieve more than you expect. You also have developed some priorities to guide you if it becomes necessary to scale back your number.

Step 3: Estimate the Total Savings Needed

Now that you have set monetary goals for each period, you must work backwards to estimate the savings needed to reach each goal in the time allotted. Most people have a variety of investments that are earning different rates of return, depending on the risk they are willing to accept in saving for each goal and the time available before reaching that milestone. Refer to part III of this book for an in-depth discussion of how best to match a particular savings goal with the most appropriate type of investment.

For now, matters will be kept fairly simple. An assumed real return of 3% each year will be used in order to illustrate the basic procedure for estimating the necessary savings. The math required to estimate the savings needed is simple. As illustrated in Table 1-3, a $1,000 investment today is worth $1,344 in ten years, assuming a real rate of return of 3%. We found that number by multiplying the initial savings of $1,000 by the real compounding factor of 1.344, based on the following formula:

$$\text{future monetary goal} = \text{today's savings} \times \text{real compounding factor}$$

This expression can be rearranged to show that the future monetary goal divided by the real compounding factor predicts how much must be saved today to achieve a particular goal.

$$\text{future savings goal} \div \text{real compounding factor} = \text{today's savings}$$

The longer you can wait and the higher the expected real rate of return, the more powerful is your savings today. As Table 1-5 shows, if you need $1,000 in forty years, then you must make a $142 investment today *if* you can find an investment that yields an average real return of 5% annually. If you need the money in ten years, you must make a much larger investment today, about $614.

TABLE 1-5
WHAT YOU NEED TO SAVE TODAY TO REACH A FUTURE GOAL

Real rate of return	If you need $1,000 in 10 years, then today you must save	If you need $1,000 in 20 years, then today you must save	If you need $1,000 in 40 years, then today you must save
1%	$905.29	$819.54	$671.65
2%	$820.35	$672.97	$452.89
3%	$744.09	$553.68	$306.56
4%	$675.56	$456.39	$208.29
5%	$613.91	$376.89	$142.05

Note. Real compounding factors are given in Table 1-3

Step 4: Account for Your Taxes

With the exception of saving for retirement, which is often tax-exempt, much of your individual savings must be taken from after-tax income. Therefore, to gauge how feasible a particular savings goal is, you must account for the taxes you will owe on your earned income. The good news, however, is that large components of military pay are not subject to taxes. Moreover, the government provides numerous investment options that can reduce or eliminate the tax on your savings. The details of military pay—taxable and nontaxable components—are discussed in the following section on budgeting. The details about tax rates are discussed in chapter 4. Tax-friendly savings plans are discussed in chapter 12.

> *Make sure to review the tax-friendly types of investments in chapter 12. Careful use of these investments can reduce the future cost of many important expenses, such as certain college, housing, medical, and child car costs.*

Again, a simple example is used here to illustrate the basic principle. In three years, a household expects to replace the roof on a home it owns. The expected cost is $3,500 (in today's dollars). At a real return of 3% annually, there must be $3,203 in the bank today to cover this future expense. This savings is from after-tax income, however. At a marginal tax rate of 25%, the family must have $4,271 in gross (pre-tax) income available today to consider making this investment.

$$\frac{\text{after-tax}}{\text{savings goal}} \div (1 - \text{marginal tax rate}) = \frac{\text{gross (pretax)}}{\text{sum needed}}$$

Once you understand the principles, you can perform these operations quickly using a financial calculator or spreadsheet program.

Step 5: Calculate the Monthly Allotment

Apart from winning the lottery (a contingency that should *not* be part of your financial plan), you probably will not have large lump sums to invest today. Instead, you will have to meet your future goals in steps. A monthly contribution is usually called an annuity plan, which is a series of regular deposits into a savings instrument. Because the savings earn an expected rate of return every year, the cumulative effect of these monthly payments is highly significant. For military personnel, an allotment from your monthly paycheck to a mutual fund is an example of such an annuity plan.

The two tables below provide a guide to the monthly payments needed to save $10,000 by a given future date. Lower rates of return are used in Table 1-6 because short-term investments tend to be invested more conservatively. Higher rates of return are used in Table 1-7 because long-term investments are often invested more aggressively. Again, time is a powerful ally. At a 4% annual return, you must save $261.91 each month to reach $10,000 in three years but only $67.91 each month to reach $10,000 in ten years.

TABLE 1-6
MONTHLY PAYMENTS NEEDED TO SAVE $10,000
OVER A SHORT PERIOD

NUMBER OF YEARS

Real rate of return	1	2	3	4	5
1%	$829.52	$412.69	$273.75	$204.28	$162.60
2%	$825.72	$408.74	$269.76	$200.28	$158.61
3%	$821.94	$404.81	$265.81	$196.34	$154.69
4%	$818.17	$400.92	$261.91	$192.46	$150.83
5%	$814.41	$397.05	$258.04	$188.63	$147.05

TABLE 1-7
MONTHLY PAYMENTS NEEDED TO SAVE $10,000
OVER A LONGER PERIOD

Real rate	NUMBER OF YEARS				
of return	10	15	20	30	40
4%	$67.91	$40.64	$27.26	$14.41	$8.46
6%	$61.02	$34.39	$21.64	$9.96	$5.02
8%	$54.66	$28.90	$16.98	$6.71	$2.86
10%	$48.82	$24.13	$13.17	$4.42	$1.58
12%	$43.47	$20.02	$10.11	$2.86	$0.85

Saving $67.91 each and every month is challenging, but it is considerably easier than finding $6,756 to invest all at once, which is the lump sum you would need to invest today to reach $10,000 in ten years. Further, because your income is likely to rise over your lifetime, your savings plan should become easier over time.

Step 6: Determine the Appropriate Investment
Finally, with the help of this book, you must determine the investment vehicle you will use for each goal. As noted earlier, a person with a long horizon and some tolerance for risk may be comfortable with aggressively invested funds. A person with a shorter horizon or lower tolerance for risk may be more comfortable with safer bonds and savings instruments. As you will see later, a diverse portfolio brings greater stability and ensures somewhat higher returns than a straight savings account.

MONTHLY BUDGET AS A PLANNING TOOL
Many of us cannot seem to keep our future goals firmly in mind today: we get sidetracked, spending impulsively and unwisely. We leave ourselves too little savings to reach our future dream of financial security. We fail to plan and prepare; we do not set limits for ourselves; we do not communicate with our families about our shared goals.

The monthly budget is *the* key tool in establishing a financial routine and reaching your financial goals. A monthly budget brings financial self-awareness by providing answers to central questions that you should ask yourself about your habits, such as (1) How do I currently spend my income and what could I do differently? (2) How much do I currently save and how much could I save?

Three Common Excuses

1. Negative attitude: "Budgets are depressing and constricting."
2. Unrealistic expectations: "Budgets are easy—just save half income!"
3. Low motivation: "This budget is not really my problem."

Budgeting, despite its usual connotation as an exercise in self-deprivation, is better viewed as a necessary step toward financial well-being. Instead of thinking of a budget as a financial diet, it might be better to consider it more as a set of well-balanced meals. Attitude is the *key* to successful budgeting. If you approach your monthly budget as unachievable and as an external constraint, you are likely to fail. If you consider it a personal choice and a path toward meeting a personal goal, you are more likely to succeed.

The structure of a monthly budget is simple: You develop a measure of your disposable income—what is left after all your taxes have been paid. You develop a measure of your monthly expenses—where all your disposable income goes. In a financially healthy household, monthly expenses are less than monthly income, and the household saves to reach its financial and personal goals. In an unhealthy situation, it spends much more than its income and accumulates stressful credit card debt or falls behind on bills.

Ten Good Reasons to Establish a Monthly Budget

1. Take control of your financial destiny.
2. Feel financially secure during an overseas deployment.
3. Know when you are getting off track.
4. Focus on shared family goals and improve family communication.
5. Keep yourself honest.
6. Get out of debt and stay out of debt.
7. Feel confident that you can manage unexpected changes in unit or duty station.
8. Give your family a financial plan while you are deployed.
9. Be responsible.
10. Realize your dreams.

The following sections will show how a budget can accurately account for all your income, both taxable and nontaxable. The focus will be on special issues involving military pay, because of its complexity. You will also learn how a budget can guide monthly spending for your household, yielding many positive results: financial security, reduced friction among household members, the knowledge that you and your family could survive a financial emergency, and a sense of financial confidence for you and your family when you deploy.

Understand Your Military Income
While serving in the armed forces, your total "pay" is a sum of numerous forms of monetary and nonmonetary compensation. Several elements of pay apply to everyone in the military; other elements are specific to a servicemember's personal circumstances. In addition, some components of your income are taxable, while others are not. It is crucial that you have a complete grasp of your total after-tax income when you develop your financial plan and household budget.

Your basic monthly pay varies with rank and length of service. Consequently, when you develop a financial plan—complete with current pay and expected future pay—you must account for expected changes in base pay. Fortunately, over time, basic monthly pay follows

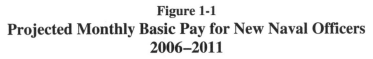

Figure 1-1
Projected Monthly Basic Pay for New Naval Officers
2006–2011

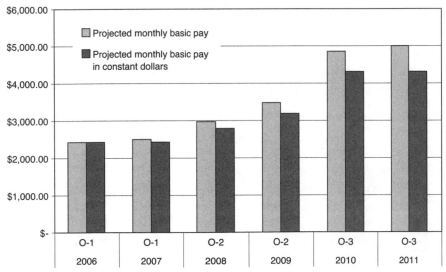

a fairly predictable path, which is valuable in financial planning. Figure 1-1 displays the trend in pay that could be anticipated by a Navy ensign (O-1) commissioned in 2006 over the first five years of service. For budgetary purposes, we estimate that her nominal pay will increase by 3% each year. Monthly basic pay is taxable.

In case of occupations and duties deemed of critical need to the armed forces, the Department of Defense has approved incentive pay to augment monthly basic pay. Personnel in highly skilled branches— such as medical officers and aviation—receive incentive pay, as do personnel performing particularly hazardous or onerous duties. This form of compensation is taxable.

Other forms of pay are less straightforward. Your basic allowances for housing and food vary by the size of your household and the location of your current duty station. For example, your housing allowance is more generous if you are assigned to a high-cost area of the country.

In other assignments, military personnel are eligible for many additional forms of pay—usually temporary in nature. Foremost, a servicemember receives additional pay during deployment to a hostile theater of operations, and most military income becomes nontaxable during a deployment as well.

In addition to basic pay, you are likely to receive specific monetary allowances to cover living expenses as well as compensation "in-kind," meaning that the good itself (such as food or housing) is provided for you. For example, you can receive additional income to cover the expenses of a relocation (permanent change of station, or PCS).

Table 1-8 summarizes the many forms of military compensation. Because of the huge number of permutations, it is unproductive to print all of the pay and allowance tables here. They are easily available on the Department of Defense's website governing military pay. The website offers a convenient calculator for helping you to determine your pay under different scenarios.

Defense Finance and Accounting Service

Home page: *www.dod.mil/dfas/*
Military pay: *www.dod.mil/dfas/militarypay/cchelpcustomer*
service.html
Ask questions: *corpweb1.dfas.mil/askDFAS/askMilPay.jsp*

TABLE 1-8
MAJOR COMPONENTS OF MILITARY COMPENSATION

Components	Purpose	Factors	Tax implications	Keep in mind	More information
Basic monthly pay	Monthly pay for services	Rank; years of service	Taxable unless deployed to a hostile theatre (limits may apply)	Periodically adjusted to keep up with inflation	DFAS
Basic Allowance for Subsistence	Compensation for basic food expenses	Rank; availability of rations and mess permissions	Not taxable	Periodically adjusted to keep up with inflation	DFAS
Basic Allowance for Housing	Compensation for basic housing expenses	Location of duty station; deployment status	Not taxable	Periodically adjusted to keep up with inflation	DFAS
Uniform and clothing allowances	Compensation for expenses related to duty uniform	Rank	Not taxable	Limits apply	DFAS
Duty-related travel and relocation (TDY)	Compensation for travel related to official duties and for expenses related to permanent change of station	Reason for travel; type of expense	Taxable; some TDY not taxable	Limits apply	DFAS; Joint Forces Travel Regulations and Defense Travel System (DTS)
Occupational incentive pay	Encourage personnel to choose assignments in critical areas		Taxable unless deployed to a hostile theatre (limits may apply)	Types of incentive pay include: aviation pay, hazardous duty incentive pay, medical officer special pay, and Career Sea Pay	DFAS

TABLE 1-8 (*continued*)
MAJOR COMPONENTS OF MILITARY COMPENSATION

Components	Purpose	Factors	Tax implications	Keep in mind	More information
Hostile Fire Pay	Additional compensation for deployment to a hostile theatre of operations	Length of deployment	Not taxable	Hostile theatre is determined by your orders —issuing authority	DFAS
Family Separation Allowance	Additional compensation for your dependents during an assignment that takes you away from your permanent duty station	Length of assignment; number of dependents	Not taxable		DFAS
Enlistment Bonuses	Additional compensation available at time of enlistment and/or reenlistment	Prior service; length of active duty service obligation	Taxable, unless awarded in a combat zone	Periodically changes to encourage entry into specific branches and occupations	DFAS
Disability Severance Pay	Entitlement for duty-related injury or illness, received upon separation	Source of disability	Taxable, unless injury or illness related to combat	Requires official action by VA	DFAS

Understand the Tax Implications of Military Pay

As you can see, many components of military compensation are exempt from federal or state taxation. In addition, some taxable components of pay become exempt from taxes when you are deployed to a combat zone. This tends to complicate the ability to develop estimates of income that are comparable to regular civilian pay, often called gross income. Chapter 4 explains the calculation of taxes and proce-

TABLE 1-9
CONVERTING NONTAXABLE INCOME INTO
"GROSS-EQUIVALENT" INCOME

Marginal tax rate	Conversion factor	$100 in tax-exempt income is equivalent to gross (pretax) income of ...
10%	1.111	$111.11
15%	1.176	$117.65
25%	1.333	$133.33
28%	1.389	$138.89
33%	1.493	$149.25

dures for managing your taxes in great depth. Here you simply need to become familiar with a few key points.

Taxable income and nontaxable income cannot be compared directly because tax-exempt income is worth more to you than regular, taxable pay. To convert a nontaxable payment into the equivalent amount of taxable income, you need to use your marginal tax rate, which is the amount of tax you must pay on your last dollar of income earned.

For most civilians, wages and salaries are fully taxable and constitute the vast bulk of their total taxable income. Such income is frequently called gross (pretax) income. Total after-tax income refers to the income remaining after all taxes have been paid. It is also called disposable income, which is the money available to your household to meet expenses and to save to meet your financial goals. For military personnel, disposable income is the sum of after-tax regular income and any nontaxable income:

$$\text{disposable income} = \left(\begin{array}{c} \text{all taxable income} \\ - \text{ taxes} \end{array} \right) + \left(\begin{array}{c} \text{all nontaxable} \\ \text{income} \end{array} \right)$$

For sound financial planning and budgeting, you must develop an accurate estimate of your monthly disposable income. This number becomes the natural limit on your monthly expenses within the framework of your budget. To derive that figure, you should review your information by using the new electronic system MyPay. On MyPay, you can view your leave and earnings statements for the past year and your W-2 statements documenting the taxes you have paid. The website for MyPay is at *https://mypay.dfas.mil/mypay.aspx*.

If you have income from other sources, such as investment and savings accounts, rental income, or spousal income, you should also collect statements reflecting these income sources for the past year. If your other income is not paid on a monthly basis, estimate an average for each month by creating a total for the year and dividing by twelve. Place your best estimate of your monthly disposable income in your budget table.

As a result of deployment, Table 1-10A estimates a naval ensign's monthly basic pay that will become exempt from taxes. For simplicity, assume a basic pay of $2,450 each month. Also, other sources of income are included in the table.

Income, especially military income, is relatively predictable. There can be surprises, however, and it is useful to track your expected income and actual income—at least for a few months—until you become fully aware of everything going into your bank account each month. The second column of Table 1-10A illustrates this procedure.

The next step in creating a viable household budget is developing realistic spending goals. To get started, collect your bank statements, credit card bills, and other receipts of your expenditures for the past twelve months. Begin to review your spending patterns with your family, sorting the spending items into categories as you go. Table 1-10B provides a set of spending categories to help with this step. When you have finished reviewing your bills and records, add up all expenditures within each category. Divide your total by twelve to calculate a monthly average for each item.

The list in Table 1-10B is not exhaustive, and you should add lines to account for spending on items not found here. The point of this

TABLE 1-10A
DISPOSABLE INCOME FOR NAVAL ENSIGN
(DEPLOYED) DURING A TYPICAL MONTH

INCOME	Estimated after-tax income	Actual after-tax income
Basic and special pay (after taxes)	$2,450.00	$2,450.00
Allowances (tax-exempt)	$450.00	$415.20
Spouse's income (after taxes)	$2,100.00	$2,160.00
Interest and investment income	$75.00	$75.00
Other income (such as rent on property, gifts)	$0.00	$100.00
TOTAL	$5,075.00	$5,200.20

TABLE 1-10B
HOUSEHOLD SPENDING FOR NAVAL ENSIGN (DEPLOYED)
DURING A TYPICAL MONTH

EXPENSES	Planned spending	Actual spending	Notes
Housing			
Mortgage or rent on primary residence	_____	_____	_____
Homeowners/renters insurance	_____	_____	_____
Property taxes	_____	_____	_____
Home repairs/Maintenance/Lawn	_____	_____	_____
Household Supplies	_____	_____	_____
Home improvements	_____	_____	_____
Utilities (phone, electricity, water, gas/oil)	_____	_____	_____
Expenses on any secondary properties	_____	_____	_____
Food			
Groceries	_____	_____	_____
Eating out	_____	_____	_____
Family obligations			
Child support	_____	_____	_____
Alimony	_____	_____	_____
Day care, babysitting	_____	_____	_____
Health and wellness			
Insurance (medical, dental, vision)	_____	_____	_____
Unreimbursed medical expenses (co-pay)	_____	_____	_____
Fitness (club memberships, classes, equipment)	_____	_____	_____
Personal grooming	_____	_____	_____
Toiletries	_____	_____	_____
Habits (smoking, coffee, alcohol)	_____	_____	_____
Transportation			
Car payments	_____	_____	_____
Gas	_____	_____	_____
Auto repairs/maintenance	_____	_____	_____
Auto insurance	_____	_____	_____
Other costs (tools, public transportation)	_____	_____	_____
Travel—deployment related	_____	_____	_____

TABLE 1-10B (*continued*)

EXPENSES	Planned spending	Actual spending	Notes
Entertainment/Social			
Cable TV/Videos/Movies			
Internet expenses/online accounts			
Computer equipment			
Hobbies			
Subscriptions/dues (clubs, church, other)			
Vacations			
Cell phone			
Celebrations/parties			
Pets			
Food			
Grooming, vet			
Moving/relocation			
Packing supplies			
Moving expense			
Clothing			
Casual/personal			
Professional			
Charity and gifts			
Debt payments			
Credit cards			
Loans (home equity, student)			
Other loans			
Direct Allotments from Military Pay			
Allotment A			
Allotment B			
Allotment C			
Contributions to savings and investments			
401(k) or IRA			
Stocks/bonds/mutual funds			
College savings			
Emergency fund			
Other savings			

exercise is to create an accurate picture of how you and your family are spending the household income in Table 1-10A. This process should generate a frank dialogue about household finances. These conversations require honesty and patience, as you assess, without hurtful recrimination, what everyone is currently spending.

In some cases, current spending exceeds current income, meaning that the family is accumulating debt, often on credit cards. In many other cases, current spending (excluding contributions to savings and investments) is barely covered by current income, meaning that the family is living paycheck to paycheck. When these patterns exist, the household cannot meet its future financial goals.

If you find yourself in this situation, you must carefully consider ways to reduce your current spending. These solutions should be concrete and realistic. Telling yourself, "I will cut my spending by 20%" is less likely to succeed than more specific changes like, "I will do more of our grocery shopping at the cheaper, local store; I will look for a used barbeque grill at the upcoming church sale before buying a new one; I will stop the fitness club membership and use the local running track instead; or I will be more careful to eat out only once a week."

The ultimate goal is to derive a spending limit for each category that will allow you to increase your capacity to save each month. It will require kind, honest, and patient negotiation with all members of your family to change ingrained spending patterns, but it is imperative for your collective future well-being that you save today. It is common for people to feel anxious about spending limits because today's culture often confuses moral worth with material wealth. One way to alleviate these frictions is to keep your financial goals handy (Table 1-4B) and remind everyone that today's saving will bring a sense of achievement and security in the future. Your family is not "losing" its standard of living, it is working to secure it.

As you work through the spending goals, you must also consider your monthly savings goal and ask yourself, "What is possible? What is desirable?" Again, it is common to feel concerned about your capacity to reach your goals. How can $50 each month really make any difference? The simple answer is that *any* monthly savings is useful. As Table 1-7 showed, a regular monthly saving of $61, invested at a 6% (real) rate of return, would generate $10,000 in ten years (in today's dollars). If you could double that amount to $122, you could double your future savings to $20,000.

When you abide by a budget, you are taking full responsibility for your future and for that of your family. You are saving for your household and creating a sustainable pattern of spending, one that they can maintain even in your absence. Imagine the naval ensign's peace of mind, *knowing* that when she is deployed, her husband and children will have the tools they need to manage the household finances and maintain the family's financial security. Imagine the sense of financial independence and satisfaction you will feel at reaching one of your financial goals. It is your future and your life. Take control of it through careful financial planning and budgeting.

USEFUL RESOURCES AND SUGGESTED READING
financialplan.about.com/
www.aarp.org/money/financial_planning/
www.nefe.org/wealthcarekit/index.html
money.aol.com/pfhub
moneycentral.msn.com/planning/home.asp

ADDITIONAL SUGGESTED INVESTING GUIDES
Faerber, Esme E. *The Personal Finance Calculator: How to Calculate the Most Important Financial Decision in Your Life*. New York: McGraw-Hill, 2003.

Gardner, David, and Tom Gardner. *The Motley Fool Personal Finance Workbook: A Foolproof Guide to Organizing Your Cash and Building Wealth*. New York: Fireside Books, 2003.

Tyson, Eric. *Personal Finance for Dummies* (4th Edition). New York: Wiley, 2003.

2

Smart Banking

An effective and convenient relationship with a bank is essential for military families. Understanding what banks offer and how to choose the best one is an important first step toward responsible financial management. Banks are an essential part of the economy for many reasons: They hold deposits of people's paychecks and their savings. They make commerce possible by allowing account holders to write checks or make debit payments to purchase goods. They make loans to homeowners and businesses.

Banks themselves are businesses that make money by paying account holders a nominal rate of interest to keep deposits at the bank and then loaning that money to others for a higher rate of interest. They can vary in type, size, and capabilities (see Table 2-1).

TABLE 2-1
BANKING CHOICES

Type of Bank	Advantages	Disadvantages
Commercial Bank	Complete range of services, including online banking Multiple ATMs and Branches	Higher Fees
Credit Union (Not-for-Profit)	Low Fees Limited hours	Fewer ATMs
Savings & Loan	Lower Fees Personal service	Fewer branches
Virtual Bank (Online Only — No branches)	Higher interest rates on deposits Time-saving	Must mail in deposits No check cashing service
Brokerage Firm or Investment Company	One-stop shopping	May require higher minimum balances

SELECTING A BANK

There are several factors to consider when selecting a bank. Convenience and cost of services are the most important considerations.

Convenience

People use banks because they want to make purchases conveniently and because they want to ensure that their money is quickly available. Since convenience is a major reason for using a bank, it is a major factor to consider when choosing a bank.

> *Choose a bank that is convenient and cost-effective and has online banking services and ATMs worldwide.*

Today cash is instantly available at twenty-four-hour automatic teller machines (ATM). The better ATM networks share sites and allow you to obtain cash from machines far removed from your individual bank; many include international access. Look for a bank that has the option of ATM service and that has ATM access convenient to your home or workplace. Keep in mind that there is normally a fee charged for using an ATM that is not associated with your bank.

Another way to get money is to write a check. A check is simply a note to your bank telling it to transfer some money from your account to someone else. In this function, most checking or share draft accounts differ little, if at all. There is a major difference, however, when you need to convert that check to cash for yourself. Depending on your bank's branch locations and operating hours, it may be difficult for you to cash a check close to work or home and after hours.

A more convenient method to make purchases is to use a debit card. A debit card looks exactly like a traditional credit card and is used in the same manner. The fundamental difference is that the use of a credit card is a loan—a loan that eventually must be repaid. A debit card acts much like a check in that it draws against a current balance in either your savings or checking account.

One of the most important convenience features that banks offer servicemembers is direct deposit of military and federal government paychecks into checking or savings accounts. A direct deposit arrangement sets up a direct link between the military or governmental pay system and your bank. On payday, your pay is automatically sent to the bank and deposited in your account; you simply receive a Leave and

Earnings Statement (LES) telling you exactly what was deposited. The important consideration is that your paycheck is deposited and your money is made available even if you are away from your duty station—on leave, TDY, or deployment.

Many military families maintain bank accounts in the locality where they are assigned. If this is the case, then old accounts must be closed out and new ones must be opened at the new duty station. To say the least, closing and opening bank accounts and shopping for the best banking services are time-consuming tasks. It is worth considering whether a local bank is really necessary. An alternative to transferring banks with each change of duty station is to maintain a permanent or hometown bank so that you can continue to write checks and maintain savings balances while in transit from one assignment to the next. The disadvantage to this option is that your permanent bank may not have a branch near your new duty station, preventing you from making deposits and cashing checks in person. It is worth your time to investigate the number and locations of branches before committing to a permanent bank. Some banks such as Bank of America, Citibank, and Washington Mutual have nationwide branches that may make it easier for servicemembers to maintain a more permanent relationship.

Similarly, with technological advances in online banking, it may be most convenient to use a virtual bank, such as USAA (*www.usaa.com*) or Etrade (*www.etrade.com*), that you can use regardless of where you are stationed. As long as you are comfortable dealing with your bank by computer, phone, and mail, you may not need a local or hometown bank. To determine if you are a good candidate for virtual banking, ask yourself these questions:

- Do I use credit or debit cards instead of checks for local retail purchases?
- Can I conveniently get cash without going to a branch to cash a check?
- Is your bank a member of a national ATM network?
- Does my bank offer online banking, and do I have a computer to access the Internet?
- Does my bank offer convenient loan service by Internet, mail, or phone?
- Can I easily move savings balances into my checking account by Internet or phone?

If you can answer yes to most of these questions, you may prefer to bank virtually. At most banks, online banking is free; however, there is usually a monthly fee for paying your bills using the bank's online service. But considering the time and postage savings it provides, it is a valuable tool that is just a few keystrokes away. Judge a bank with computer banking just like you would any other bank; the fundamental analysis remains the same. Remember, you are trying to find the bank that meets your banking needs at the lowest cost.

Cost of Services

You should shop around to compare the fees different banks charge and the interest that they pay you on your deposits before committing to a financial institution. Banks compete with other banks in both price and service to earn you as a customer. In developing a price strategy, most banks try to attract the most profitable customers; therefore, their pricing schemes encourage or discourage specific types of customers. You should understand these pricing schemes and seek a bank desiring accounts like yours. Additionally, by minimizing the number of accounts you open with a bank, you can not only simplify your life, but hold down the cost of your financial services as well. Finally, if you can establish a long history of reliable credit with a single bank, it may be easier to qualify for a large loan or mortgage at a lower interest rate.

TYPES OF BANK ACCOUNTS

There are a number of major services that banks offer to meet your basic needs, such as checking and share draft accounts for transactions; savings accounts or money market deposit accounts for emergency funds; and certificates of deposit for short- and medium-term savings. Investment options for meeting your short-, medium-, and long-term financial goals are discussed further in part III of this book.

Checking Accounts

No banking service meets your need for transactions as well as a checking or share draft account (a checking account at a credit union). A checking account or a share draft account is a transactions account. Checking accounts come in two basic varieties: noninterest-bearing and interest-bearing. As their name implies, noninterest-bearing accounts offer no interest on the deposited funds. Since there is no interest cost to the bank, these accounts are cheaper to run. Banks generally encourage depositors who plan to keep very small balances (less than $500 or $1,000) to use noninterest checking accounts.

Some banks charge a per-check fee along with a service fee for a checking account. Per-check fees are levied on each check written on the account; they are intended to cover the expenses involved in processing and clearing checks. Service fees, designed to compensate the bank for the costs of maintaining small accounts, are levied every month on some checking accounts. Many banks will waive these fees for direct-deposit customers, and most credit unions associated with the military do not have them at all. These fees can really add up, so it is worth shopping around.

You will often see advertisements for "free" checking accounts, with no per-check or service fees. The catch on most free checking accounts is that the fees are waived only if the average balance in the account is greater than a minimum amount, sometimes $1,000 or more. In other cases, free checking is offered if the depositor has savings accounts or time deposits greater than a required minimum, which again could be $1,000.

Overdraft Protection

It is essential that all military personnel have overdraft protection on their checking accounts. If you write a check for more than the balance of your account, you are said to have "bounced" a check. A bounced check, or a check presented for insufficient funds, can be detrimental to a military career. Good money management and fiscal responsibility are attributes of good military officers and noncommissioned officers. The military chain of command will generally view a bounced check as an irresponsible or careless act. Bouncing a check is also expensive. Your bank will generally charge you $25 to $50 for the administrative cost of handling the check, and the retailer where you wrote the check will likely charge $30 as well.

> *A basic financial goal should be to find a bank that offers overdraft protection along with free checking: the best bank may also pay interest on larger balances.*

All this can be avoided, however, with overdraft protection. Overdraft protection is simply a money transfer and/or a short-term loan. For example, if you write a check for $100 but have a balance of only $50 in your checking account, with overdraft protection, the bank would immediately transfer $50 from your savings account to your checking account and then process the check. Some banks require you to get a bank-issued credit card from them in order to qualify for overdraft protection. They would then link your checking account to your credit card to cover any overdrafts. Although the credit card will charge you interest on this "loan," the cost will be minimal compared with the charges associated with bouncing a check. Simply put, do not bank without overdraft protection.

Savings Accounts

An essential part of your financial plan is savings. Unlike checking account deposits, you should not need constant access to your savings, so the banks provide two basic choices for these funds: money market savings accounts and certificates of deposit (CDs). These accounts are relatively low-risk instruments for achieving your short- and medium-term financial goals. Generally, savings accounts are not appropriate for long-term financial goals because interest rates are so low.

Money Market Accounts. Competitive savings accounts, often called money market deposit accounts (MMDAs), offer rates of interest close to the money market rate. Frequently, the rates are tied to those currently prevailing in the money markets. The rates earned in savings accounts are not guaranteed for any length of time, but are adjusted up and down with market rates. The easiest way to access the most up-to-date information about the best savings accounts and trends in banking is *www.bankrate.com*.

Savings accounts that pay money market rates (MMDAs) and money market funds with check-writing privileges are ideal for emergency funds. With emergency funds, you are much more concerned with the ability to use your money quickly than in the interest earned on such funds. You should be willing to trade higher rates of interest for liquidity (the ability to have access to it quickly, if necessary) and safety. If you cannot manage to accumulate an emergency fund, you should have a credit card with a sufficient line of credit to provide you with the peace of mind that you can pay for your family's immediate emergency requirements.

The emergency fund provides immediate cash if a disaster or adverse event occurs. You must first determine the size of your needs. Most financial advisors suggest between two and six months' worth of income. Two months' base pay may be sufficient if you have quick and easy access to credit. Ask yourself what emergencies might arise that would require immediate payments. Certainly you would want a fund large enough to buy plane tickets home for the entire family. In other cases, you would want to be able to cover the deductible on your automobile insurance in case of an accident or to be able to pay for a significant automobile repair. You may need much more if you anticipate a loss of income due to illness or lost employment. Even though you may pay for these emergencies with a credit card, you need access to emergency funds to "pay off" the credit card balance immediately.

> *Open a savings account that earns interest, and immediately start saving two to sixth months' worth of income as an emergency fund.*

Certificates of Deposit. For your medium-term investments, you might want to consider certificates of deposit (CDs). Certificates of deposit pay higher interest rates than regular savings accounts but levy an early withdrawal penalty if the funds are removed before the maturity date. CDs are usually available in six-month to five-year increments. Interest rates are usually higher for longer maturity periods. Generally, you should use CDs when you have funds in excess of your requirements for emergencies and short-term needs. For example, if you have already established an emergency fund with a balance two times your monthly pay and you have no other short-term need for the excess funds, a CD that pays higher interest than the savings account is one way to save.

A great advantage of CDs is that the interest is guaranteed for the entire life of the certificate, so a CD enables you to "lock in" an attractive rate of interest for a known amount of time. Savings accounts do not offer this advantage, typically paying very low interest rates or money market rates that fluctuate up and down weekly or monthly. Being able to guarantee a rate of interest for several years is a double-edged sword, however, because you can never tell what will happen to money market rates in the future. For example, a CD rate of 4% guaranteed for five years (and locking in your deposit in for five years) may seem attractive today if savings deposits are paying 3%; but your guaranteed 4% rate is much less attractive if money market rates go to 6% next year.

Don't worry about your money being locked up in a CD, however. If you really need the money or if interest rates shoot way up, you can always get your deposit out of the CD by paying the withdrawal penalty. The penalty may take away some interest earned, but the principal remains intact. As with all bank deposits, it is important to understand fully the terms of a CD before you invest in it. Chapter 11 discusses how a CD may fit into a portfolio of financial assets.

LOANS

Most people find it necessary to borrow money from time to time. You may not have the cash available to pay for expensive items like major appliances or cars, and you certainly will need to borrow money to buy a house. It often makes sense to spread the cost over the period of time you anticipate using the purchase, and to do so you must borrow and pay interest for that convenience. A credit card is a type of loan, and banks are just one type of institution that issue credit cards. You should make comparisons among different credit card companies before you select one. Chapter 3 will help you evaluate the credit services offered by banks and other credit card companies, and part II of this book addresses borrowing money to finance major purchases like a home or automobile.

3

Using Credit Wisely

Borrowing to finance the purchase of durable goods such as cars, furniture, and appliances has long been a traditional feature of American life. This chapter discusses the wise use of consumer credit, the operation of traditional bank-loan services, and some of the different types of loans available to consumers. It concludes with a review of the uses, abuses, and costs of consumer credit and debit cards. *If you have credit problems, skip to the last two sections of this chapter now.*

THE ROLE OF CONSUMER CREDIT
IN A PERSONAL BUDGET

Today, consumer credit is easy to get—so easy that many families find themselves in financial distress. The danger of too much debt is that there is not enough income both to pay off the debt and to provide for the basic needs of food and shelter, much less save for future needs. As emphasized in chapter 1, success in personal financial management requires planning and perseverance. An absolute requirement for any family is a regular savings plan. If large monthly installment debt payments make regular saving impossible, take immediate steps to reduce the amount you owe. Although this situation is easier to prevent than to cure, it is never possible to get out of debt.

This is not to say that military families should never borrow. Virtually everyone needs to borrow money to finance major purchases, such as automobiles and furniture, or to pay educational expenses. Additionally, very few people can afford to buy a house with cash alone. Without credit, a family could not buy some of these costly items unless they had saved enough money to pay for these purchases outright. If you have the money available to cover such purchases from your own resources (even if intended for some other long-range goal), it is usually more advantageous to use your own funds, which is really "borrowing from yourself," rather than to borrow from a lending institution. The interest rate you forego on the savings is often lower than the interest rate a lender would charge you on a loan. You can then replenish your savings by "repaying" yourself each month with the amount you would have paid the lender.

It is inappropriate to use consumer credit to finance routine day-to-day needs. A good practice is to ensure that any item you finance has a useful life for at least the time it takes to repay the debt (for example, durable goods such as cars and furniture and long-lasting assets such as education). You should not routinely carry unpaid credit card balances for purchases of clothes, entertainment, groceries, and other such nondurable items. Cover this spending with current income. Using credit to finance routine purchases or to splurge on extras is a sure sign of personal financial mismanagement.

While one appropriate use of consumer credit is to defray the costs of the occasional emergency (such as airfare for a funeral or a major automobile repair), even these situations can be handled best by using your savings or seeking assistance from aid agencies that make low-cost loans and grants to servicemembers and their families in times of crisis. One such agency is Army Emergency Relief.

Since not everyone reading this book will likely adhere to this strict view of consumer credit, the following paragraphs offer some guidance on how much consumer debt is too much. Consumer debt refers to all debts incurred to finance purchases, including car loans and credit card debt but excluding real estate mortgages. One useful rule of thumb is that monthly payments on consumer debt should be no more than 20% of monthly disposable income (income after subtracting mortgage or rent, food, utilities, and taxes). Another guideline is that the total outstanding consumer debt should be less than one-third of your annual disposable income. The important point is that you must carefully plan for consumer debt as one component of a monthly budget that includes adequate provisions for regular savings and an emergency reserve. To see how to apply these guidelines, consider the following examples.

Debt-Payment Guideline Example. A family that occupies government quarters has after-tax take-home pay of approximately $2,500 per month. If the family has no utilities or other housing expenses, they need only estimate spending for food to find disposable income. Assuming that the family's food costs are $500 per month, this means that the family has $2,000 a month in disposable income. According to the first guideline, installment debt payments should not exceed $400 per month (20% of $2,000). How long would it take a family with $12,000 in credit card debt charging 18% APR for $400 per month to repay the money? Approximately forty-one months would be required. Similar calculations based on your family's debt situation can be made using the calculator at: *www.bankrate.com/brm/calc/creditcardpay.asp* or by typing "credit card calculator" into your Internet search engine.

Total-Debt Guideline Example. This rule is a bit more constraining than the debt-payment guideline. Modifying the preceding example, the family living in government quarters with an annual disposable income of $24,000 should not owe more than one-third, or $8,000, in consumer debt. Either method of figuring will provide a ballpark figure for the maximum debt you should carry.

TYPES OF CONSUMER LOANS AND THEIR COMPONENTS

The most common type of consumer loan arrangement is the installment loan, in which consumers repay the amount borrowed, plus interest, over a predetermined period in equal monthly payments. Automobile loans and home mortgages are common examples of installment loans.

Some lenders also use single-payment loans, but this is less common. In a single-payment loan, borrowers must repay the full amount plus interest at the loan's maturity date. A loan with a combination of periodic payments and a large repayment at the end is called a balloon loan. It is important to be aware of a common variety of this type of loan, the "same as cash" terms offered by retailers for large-ticket items such as electronics, appliances, and furniture. In this case, you apply for a retailer's credit card and commit to making nominal payments during the course of the "same as cash" period, which ranges typically from six months to two years. If you repay the entire balance of the loan in this period, the interest is waived. *However, if you have not paid off the loan in full when the terms expire, you will be charged back interest for the entire period of the loan, usually at an interest rate approaching the maximum allowed by law.*

The following section will primarily focus on variants of install-ment loans because they are more common.

The "True Interest Rate"

Consumers shopping for installment loans should compare three features: the annual percentage rate (APR), the term (length) of the contract, and any prepayment penalties or other fees. The APR's effect on a loan contract is straightforward: A higher APR will yield a higher monthly payment for the term of the loan and will increase the total interest you will pay over the loan's life. The impact of the loan's term is more subtle. The longer the period for installment payments, the lower the required monthly payments. However, the total interest you pay will be higher because you are using the money longer. In loan contracts, the total amount of interest over the life of the loan is called the total finance charge; it is one of the items, along with the APR, that lenders must disclose in every loan agreement, as required by the Truth in Lending Act.

Lenders use several different methods to compute the monthly payment on an installment loan. Two loans that appear to be the same (and they are for the same amount, duration, and interest rate) can have different monthly payments, finance charges, and APRs, based on how the lender calculates the interest. Consumers typically must choose among loans with different durations, different lengths until the first payment is due, and any number of other variables. The APR is a standardized calculation that allows consumers to compare the true interest rate for different loans in order to determine which loan has the lowest cost of borrowing.

Tables 3-1 and 3-2 illustrate the differences between the monthly balance and the add-on interest methods of charging interest on a loan for $2,000 at 12% interest per year, repaid in twelve equal monthly payments. These two loans sound identical, but they are not. The monthly balance method is the usual way that loans are repaid. When interest is computed using the monthly balance method, the monthly payments are $177.70 and the APR is 12% per year. The add-on interest method charges interest on the entire amount borrowed over the whole year, even though some of the principal is being repaid each month. When interest is computed using the add-on interest method, the monthly payments are $186.67 and the APR is 21.3% per year.

> *Consumers do not have to calculate the APR; they need only compare the APRs that the law requires lenders to reveal.*

Tables 3-1 and 3-2 show two different formulas for the APR, and there are many others (one for every type of consumer loan). Every APR formula is an approximation of the same thing: the true interest cost of the loan. The bottom line is that all APR formulas are very good approximations of the true interest cost of the loan. Consumers do not have to calculate the APR; they need only compare the APRs that the law requires lenders to reveal.

It is clear that the monthly balance interest method is less costly than the add-on interest method. The point of the example in Tables 3-1 and 3-2 is to show how much difference the method of computing interest can make. Do not rely on the advertised interest rate in a loan contract. Find the APR in the Truth in Lending Act section. Compare the APR the lender is offering you to typical loan rates reported at websites in the "Money Rates" section of either the *Wall Street Journal* at *online .wsj.com* or *Barron's* at *www.barrons.com*, or in frequent surveys published in *Money* at *money.cnn.com* or *Consumer Reports* at *www.consumerreports.org*. It pays to shop around for various loan terms.

TABLE 3-1
MONTHLY BALANCE INTEREST METHOD
$2,000 AT 12% FOR 1 YEAR, 12 MONTHLY PAYMENTS

Month	Payment	Interest	Principal	Outstanding
				$2,000.00
1	$177.70	$20.00	$157.70	1,842.30
2	177.70	18.42	159.28	1,683.02
3	177.70	16.83	160.87	1,522.15
4	177.70	15.22	162.48	1,359.67
5	177.70	13.60	164.10	1,195.57
6	177.70	11.96	165.74	1,029.83
7	177.70	10.30	167.40	862.43
8	177.70	8.62	169.08	693.35
9	177.70	6.93	170.77	522.58
10	177.70	5.23	172.47	350.11
11	177.70	3.50	174.20	175.91
12	177.70	1.79	175.91	0.00
	$2,132.40	$132.40	$2,000.00	$1,103.08*

*Average outstanding balance (sum of last column divided by 12).

$$APR = \frac{\text{finance charge}}{\text{average balance}} = \frac{\$132.40}{\$1,103.08} = 0.12\ (12\%)$$

TABLE 3-2
RESULTS WITH ADD-ON INTEREST METHOD
$2,000 AT 12% FOR 1 YEAR, 12 MONTHLY PAYMENTS

Month	Payment	Interest	Principal	Outstanding
				$2,000.00
1	$186.67	$20.00	$166.67	1,833.33
2	186.67	20.00	166.67	1,666.66
3	186.67	20.00	166.67	1,499.99
4	186.67	20.00	166.67	1,333.32
5	186.67	20.00	166.67	1,166.65
6	186.67	20.00	166.67	999.98
7	186.67	20.00	166.67	833.31
8	186.67	20.00	166.67	666.64
9	186.67	20.00	166.67	499.97
10	186.67	20.00	166.67	333.30
11	186.67	20.00	166.67	166.63
12	186.63	20.00	166.63	0.00
	$2,240.00	$240.00	$2,000.00	$1,083.32*

*Average outstanding balance (sum of last column divided by 12).

$$APR = \frac{\text{finance charge}}{\text{average balance}} = \frac{\$240.00}{\$1,083.32} = 0.22 \ (22\%)$$

> *Do not look only at the advertised interest rate in a loan contract. Find the APR in the Truth in Lending Act section.*

Not knowing the market for consumer loans can cost you a lot of money. It is common today for auto loans to offer low APRs, but as discussed in chapter 6, the low-rate loans are often available only if other purchasing conditions are met. To determine whether the offered interest rate is attractive, identify the costs of purchasing conditions placed on the loan. One example might be that you must qualify for the advertised APR by having a high-enough "credit score" (to be discussed later in the chapter).

The loan conditions of particular banks may also be important criteria in the selection of the financial institution in which you deposit your paycheck. Loan approval and repayment options will often be easier in conjunction with the bank that receives your direct deposit. This includes the ability to establish monthly automatic deductions from your account; however, this is often possible with many financial institutions simply by providing a voided check and signing an agreement to allow such automatic deductions. Such methods save both you and the lender from monthly hassles and add credibility to your repayment commitment.

Prepayment Penalties

You should also investigate loan contracts for any prepayment penalties. Strangely enough, if you decide you want to repay your loan in a shorter period than the contract specifies, you may have to pay more interest on the loan than originally stated in the terms. Your lender must tell you, in writing, how much it will cost you to "pay off" your loan early. Seek loans without prepayment penalties.

The Role of Collateral in Consumer Lending

For many loans that consumers use to finance major purchases, the item purchased becomes the collateral for the loan. That is, the bank takes a lien against the item, so that if repayment is not made as agreed, the bank may repossess the property and sell it for cash; the two best examples are auto and home loans. Remember that banks are lending their depositors' money and want to have some protection if a borrower fails to repay. Collateral for loans can also include other property, such as stocks and bonds, equity in a home, and sometimes jewelry. In some cases, the bank will insist on taking physical possession of the collateral.

Collateralized, or secured, loans are less risky for banks because they offer some protection in the event the borrower defaults. As a result, the interest rate on a secured loan tends to be lower than for an unsecured or "signature" loan. This is worth remembering if you want to borrow for some purpose (such as a child's education) where the asset you are financing cannot be used as collateral. It may be worthwhile to use some of your other assets to secure a loan in such cases (for example, equity in your home). Also consider selling the assets for cash, since this may be cheaper than borrowing; however, bear in mind that some depreciated assets may have a great deal more use and value to you than the cash that you will receive on the open market.

Home-Equity Loans

A popular form of collateralized borrowing involves second mortgages and lines of credit secured by the borrower's equity in a home. Equity in a home is the difference between the value of a home, as determined by an appraiser, and what the homeowner still owes the mortgage holder.

Second mortgages and home-equity lines of credit allow homeowners to borrow money at interest rates lower than those of normal consumer loans because the loans are secured by the property. The interest on home-equity loans is usually tax deductible. (Please consult your unit tax advisor or some other knowledgeable source.) Another advantage of home-equity loans is that relatively large amounts of money can be borrowed for long periods of time, often up to fifteen years.

Home-equity loans have several disadvantages, however. They can be fairly expensive to set up, because the closing costs—transaction fees—involved in real estate lending can run into several hundreds or thousands of dollars. In addition, lenders can charge points—a point is one percent of the amount borrowed—on second mortgages, further adding to the cost. Finally, the interest rate on a second mortgage will be a few percentage points higher than the going rate on first mortgages.

If you need to borrow a large amount of money with a reasonably long period to repay (for example, to finance college education costs for children), a second mortgage on your home may be a good alternative. For smaller amounts and shorter repayment periods, shop carefully for more conventional loans before committing yourself to a second mortgage. Weigh the tax and interest rate advantages against the sizable upfront closing fees.

Home-equity lines of credit are similar to second mortgages in that the borrowing is secured by the equity in a home, and there are closing costs when the credit line is established. However, once you establish the credit line, there is a great deal of flexibility for use of the credit. In most cases, you can draw cash against the credit line by simply writing a check, and you can repay on any schedule that is convenient. Borrowers pay interest monthly on the outstanding credit, but some institutions make the interest rates fairly attractive. The closing costs and other fees on a home-equity line of credit will be lower than on a second mortgage for most lending institutions. Some consumers use home-equity credit lines to finance cars, appliances, educational expenses, and many other needs that have traditionally been financed by conventional bank loans. An obvious potential danger in using your home's equity as a source of funds is that you risk losing your home if you default on your loan obligation.

> *An obvious potential danger in using your home's equity as a source of funds is that you risk losing your home.*

Common Sources for Consumer Loans

Banks are often the first source of credit that comes to mind. However, banks are not the only source of consumer credit. As mentioned in chapter 5, the financial sector of the economy is becoming increasingly competitive as different kinds of institutions enter the market for consumer financial services. Therefore, you should also consider credit unions, savings and loan associations, or mutual savings banks. Many of these institutions are consumer-oriented and may offer better loan rates than banks in your area. In addition, some stockbrokers will lend money using your stocks, bonds, or other qualifying assets as collateral. These "margin loans" are usually used by aggressive investors to leverage their stock portfolios when they believe stock prices are about to rise, but in some cases they may be used for other purposes, too. The rate of interest on broker loans is generally very close to the short-term Treasury bill rate—the theoretical "risk-free" interest rate used as a reference by financial institutions. A loan from your broker may be cheaper than a loan from any other institution. In addition, the repayment terms on loans from brokers are typically flexible: You repay when you want, but you pay interest on the amount borrowed as long as you have it.

The military provides servicemembers an interest-free loan in the form of an advance on future pay. This is available only in conjunction with a permanent-change-of-station (PCS) move. With appropriate justification and command approval, servicemembers can obtain one month's advance pay from the departing station and two months' advance pay at the new assignment location. Repayment by payroll deduction will take place over a twelve- to twenty-four-month period. Servicemembers are not charged interest for advance-pay transactions.

Finally, if you own permanent life insurance (whole life), you can borrow against the cash value of your policy at very attractive rates. If you already own a whole life policy with a substantial cash value, this may be your best alternative for borrowing small amounts cheaply. See chapter 13 for details on borrowing against a whole life policy.

USING CREDIT AND DEBIT CARDS

One of the most familiar and popular forms of consumer credit is the credit card. Banks, credit unions, and thrift institutions usually offer either MasterCard or VISA, and sometimes both. Most military credit unions and financial services companies such as USAA offer these cards with no annual fee and very low interest rates; in fact, shopping around will reveal this to be the case with most credit cards today.

Bank credit cards are available to a broad range of consumers. Furthermore, gasoline companies, major department stores, and financial service conglomerates (e.g., Discover is backed by investment bank Morgan Stanley) also offer credit cards. American Express, Diner's Club, and Carte Blanche offer travel and entertainment cards that extend credit but under quite different terms than banks, stores, and gasoline companies. Most of the long-distance phone companies now offer combination credit and calling cards. Additionally, most financial institutions offer automatic teller machine (ATM) cards that provide access to savings and checking accounts from machines throughout the world. Often these ATM cards are also debit cards that can be used anywhere a credit card is accepted.

The term *credit card* comes from the nature of the arrangement between the lender and the holder of the credit card. When you make a purchase with a credit card, the lender, in effect, makes a loan to you. The lender agrees to pay the merchant quickly for the goods you bought and to bill you later for the purchase. Credit cards represent preapproved lines of credit, up to a specified limit.

From the cardholder's perspective, the credit card is a very effective substitute for cash or checks in making routine purchases. The insecurity and inconvenience of carrying currency and the uncertainty about the acceptance of personal checks are eliminated, since so many retail establishments (including post or base exchanges) accept the nationally known credit cards. Use of a credit card allows the cardholder to make a single payment for all the small purchases made during the month. A cardholder could buy nearly everything needed during the month with credit cards and then repay the entire balance right after payday. However, the constant danger is in spending outside your means, carrying a balance and paying interest on routine purchases.

One of the best features of credit cards is that they represent a reserve of purchasing power that can be tapped immediately in an emergency. When applying for a credit card, ask for a credit limit that is high enough to allow you to finance emergency expenditures. Remember that only the unused portion of your credit line serves as an effective source of reserves. This is a good reason to repay the entire balance on the card each month. Some cards, like those typically offered by American Express, exist only for convenience and do not allow you to carry a balance. This will be discussed later under Travel and Entertainment cards.

Credit cards can also prove particularly useful during international travel. They reduce the need for converting currency because they are so widely accepted. Furthermore, the exchange rate used by the card companies to convert foreign currency charges into dollars is generally competitive and often better than the exchange rate you would receive at a bank or exchange office.

The Cost of Credit Cards

Most credit cards provide free credit, as long as the cardholder pays the entire balance of the account within a grace period—usually twenty-five days from the end of the monthly billing period. However, if the cardholder fails to repay the full amount, the lender charges interest on the unpaid balance. Although credit cards offer great utility to consumers, their misuse costs cardholders many millions of dollars in needless interest expenses. Accumulating credit card debt is an easy trap for an undisciplined consumer and a sure sign that he or she has become dangerously overextended on credit. It is best to repay the entire balance during each billing cycle.

While the convenience and free credit feature of credit cards make them potentially useful to everyone, many consumers accumulate large unpaid balances on their card accounts and continually make sizable interest payments. The card issuers make this easy by asking that the cardholder repay only a minimum monthly amount, which is usually far less than the unpaid balance. This minimum payment can be little more than enough to cover the finance charge of the previous month and 1% or 2% of the principal. Making only the minimum payment ensures that it will take a long time to repay the debt and guarantees the card companies a hefty return in interest payments. Occasionally, often right after Christmas, credit card companies encourage consumers to "take a payment holiday" and skip a month's payment. The interest charges, of course, accrue on the unpaid balance, making it a very expensive holiday for the consumer when he or she eventually has to pay the bill with additional interest.

Lenders are eager to have cardholders maintain unpaid balances, because the interest rate on these balances is typically much higher than lenders earn on regular loans and investments. Typically, credit card agreements specify that interest on the unpaid balance will be 1.5% per month. This may seem like a low rate, but consider that if you maintained a $1,000 unpaid balance on your credit card for a year, you would pay more than $195 in interest. Thus the effective annual interest rate exceeds 19.5%, which is much higher than you would pay for even an expensive signature loan. Even worse, if the unpaid balance reaches the credit limit, the card is essentially worthless. At that point, all you have is a very expensive loan.

If you find yourself in this situation, consider getting a signature loan from your bank or another financial institution and consolidating your debts at the lower signature loan rate. Such a loan adds the discipline of fixed monthly installment payments. Banks will consider the credit limits of all your active credit cards—even if the intent is to pay them down to zero balance—when they decide whether to approve a loan. After all, there is nothing that stops you from immediately going out and incurring new charges on a credit card once you have used the signature loan to repay the balance.

How Balances Are Computed
When comparing credit cards, keep in mind that you cannot simply compare the interest rates charged. Card issuers use different methods to determine the balance on which they charge interest. As with bank deposits and loans, the method used to calculate the outstanding balance can have an important effect on the total interest expense. The most common method used by card issuers is the average daily balance (ADB) method. This method applies the daily interest rate to the average of your daily balances during the billing cycle.

Two other methods are frequently used. In the "previous balance" method, finance charges are levied on the previous balance due as of the beginning of the billing period. The "adjusted balance" method levies the charge on the amount of the previous balance minus any payments made during the billing period. Thus, the adjusted balance method results in the lowest finance charge, the previous balance method has the highest charge, and the ADB method falls somewhere in between.

One other method of billing that has come to light is a two-cycle billing method. This is a more costly method than the others. This method takes the average of your balance over the previous two billing cycles—two months—and applies the finance charge to that. Using this method, it is possible to carry no unpaid balance for a month and still be charged interest based on the balance of the previous month.

Credit cards also allow cardholders to get cash advances from any bank around the world that services the card. Most cards also allow you to get a cash advance by writing a check on your account or using your card in a participating ATM machine. This service can be a real convenience for travelers who run short of cash. However, lenders assess finance charges on the cash advances even when the balance is fully paid within the twenty-five-day grace period. Usually, interest is charged from the day of withdrawal at the normal credit card rate. Many cards also charge a sizable fee, often 3% of the cash advance, along with the finance charge. Some cards apply a higher interest rate to cash advances than they do to purchases; this appears to be a common feature for cards issued under attractive introductory offers. Because of the high additional cost of cash advances, you should use this service only in emergencies.

If you have to use a credit card to help you through a tough time, such as emergency leave or unexpected major car repairs, repay the balance as soon as possible. In most cases, it is more cost effective to use your savings to pay off credit card debt, since the APR of the credit card is likely to exceed the return on the savings you have available.

If you do not have adequate savings available to pay an entire credit card balance after the emergency, figure out a way to repay it at a rate greater than the minimum requirements established by the lenders. To help discipline yourself, consider establishing your own repayment goals to pay down the balance on credit card charges. For example, treat a particular credit card balance as a closed-end loan (like those a bank might approve) by establishing a time period for repayment, and faithfully making regular monthly payments.

A quick way to establish a reasonable payment plan is not as ominous as you might think. Divide the balance on your card by the number of months you need to repay the balance and add estimated finance charges. This is your monthly payment. For example, to repay an entire

$2,000 balance in ten months requires that you pay $200 of the principal each month. This means that you must add $200 to the finance charge for the previous month to come up with the appropriate payment. It is also generally wise to use any leftover funds from other parts of your budget to reduce credit card debt as quickly as possible.

In summary, avoid carrying a balance on credit cards, but if you are carrying a balance, make it a priority to reduce or eliminate it. In general, repay your debt before trying to save. If you have more than one credit card carrying a balance, pay the minimum on the cards with the lowest APR and concentrate on eliminating each credit card, one at a time, starting with the card with highest APR.

> *Repay your credit card debt as quickly as possible before trying to save.*

Credit Card Insurance

Occasionally, credit card issuers will encourage you to buy credit card insurance. There really is little reason to pay for such insurance, because your liability for unauthorized use of your cards is generally limited to $50, and few issuers actually attempt to get their cardholders to pay even that. Just make sure that you report any lost credit card within twenty-four hours. One technique to keep track of your cards in case your purse or wallet is lost or stolen is to empty its contents onto a copy machine and make a copy. Do this now and on each birthday. Put the copy in a safe place at home. This provides a quick and convenient record in case of a loss or theft.

> *Make sure that you report any lost credit card within twenty-four hours.*

Choosing a Credit Card

Today, virtually anyone in the military who wants a credit card can get one, and many servicemembers have more than one. This has changed the competition among card issuers from one of simply reaching new credit users to one of trying to lure credit card customers away from one another. A common technique for lenders is to offer a low introductory APR (such as 0.9%) for a six-month to one-year period. At the end of the introductory period, the APR often will jump up significantly. It is common for lenders to exclude cash advances from these introductory rates and to convert to the higher, "regular" APR if cardholders exceed the credit limit or have a late payment.

Credit cards with no annual fee are common today. Better-educated consumers caused many financial institutions to offer credit cards with no annual fees and to compete for credit card holders in other ways. Many banks offer free credit cards for a brief period as a competitive offer to lure new customers. It is common for a credit card issuer to change its terms or rates and even to change a no-fee card to one with an annual fee. Since there is really no reason to have your credit card issued by your regular bank, feel free to shop for the best deal. There are so many no-fee cards available to servicemembers that you should never pay an annual fee without a very good reason. If you repay your balance nearly every month, you should select a card with no annual fee and no charges if you pay your balance within the grace period. Select credit cards with no annual fees, long (twenty-five days) grace periods, and the lowest regular interest rates—as opposed to introductory interest rates. Many military credit unions have cards with lower rates, often some of the lowest rates in the nation.

If for some reason you have to carry a credit card balance for a while (because of an emergency or other high-cost event), consider taking advantage of low introductory rate offers; if necessary, transfer any remaining balance to another low-rate introductory offer when the original introductory period expires. However, keep in mind that there may be a "transfer fee" to take advantage of such an offer; and if not, check to see if interest will accrue immediately. With the competition among lenders, such offers will generally show up in your mailbox with little or no effort on your part. You should also maintain a card whose regular APR is lower than the rate that takes effect after the introductory period of other cards expire. *Money* magazine at *money.cnn.com* and other financial websites and periodicals are the best sources of credit card interest rate information.

Also keep in mind that the number of credit cards you have, their limits, and current balances all affect your credit score and appear on your credit report. This information is readily available to anyone making a decision on whether or not to offer you more credit. Because nothing stops you from going out and maxing all credit cards after you have received a new loan (and thus increasing your risk of default), creditors take your available credit on revolving accounts into consideration before extending you a new line.

To obtain information about credit card offers, contact one of the agencies that will sell lists of institutions and their comparative credit card offers. A list is available for a nominal fee from *www.myvesta.org*.

Other Specialty Cards

Travel and Entertainment Cards. The travel and entertainment (T&E) cards issued by American Express, Diner's Club, and Carte Blanche are used just like credit cards but differ in a very important way from credit cards such as VISA or MasterCard. Issuers of the T&E cards expect you to use the cards only for the convenience of eliminating cash and check purchases—not for revolving credit. That means you must pay the full balance when it is due. Failure to use the cards as prescribed may result in very stiff penalties, including interest rates of up to 2% per month and probable cancellation of the agreement. Use these cards only if you will pay off the entire balance each month.

Since these cards are most useful to those who travel and entertain away from home frequently, most military people will not find much extra benefit from having one if they already have conventional bank credit cards. Besides the requirement that the balance be paid in full each month, the annual service or membership charges are rather high ($50 to $75 per year). Along with its traditional travel and entertainment card, American Express also has marketed a regular credit card with revolving credit, and now allows the balances to be repaid over time.

Government Travel Cards. For servicemembers who travel often on temporary duty, the government has arranged for VISA to provide government cards for official travel. Rather than provide cash advances, servicemembers are encouraged (and in most cases required) to apply for the government travel card through appropriate channels. Contact your unit finance office to learn how to get the official card. The restriction on the card is that it may be used only for official purchases and expenses in conjunction with official orders. Upon completion of temporary duty, you must still file your TDY claim and then use the proceeds from the reconciliation to pay the travel card balance. If the TDY is of extended duration (more than thirty days), then the servicemember should file interim vouchers so that he or she can pay the monthly balance of the government travel card. Failure to do so will increase the cost to the servicemember and will harm his or her credit score.

Premium Credit Cards. Another service that has been growing in prominence is the premium credit card. Card issuers market "gold" or "platinum" VISA, MasterCard, and American Express cards to customers as signs that an individual has achieved a high economic standing. The premium cards are usually tied to a larger line of credit ($5,000 to $100,000 or more) and offer a variety of other services to cardholders. The main allure of these cards is their reward programs, but the primary disadvantage is their high annual cost, which can be $50 or more. Although issuing financial institutions may offer expanded services to premium cardholders, you should determine whether the additional services are worth the extra cost. The competition by card issuers to obtain more customers has led to relaxation of the criteria for their issue and to a tremendous proliferation of gold cards, many of which do not have annual fees. If you need to obtain the higher credit limits associated with a gold card, a little comparative shopping goes a long way.

If You Have Credit Problems
Credit and some people just do not mix. Through bad luck, bad management, or just lack of willpower, some people either cannot get credit or cannot handle it well once they do.

If you cannot get either a VISA or MasterCard, it is probably because your credit is bad. This could mean several different things, from having a history of bankruptcy or unpaid bills to just being too young or inexperienced to be offered a credit card. This does not happen much anymore, since issuers are trying hard to get new card customers. If you cannot get a card and you do not have any credit history, then take some measures to build a credit history. Start with a gasoline company credit card—practically anyone can get one. Use it and pay the entire balance immediately. Then work your way up to a department store card and eventually to a bank card. Try your bank or credit union—most military credit unions will give you a low credit limit, even if you have no credit history.

If all else fails and you just cannot wait, you can get a secured credit card, which is usually very expensive and operates more like a debit card. If you have destroyed your credit rating and have exhausted your other options, there are some banks that will issue you a card secured by a sizable deposit. If you prove that you can use this for a while, you could "graduate" to a normal credit card. A list of banks with secured cards is available from *www.myvesta.org.*

You may be tempted by an offer (for a fee, of course) from some direct mailer to check your credit rating or "score." You should not pay for something like this. By law, the leading credit agencies must disclose your score for a capped fee. This fee includes your three-digit credit score, how it was derived, and advice on how to improve it. This service also includes a full credit report. Explore *www.MyFICO.com* for further information.

If you wish to get the full credit report without your three-digit credit score, you are entitled by law to receive a free one annually. The official website that you can use to get your free annual credit report, but without the three-digit credit score, is *www.annualcreditreport.com.*

Furthermore, if you are ever refused credit, you can get your credit rating information for free. (See point 9 under Borrowers' Rights, below.)

If you get out of control with high, unpaid credit card balances, you have a serious problem. Each service has trained financial counselors to help structure a way out of debt. There are also other agencies in the civilian community, such as the National Foundation for Consumer Credit at 800-388-2227, that can assist with personal budgeting and debt management. Moreover, the sooner you get some help with working your financial problem, the easier it will be to get out of debt.

BORROWERS' RIGHTS

When considering whether to take advantage of any of the various forms of consumer credit outlined in this chapter, you should know your legal rights as a borrower. Over the years, the U.S. Congress has passed two major pieces of legislation that protect the borrower's rights: the Consumer Credit Protection Act of 1968 (better known as the Truth in Lending Act) and the Fair Credit Billing Act of 1975. Under these two acts, you, as a borrower, have the following rights:

1. You have the right to know the true interest rate (in APR terms) and total finance charges before signing any loan agreement.
2. Credit card issuers must advertise the true interest rate (in APR terms) charged on their cards.
3. You must be given at least fourteen days from the postmark on your credit card statement to pay off your balance and avoid paying any interest.
4. When considering your application for a loan or a credit card, a financial institution cannot ignore income from child support, alimony, or a pension.

5. In the event that you purchased goods or services in excess of $50 with your credit card and you are dissatisfied, you have the right to cancel the charges if you make a genuine effort to settle matters with the seller and the purchase was made in your home state or within one hundred miles of your home.

6. In the event that your credit card is used against your will or without your permission (that is, it is stolen or lost), your liability for the unauthorized purchases is limited to $50. If you are able to notify the credit card issuer of the loss or theft of the card before anyone tries to purchase something with it, you will not be liable for any unauthorized purchases.

7. In the event that a debit card is stolen or lost, you must notify the bank within two business days in order to limit your liability to $50. If you fail to do so, you can be liable for the first $500 taken from your account. If sixty-one days pass after the mailing date of your first bank statement showing unauthorized withdrawals, you may be liable for all the money taken from your account.

8. In the event you are applying for a credit card or loan on your own for the first time (in other words, you have no credit record of your own), you have the right to have your spouse's unblemished credit record considered as your own.

9. Should you ever be denied a loan or a credit card, you have the right to be told the specific reasons why you were turned down. You cannot be denied access to what has been reported about you to a credit bureau. If the credit bureau's report was instrumental in your being rejected for a loan or a credit card, you must be provided access to your file at no charge. If you wish to find out what is in your credit record without having been rejected for a credit application, you can contact the three major credit bureaus: Experian (formerly TRW), Equifax, and TransUnion. Any or all may have a file on you, and your report may be accurate at one and inaccurate at another. Therefore, you should check your credit report at all three bureaus. To find out how to get your credit report, contact credit bureaus directly by checking the following websites: *www.experian.com*, *www.equifax.com*, *www.transunion.com*.

4

Paying Your Taxes

The information provided in this chapter is by necessity general in nature. Each family's financial situation is different, and tax law is complex. In addition, many of the dollar values for exemptions, credits, exclusions, and deductions change annually. To help, all military installations have legal assistance offices that provide tax forms and offer professional help in tax matters at no charge to you and your family. In addition, the Volunteer Income Tax Assistance (VITA) program at each base provides unit-level volunteers with training to assist with simple tax preparation. Finally, the Internal Revenue Service (IRS) maintains local offices around the country, a toll-free phone number, and assistance over the internet at *www.irs.gov*.

Tax-Help Websites

www.MilitaryOneSource.com
www.irs.gov
www.mypay.dfas.mil
www.taxslayer.com

With regard to taxes, military compensation has peculiarities that distinguish it from typical civilian pay systems. For example, many military allowances are exempt from income taxation by all three levels of government: federal, state, and local. Considering the housing (BAH) and subsistence (BAS) allowances alone, about one-fourth of military compensation is tax exempt. In addition, several states either have no state income tax or allow military incomes to forgo state income taxes. Thus, by exempting military income from taxation, the tax code raises the value of military compensation by providing a "tax advantage" to servicemembers. However, basic military pay, investment income, and your spouse's income are fully taxable by all levels of government. As a result, you need to understand tax laws so you can ensure compliance, incorporate tax considerations into your financial planning decisions, and understand the value of your military compensation.

This chapter will discuss the military member's personal tax responsibilities and the peculiarities of federal, state, and local taxation that apply to servicemembers. You will learn how to prepare your tax returns and how to tackle the myriad of roadblocks that discourage many Americans from preparing their taxes themselves. Information in this chapter will provide some general tax planning guidance that should be useful in your overall financial plan and help you avoid over-paying taxes.

FEDERAL INCOME TAX

This section will begin by providing a summary of the general provisions of the complicated federal tax code, because federal income taxes are the largest tax burden on the average American. Luckily, every IRS form has detailed instructions, and the federal tax computations for the typical servicemember are relatively straightforward. You should be able to calculate your federal income tax liability without professional assistance, although experts say it may take you up to twenty hours to gather the appropriate information and complete the forms. Besides completing Form 1040, you may also have to prepare many other schedules and forms, depending on whether or not you itemize deductions, receive investment or rental income, or are eligible for various credits.

Before you tackle the mechanics of completing the actual tax return, you will need the answers to some basic questions about you and your family. Common questions include the following: How many exemptions should I have? What is my filing status? Which forms do I use? As a military member, do I have to pay state taxes? Should I item-ize deductions or take the standard deduction? All of these are valid questions, and taxpayers must understand their answers to them prior to preparing their tax return.

Tax Basics

One of the first things to do in the military is to file Form W-4 with your local finance office. This form basically records your marital status and the number of exemptions you wish to claim for withholding purposes. An exemption reduces taxable income by a specified amount of income ($3,300 in 2006) based on the idea that a taxpayer with a small amount of income should pay less tax. Thus, with a greater number of exemptions, more income can be "exempt" from being taxed. Tax codes provide one personal exemption for the taxpayer and an exemption for the spouse if a joint return is filed. In addition, a taxpayer may claim an exemption for each dependent (e.g., child). Thus, a married soldier with two children is allowed four exemptions if he or she files a joint return with his or her spouse. An unmarried soldier without responsibility for children would be allowed one exemption. There are many situations where it is not clear whether or not a person is a soldier's dependent. Some servicemembers care for elderly parents, have stepchildren, or are the primary caregiver for nephews and nieces. Consult the IRS website to determine the eligibility requirements for dependency.

Servicemembers should consult their tax office before claiming an exemption because failure to meet the criteria for any of these tests results in the disallowance of an exemption. If the IRS determines you inappropriately claimed an exemption, you will be subject to back taxes, interest, and possibly penalties.

Filing status is a much more straightforward issue. There are five categories of filing status: single, married filing joint return, married filing separate return, head of household, and qualifying widower. Each filing status carries different tax rate schedules and standard deductions and hence has a significant effect on tax liabilities. In general, if you are legally married by a state law, you have the choice to file a joint return or a separate return. If you are separated from your spouse by a decree of divorce or separate maintenance and do not qualify for another filing status (i.e., head of household or dependent), you must use the rates for single taxpayers. A single parent who chooses not to live with his or her spouse should consult with the IRS to see if he or she qualifies as a head of household under the abandoned-spouse provisions. Marital status is determined as of the last day of the tax year—except when a spouse dies during the year.

This brings us to questions about itemizing deductions or taking the basic standard deduction. You should itemize only if your deductions exceed the standard deduction shown in Table 4-1. Given the large standard deduction, itemizing typically applies only if you own a home because the interest paid on the mortgage debt is deductible. (This feature is explained in more detail in chapter 5.) If you decide to itemize,

TABLE 4-1
STANDARD FEDERAL INCOME TAX DEDUCTION

Filing Status	2006 Standard Deduction
Single	$5,150
Married Filing Jointly	$10,300
Qualifying Widow(er)s	$10,300
Head of Household	$7,550
Married Filing Separately	$5,150

Note: These rates change from year to year, so be sure to consult *www .jklasser.com* or *www.irs.gov* for the most accurate information.

be sure to include all possible deductions, many of which are listed in Table 4-2. Common deductions include mortgage interest, contributions to charities, special uniform costs, employee business expenses, tax preparation fees, and investment expenses. Besides mortgage interest and charitable contributions, servicemembers often try to deduct unreimbursed moving expenses. According to IRS Publication 3, *Tax Information for Military Personnel*, servicemembers can deduct expenses that *exceed* dislocation and travel allowances. Most servicemembers do not qualify, however, because the Army normally reimburses legitimate moving expenses. If you do qualify, you will need to file Form 3903, "Moving Expenses." Remember, you may only deduct *unreimbursed* expenses. For National Guard and reserve members, certain business expenses for travel more than a hundred miles from home to perform services as a National Guard or reserve member are deductible. As is required with all deductions, be sure to save receipts, canceled checks, and mortgage records as evidence to support your deductions.

Preparing Your Tax Return
Once you have an understanding of filing status, standard deductions, and how to determine the number of dependents, you are ready to begin calculating taxable income as shown in Figure 4-1. During January of each year, you should receive a Form W-2 from the Defense Finance and Accounting Service, which documents your taxable income, income tax withheld, and Social Security (FICA) tax withheld for the prior calendar year. You can also access this information via the internet at *www.mypay.dfas.mil*. You should receive Form 1099-Div for any dividend and capital gains income from your investments and Form 1099-Interest for interest income from your banks. If you are

TABLE 4-2
TAXABLE AND NONTAXABLE INCOME AND DEDUCTIONS

Taxable Income	Nontaxable Income	Deductions
1. Basic pay, including longevity pay	1. Basic Allowance for Housing (BAH)	1. Medical and dental expenses in excess of 7.5% of AGI
2. Special pay	2. Subsistence allowance	2. Local and state taxes
3. Incentive pay for hazardous duty	3. Value of quarters and subsistence received in kind	3. Charitable contributions (cash or property)
4. Special pay	4. Overseas COLA	4. Home loan interest
5. Military retirement pay	5. Uniform, travel, and family separation allowances	5. Investment margin interest
6. Accrued leave and separation pay	6. Dividends on veterans insurance	6. Student loans
7. Armed services academy pay (cadet and midshipman pay)	7. Death gratuities	7. Fees for investment advice and management
8. Personal money allowances	8. Dislocation Allowances	8. Fees for administration
9. Bonuses (enlistment, reenlistment, overseas extension)	9. Combat zone pay (when combat zone exclusion applies)	9. Subscriptions to publications on investing
10. A portion of DITY—move incentive payment (you will receive a separate W-2 form that details the taxable income and taxes withheld)	10. Sick pay (after the first thirty days not combat connected)	10. Unreimbursed business expense in excess of 2% AGI
11. CONUS cost-of-living allowance (COLA)	11. Forfeiture/detention of pay	
12. Spouse's income if filing a joint return)	12. Professional education (paid by U.S. government)	
13. Interest received on investments	13. Evacuation/interment allowance	
14. Dividends	14. Medical benefits (including dental)	
15. Capital gains (requires a Schedule D)	15. Veterans benefits	
16. Rental income (requires a Schedule E)	16. ROTC allowances	
17. Royalties	17. Moving and storage (in kind)	
18. Alimony	18. Group term life insurance	
19. Prizes, awards, and gambling winnings	19. Medal of Honor pension payments	
20. Gains realized on the sale of assets*	20. Child support payments you receive	
	21. Value of scholarships and grants	

*Realized gain (or loss) on asset = amount realized from the sale − adjusted basis of the property.
  Adjusted basis of property = cost + capital additions − depreciation property.

Figure 4-1
Form 1040 Process

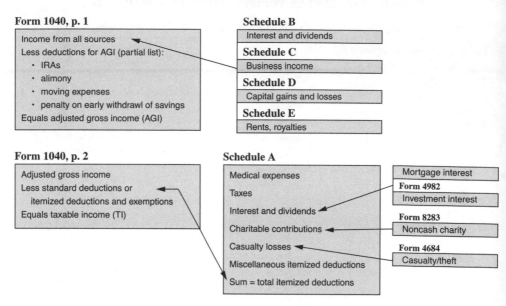

using the married-filing-jointly status, ensure that you have the W-2s for your spouse as well. Next, choose the correct filing status and number of exemptions. You must provide the IRS with the Social Security numbers for all exemptions, so make sure you have obtained these for dependents. Use the long Form 1040 unless you are single and cannot claim any dependents or have a taxable income of less than $50,000 and are not itemizing, in which case you would use Form 1040-EZ. Next, follow the four steps below:

Step 1. Tally all income that is subject to taxes. Do not include income not subject to taxes, such as inheritances, life insurance proceeds, or military allowances, outlined in Table 4-2.

Step 2. Reduce that total by the proper legal methods—adjustments, deductions, and exemptions.

Step 3. Then figure the lowest possible tax by choosing the right filing status and apply the correct tax rates to the marginal income. Table 4-3 outlines the marginal tax brackets for 2006 for the married filing jointly and single filing statuses. These are the most common filing statuses but the other income levels can be easily obtained at the IRS website. Also, the tax rates may change each year, so be sure to look up the current rates on the IRS website.

TABLE 4-3
FEDERAL INCOME TAX BRACKETS

2006 Tax Bracket	Married Filing Jointly	Single
10% income tax bracket (based on taxable income)	$0–$15,100	$0–$7,550
15% income tax bracket (based on taxable income)	$15,100–$61,300	$7,550–$30,650
Beginning of 25% bracket	$61,300–$123,700	$30,650–$74,200
Beginning of 28% bracket	$123,700–$188,450	$74,200–$154,800
Beginning of 33% bracket	$188,450–$336,550	$154,800–$336,550
Beginning of 35% bracket	$336,550 and above	$336,550 and above

Figure 4-1 summarizes these steps on how to complete the long Form 1040. After tax credits have been discussed, an example to help illustrate the process will be given.

Do not be alarmed by the complexity of the diagram. Remember to start by listing all income from all sources in order to calculate your adjusted gross income. You must include the various schedules only if you draw income from sources outside your military pay. For example, you must complete Schedule B if you have interest income or dividends in excess of $1,500. Complete Schedule D if you have capital gains from investments (mutual funds), and Schedule E if you receive rental income. Remember that it makes sense to itemize only if your deductions are greater than your standard deductions. To assist you in determining your income and deductions, Table 4-2 summarizes some of the more common sources of income, itemized deductions, and nonreportable income that can be excluded from your taxable income (step 2), as well as the most common deductions.

Step 4. After calculating your federal income tax, reduce it by any tax credits you may have.

Tax Credits
Now you are ready to attack step 4 of the process—reducing your tax by the appropriate credits. Besides merely raising revenue, our tax system is used to obtain equity as well as social and economic goals. Tax credits in particular have been enacted to make tax burdens more equitable across income levels. A tax credit is different from a tax deduction, which reduces your taxable income and depends on your filing

status and tax rate. A tax credit, on the other hand, reduces your taxes on a dollar-for-dollar basis. Spending the few minutes to determine whether or not you are eligible for tax credits could save you hundreds of dollars.

The most common tax credit is the Earned Income Tax Credit (EITC). Many younger servicemembers can take advantage of the EITC. It is intended to provide tax equity for those of modest means. Table 4-5 shows the conditions to qualify for the EITC and the maximum credit for tax year 2006. You can also consult *www.irs.gov* and use the EITC Assistant to determine if you qualify and to obtain the most updated information.

Computing the EITC is complicated, and therefore it is recommended that you consult the Post Tax Assistance Office if you suspect you might qualify, based on the maximum amount of earned income in Table 4-5. The table and example are intended for illustrative purposes only. Servicemembers and their leaders should be aware of the EITC and have a general idea of the income range. From there, they should consult the IRS web page. Each year, the IRS issues an "Earned Income Tax Credit Table" for determining the appropriate amount of credit. Claim the EITC on Form 1040, line 60a.

Credit for Child and Dependent Care Expenses. If you paid for someone to take care of your children under age thirteen so you can work, you can claim a credit for child-care expenses up to a maximum of $3,000 for one child and $6,000 for two or more children. The credit can be as much as 35% of these qualifying expenses—depending on

---

TABLE 4-5
EARNED INCOME TAX CREDIT—TAX YEAR 2006

EARNED INCOME AND ADJUSTED GROSS INCOME (AGI) MUST EACH BE LESS THAN:

- $36,348 ($38,348 married filing jointly) with two or more qualifying children;
- $32,001 ($34,001 married filing jointly) with one qualifying child;
- $12,120 ($14,120 married filing jointly) with no qualifying children.

MAXIMUM CREDIT:

- $4,536 with two or more qualifying children;
- $2,747 with one qualifying child;
- $412 with no qualifying children.

---

your adjusted gross income. Be careful. You do not qualify for this credit if you are married and your spouse does not work. It is intended to help mitigate only necessary child-care expenses. In addition, you must supply the name and Social Security number of your care provider and fill out Form 2441, "Child and Dependent Care Expenses." If you hire an in-home care provider (e.g., nanny), Form 2441 alerts the IRS and you may owe a nanny tax. If this applies to you, visit the IRS website for more information on this tax.

You may also qualify for this credit if you incur expenses taking care of any other dependent who is physically or mentally unable to care for himself or herself (e.g., an elderly or disabled parent). Again, to take advantage of the credit, the person must pass the dependency tests described earlier in this chapter.

Foreign Tax Credit. If you invest in international mutual funds, it is likely that you paid foreign taxes last year. These foreign taxes will show up on Forms 1099-Div and 1099-Interest, which must be provided to you by all mutual funds at the end of the calendar year. If your foreign taxes come to less than $300 ($600 if filing jointly), you simply claim this as credit on line 43 of Form 1040. If you paid more in foreign taxes, you must file Form 1116.

If you or your spouse receive income from a foreign country and pay income taxes to that country, you will be excused from being taxed by the United States. An example of this is a U.S. servicemember living in Germany whose spouse is a German citizen with a job earning income on the German economy. If the spouse pays taxes in Germany, the U.S. servicemember will have to declare that income on the United States Form 1040. However, filling out Form 1116 will relieve the servicemember from paying taxes to the United States government if the spouse can prove income taxes were paid to Germany.

Child Tax Credit. This allows a credit for each dependent child under age seventeen. For 2006, the amount is $1,000, but is subject to change in the future. This is perhaps the easiest credit to include on your tax return. Assuming you have dependents under age seventeen, there is no form to fill out. All you have to do is provide the Social Security number for each dependent under age seventeen on the front of your Form 1040.

Other Issues

Determining how much to withhold. The proportion of your income that is withheld as tax payment from your wage statements is determined by the number of withholding allowances you claim when you file a statement (Form W-4) with your finance office. A very rough estimate of the effects of one additional allowance is $25 (in the 15 percent tax bracket) or $42 (in the 25% tax bracket) less withheld from your pay each month.

There is good reason not to have too much withheld each month. In effect, you are extending an interest-free loan to the government—the government holds your excess tax payments until you get your refund, but pays you no interest for the use of your funds. If you consistently receive a large refund, you may want to file a new W-4 form. This will allow you to match your monthly tax withholding to your tax liability. As a result, you will have more take-home pay to use or invest as you see fit. While this approach offers the potential for additional investment income, you should be careful not to underwithhold. If you fall beneath the minimum required withholding amount, you expose yourself to the risk of an IRS penalty. To avoid this penalty, you should ensure withholdings cover 100% of your previous year's tax liability.

Filing an Extension for Tax Returns. Income tax returns and final payments become due on 15 April. Military personnel and government employees living outside the United States and Puerto Rico get an automatic extension until 15 June. This rule also applies even if only one spouse is out of the country and files a joint return with the one who is not. You must attach a statement to your return showing that you met the requirement for the extension. *Remember, this extension prevents only the assessment of penalties for a late filing and payment of tax; interest will be charged on any taxes still unpaid after 15 April.*

Serving in a Combat Zone. There is special consideration for military pay earned in a combat zone. If you are serving in an imminent danger area designated by an Executive Order for any part of a month, then your pay for the entire month falls under the exclusion. It differs for enlisted members and officers, as described below. Consult your chain of command to determine if you are unsure whether you served in a combat zone. In general, if you are receiving hazardous duty pay, then you are in one.

For enlisted members and warrant officers, all basic pay received in a combat zone is nontaxable. Specifically, if you were in a combat zone for any portion of a month, your pay for the entire month is nontaxable. For example, a sergeant earning $2,000 a month would accrue a tax savings of $300 per month ($0.15 \times \$2,000$). Over a six-month rotation in a combat zone, this would mean a pay increase of $1,800 (see chapter 9 on deployments). You do, however, pay Social Security and Medicare while in a combat zone.

Officers may deduct their monthly pay up to the maximum enlisted amount.

Tax Treatment of Servicemembers Who Die in a Combat Zone. The Internal Revenue Code provides tax forgiveness for any member whose death results from service in a terrorist or military action. This tax forgiveness applies to income for the taxable year in which the member dies and for prior years that ended on or after the first day served in a combat zone. Furthermore, any tax liability outstanding against such a member at the time of death will be canceled or reduced. Make sure that your spouse is aware of this provision and is instructed to contact the legal assistance officer in case of your death by including a note to this effect in the letter of instruction that should accompany your will. The Military Family Tax Relief Act of 2003 also increased the death gratuity paid to survivors from $6,000 to $12,000, which is not taxable.

Filing When a Spouse is Deployed to a Hazardous Duty Area. You still have to file by April 15. In this case, you should have prepared a power of attorney prior to your deployment so that your spouse can sign the joint return. If you failed to do this, IRS Publication 3 states that your spouse should simply attach a signed statement stating that the servicemember cannot sign the joint return because he or she is serving in a combat zone or qualified hazardous duty area.

Tax Implications of IRA Savings. An Individual Retirement Account (IRA) is an individual savings plan that also offers unique tax benefits. Two types of IRAs are of importance to military members: the traditional IRA and the Roth IRA. If you meet certain criteria of filing status and income level, then you may qualify to deduct part or all of your traditional IRA contribution from your taxable income. When you withdraw the money, usually at retirement, some or all will be taxable.

The Roth IRA is more flexible and a better choice for most military members. It is not tax deductible, meaning you do not reduce your taxable income by the contribution. You can, however, take your contributions out for first-time home purchases and to meet educational expenses. More importantly, your contributions grow tax exempt, which is the real benefit of contributing to a Roth IRA. In other words, you do not pay taxes on the interest, dividends, or capital gains income that your account generates during the year. When the Roth IRA funds are withdrawn, no taxes are paid since you funded the Roth with after-tax dollars.

Perhaps the only drawback to both versions of the IRA is that the Internal Revenue Code places a 10% penalty on top of normal taxes for early withdrawals. The earliest you can begin withdrawals is age 59.5, except for the limited withdrawal reasons mentioned.

As an added incentive to save, your spouse may also contribute to a separate IRA, even if he or she does not work. IRAs are a tremendous way to reduce your tax liability or save for your future. For more information, see chapter 12 on IRAs.

Tax Treatment of Additional Income. Servicemembers (or family members) running a business or earning nonwage income "on the side" will most likely have to report that income on Schedule C and pay a "double" Social Security tax on it (along with Schedule SE). As a general rule, if you receive any income (except investment or rental income) on which taxes have not been withheld, you should check on the likely requirement to report it here. Failure to do so could result in serious consequences.

Keeping Old Returns. You should keep a copy of your tax return for a minimum of seven years. Along with your tax return, you should keep copies of any supporting documents. These include W-2 forms, 1099 forms, receipts, and mortgage records. If you make nondeductible contributions to your traditional IRA, you should keep page 1 of Form 1040 and Form 8606 until you withdraw those contributions beginning after age 59.5.

This section provided an overview of the rules governing federal taxes. However, coverage has not been exhaustive. If you still have questions, your legal assistance officer, unit tax advisor, community services representative, and IRS officials can help you. Also, refer to the income tax aids listed in the references at the end of this chapter.

STATE TAXES

State tax codes change constantly, and they can be as complicated as the federal code. Before preparing your state taxes, you should check with your local legal assistance office or taxation authority in your state of legal residence. Contacting your state is now easier because most states have Internet sites that offer specific information and the necessary tax forms

Each state treats military compensation differently (see Figure 4-2). Seven states (Alaska, Florida, Nevada, South Dakota, Texas, Washington, and Wyoming) have no income tax. If you are a legal resident of one of these states, your income from any source will not be taxed. Many other states provide special breaks to servicemembers. For exam-

Figure 4-2
State Tax Treatment of Military Compensation

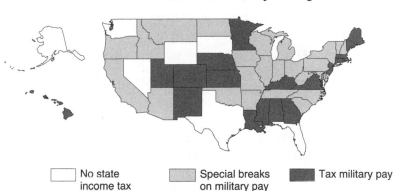

| No state income tax | Special breaks on military pay | Tax military pay |

ple, some do not tax military compensation at all while other states do not tax military pay if the servicemember is serving outside the state. The remaining states levy some form of tax on military income.

Changing Your Legal Residence

Military personnel can legally reduce state income tax by establishing their domicile of choice in a state that does not have an income tax. The servicemember must be able to show evidence of certain criteria for a change in domicile to be persuading to state tax authorities. If you are able to provide such evidence without extreme difficulty or large expenses, then you might want to consider doing so. However, tax authorities are alert for fraudulent domicile changes. Therefore, you should seek advice at your installation legal assistance office to ensure that your actions meet all of the legal requirements. They will discuss legal terms with you, including the definitions of *residence* and *legal residence* (or *domicile*).

Residence is established in a state by residing in that state. Residence involves your physical presence or the presence of your living quarters for a period of time. When you are assigned to a service installation, you are usually a temporary resident of that state.

Legal residence, which is synonymous with *domicile* and *home of record* for tax purposes, refers to the individual's permanent home for legal purposes. According to the Soldiers' and Sailors' Relief Act, servicemembers are subject to the tax laws in the state of their domicile. Everyone has only one legal residence at any given time. This legal residence may be in the state where a person was born—domicile of origin—or it may be a place he or she has chosen—domicile of choice.

Once established, legal residence continues until legally changed. Legal residence changes only by a voluntary and positive action. A mere attempt or desire to make a change is not sufficient. As a rule, to acquire a domicile of choice, you must meet the following three conditions concurrently:

1. Be physically present in the new state.
2. Have the intention of abandoning the former domicile.
3. Have the intention to remain in the new state indefinitely.

Once a person has established a legal residence in a particular state, a temporary absence does not cause that legal residence to change. Thus, it is possible for you to have a domicile in one state and a temporary residence in another.

Servicemembers can use some of the following as evidence of intent to establishing domicile of choice:

1. Place of birth.
2. Permanent place of abode.
3. Registering to vote and voting by absentee ballot.
4. Obtaining a driver's license.
5. State from which you entered the military service.
6. Filing with state authorities an approved certificate or other statement indicating legal residence.

Once you have legally changed your domicile of choice using this information, contact your finance office. The finance office must adjust your state tax withholding and pay it to the proper state.

Common Rules For State Tax Liabilities

1. Your state of domicile may tax your service income and other income (such as dividends and interest), regardless of how or where it is earned.
2. Your state of temporary residence may not tax military pay. However, your state of temporary residence (because of military orders) may tax any other income you or your family members derive from working or investing in that state.
3. Your state of temporary residence cannot tax your personal property located in the state. Your state of domicile could tax your personal property, but typically states do not tax personal property that is not physically in the state. Real estate is taxed where it is located.
4. For retirees, the state may tax your military pension only if it taxes other pensions in the same manner.

5. If you obtain your state automobile license tags from the state in which you are temporarily residing, check with your local legal assistance office. You may be exempted from paying certain fees.

Military Spouses

Under current tax law, a spouse does not become a legal resident of the servicemember's state of domicile at the time of marriage. A spouse's income is normally taxed in the state in which it is earned—the state of residence. Consequently, military spouses will often have to file non-resident state income taxes with the state in which the family is stationed. Since the servicemember's state of domicile taxes the military income, it is possible for many military families to file tax forms in two or three states:

1. For the servicemember's income in the state of domicile.
2. For the spouse's income in state of temporary residence.
3. For the spouse's income in the spouse's state of domicile.

Tax Savings That May Be Available To You

Although each state's tax code is unique, here are some rules that may exist that might reduce your tax burden. You may be eligible for one or more of the following deductions (read the rules carefully because these are not offered in all states):

1. Federal tax liability.
2. Property taxes.
3. Interest and dividend income, depending on the source of these earnings.

LOCAL TAXES

Typically, you will pay local taxes in a state of temporary residence only if you own real estate in the state. However, servicemembers may also be subject to local income or property taxes levied by town, county, or other local governments in whose jurisdiction their legal residence lies. If you are unsure, contact local government clerks for information on income taxes that may be due while you are on active duty.

SUGGESTED REFERENCES

The following IRS publications (available free from IRS publications centers and electronically from the Internet site) are particularly helpful:

- IRS Publication 3, Tax Guide for Military Personnel.
- IRS Publication 17, Your Federal Income Tax.

- IRS Publication 552, Recordkeeping for Individuals.
- IRS Publication 553, Highlight of Tax Changes.

Annual income tax supplement to the *Army*, *Navy*, and *Air Force Times*, published annually (typically in mid-February). It contains useful tax tips and information, including detailed information on state taxes.

Software packages for preparing taxes include most forms for printing and transmitting returns directly to the IRS. These include Quicken, Turbotax, and Kiplinger's TaxCut.

Tax guides are also published by the J. K. Lasser Tax Institute, Prentice-Hall, Commerce Clearing House, and accounting firms such as Arthur Young and PriceWaterhouseCoopers.

The local tax assistance office on your post and the Staff Judge Advocate (SJA) are resources.

PART II

FINANCIAL DECISIONS FOR SERVICEMEMBERS

5

Housing

This chapter discusses some of the housing choices faced by military families and suggests ways to evaluate housing alternatives. Because determining where you live is ultimately a personal decision, these guidelines must be adapted to fit your particular situation. Whether you plan to invest in a home, live in military housing, or rent a home or apartment, your decision is financially significant.

When moving to a new area, servicemembers should start by reviewing the installation's website and contacting Army Community Service (ACS) and the housing office. If you are not required to live on the installation or installation housing is not available, you can obtain information about rental and purchase options from many sources, such as your sponsor, local real estate agents, the local chamber of commerce, the Internet, and newspapers.

Your ability to purchase or rent a home will depend primarily on your personal financial situation. If you have an excellent credit history, sufficient income, and personal savings for a down payment, you may qualify for a mortgage to buy a home. Most American homeowners budget 30% to 35% of their after-tax household income for their mortgage. Your Basic Allowance for Housing[1] (BAH) may be less than your monthly mortgage payment, but homeownership has significant tax advantages that make it a financially attractive option. BAH is not taxed as income since it is an allowance. Additionally, mortgage interest is a tax

---

[1]Basic Allowance for Housing (BAH) is the monthly payment the military pays to servicemembers who do not live on the installation. Because BAH is an allowance, it is not considered part of your taxable income; thus, servicemembers do not pay income tax on BAH.

deductible item, so servicemembers accrue twice the tax benefit. Refer to chapter 4 for an in-depth discussion of tax deductions.

THE DECISION TO LIVE ON OR OFF
THE INSTALLATION

Living in quarters on the installation is not free. Because servicemembers give up their BAH in order to live on the installation, they are essentially renting from the government for the price of BAH. Servicemembers should compare the houses they could afford based on their BAH to quarters they are offered on the installation. Since dual military couples both receive BAH entitlements, their cost of living on the installation is the sum of both of their BAH amounts. Typically, this substantial monthly allowance makes living off the installation the best economic decision for dual-military couples.

The decision to live on or off the installation is more than a financial decision. Usually the local real estate market offers greater variety, but often at additional costs. Prioritizing your housing needs will help you decide where to live. In weighing your options, identify your priorities such as: quality of the school system, proximity to community facilities, taxes, availability of public transportation, and commuting costs. Each option affects your ability to choose neighbors, your sense of security, the flexibility of departure dates due to military necessity, responsiveness of maintenance workers, and other considerations. Should you decide to live off the installation, you must then determine whether to rent or buy.

> *When deciding between living on or off the installation, some things to consider include local BAH rates relative to likely rent or mortgage payments, school systems, flexibility of departure dates, commuting costs, and sense of security.*

THE RENT VS. BUY DECISION

The funds available for housing will depend on your other expenses such as transportation, food, entertainment, savings, maintenance, and other budget items. Chapter 1 provides guidance in preparing a personal budget. In addition, many budget templates are available online at sites such as *www.freddiemac.com* or *www.fanniemae.com* to assist you in your analysis.[2] It is imperative that your budget accurately depict your spending habits, priorities, and monthly cash flows. A comprehensive needs-based budget will enable you to determine the amount you can afford to spend on housing.

Rent is payment for the purchase of housing services. The decision to rent should be made after a careful review of total costs and family goals. Owning your home almost always costs more each month than renting an equivalent dwelling. However, many families decide to buy in the expectation that they will make money when they sell the home. But, homeowners do not always make money when they sell, because of the risks and costs inherent in real estate investments. Further, you may decide to rent because you do not have the savings available for a down payment or so that you can use your savings toward other financial goals or obligations.

When deciding whether to rent or buy a home, you should consider the advantages and disadvantages of each option. One important consideration is that homeownership has many tax advantages. Certain expenses associated with home ownership are tax deductible and thus reduce the amount of income taxes that homeowners pay. Servicemembers with mortgages enjoy an unusual advantage. They receive tax-free quarters allowances (BAH) to pay their mortgages. The primary tax advantage is that the interest paid on a mortgage loan is deductible from your income when computing your federal income taxes, and it offsets part of your loan payment. Other tax advantages include:

- Deduction of points[3] paid to secure an initial mortgage, either in the year of purchase or over the life of the loan. (See Internal Revenue Service Publication 936 *Home Mortgage Interest Deduction* at *www.irs.gov*.)
- Deduction of property taxes.

---

[2] In the United States, Freddie Mac and Fannie Mae (private companies with government charters) purchase the majority of mortgage loans. Thus, they set the mortgage lending criteria. They also provide a wealth of information on buying a home and interest rates on mortgages, as well as analytic tools for evaluating the rent versus purchase decision, preparing budgets, estimating how much home you can afford, and calculating mortgage payments.

[3] Discount points are often called points or loan origination fees. A point is equal to 1 percent of the loan amount. Points are considered like interest that you pay in advance, so the more points you pay when you close the loan, the lower your interest rate.

- Relief from capital gains tax on profits up to $250,000 for single tax filers and $500,000 for joint filers. To qualify you must meet certain criteria, which include that you must have lived in the home for two of the last five years on the date of sale.

> *Certain expenses associated with home ownership are tax deductible and thus reduce the amount of income taxes that homeowners pay.*

The tax advantages of home ownership are significant, and they should be thoroughly analyzed before you make your housing decision. (See IRS Publication 523 *Selling Your Home* at *www.irs.gov.*) Table 5-1 summarizes the advantages and disadvantages of renting versus buying a home.

Preparing a net present value analysis is an excellent way to compare your rent-versus-purchase options. Fortunately, you do not need a degree in finance to complete this analysis. Online tools are available to calculate the costs and benefits of each option. The following sites provide tools to facilitate your analysis: *www.freddiemac.com*, *www.fannie mae.com*, *www.mortgages-loans-calculators.com*, and *www.bankrate .com*. Using your Internet search program, type in "rent versus buy" to obtain other useful links to financial calculators. However, you will need to gather the information listed in Table 5-2 for input to the calculator. You can obtain much of this information from a real estate agent, potential mortgage lenders, or online.

In summary, if the cost of owning a house in your new location exceeds your monthly budget, renting may be your best alternative. If you have the financial resources to buy a home but you anticipate that home prices will not increase enough to offset the closing costs associated with ownership (discussed in the next section) and provide a reasonable return on your down payment, you should consider renting a home.

RENTAL AGREEMENTS

Upon finding an appropriate rental property, you should negotiate with the landlord or agent on the price and terms. Then, clearly document key rental contract terms, including responsibility for utility payments and repairs, payment terms, duration of rental contract, ability to sublet, restrictions, and deposits. All tenant-landlord agreements should be in writing and should contain a military clause releasing the servicemember from the lease in the event of transfer or deployment. Read your

TABLE 5-1
ADVANTAGES AND DISADVANTAGES OF RENTING
VERSUS BUYING A HOME

Renting	Buying
Advantages:	*Advantages:*
• Generally the monthly rent is less than a mortgage would be for a comparable home. • You will probably not be responsible for maintenance and repairs, and maybe utilities. • You will need enough cash for a deposit, but that amount is significantly smaller than a down payment or closing costs. • You will not need to sell a home or worry about housing prices when you move. • If you have a military clause in your lease, you can easily break the contract if you PCS or deploy.	• If the value of your home increases, you may sell your home at a profit. • Gains on home sales are generally not taxable taxable up to $250,000 for single tax payers or $500,000 for a married couple. • Property taxes, mortgage interest and points are tax deductible. • You can borrow against the equity in your home.
Disadvantages:	*Disadvantages:*
• You will forego the opportunity to earn a capital gain if housing prices rise. • You may have fewer rental options. • Your rent payment is not tax deductible.	• You need 10–20% of the home price for a down payment plus closing costs. • You must have a good credit history. • The home may not increase in value enough to payoff your mortgage and closing costs when you sell your home. • You are giving up the interest you could have earned on your down payment. • You will be responsible for home maintenance and repair costs.

contract thoroughly. Before signing any lease you should ask your commanding officer, your NCOIC, or the JAG office to review the contract.

> *All tenant-landlord rental agreements should contain a military clause releasing the servicemember from the lease in the event of a transfer or deployment.*

PURCHASING A HOME
If you decide that purchasing a home is your best option, you should determine how much home you can afford. Lenders want to ensure that

TABLE 5-2
INFORMATION TO HELP MAKE THE RENT VS. BUY DECISION

Personal Information	Rental Information	Purchase Information[4]
• Your Marginal Tax Rate (MTR), based on your income tax bracket (see chapter 4). • The annual return (%) you could earn on the savings you apply towards a down payment on your mortgage.[5]	• Estimated monthly rent • Projected rent increases • Renters' insurance premiums	• Estimated maintenance costs, homeowner's insurance, and property taxes • Potential home purchase price • Loan terms (down payment, interest rate, maturity, points, and closing costs) • Estimated housing price appreciation rate

you have enough monthly income to make your mortgage payments. They calculate your monthly mortgage expenses by summing your mortgage payment, insurance, and taxes. Then, they apply two general tests: the income and debt tests described below.

Income Test	Debt Test
• **Your mortgage expenses should not exceed 28% of your pretax income.**	• **Your mortgage expenses and other regular debt payments should not be more than 36% of total income.**

The lower the interest rate, the lower your mortgage payment will be; with this savings, you can afford to buy a more expensive home. Table 5-3 depicts sample down payments, closing costs, and mortgage payments for a thirty-year fixed rate loan under two different interest rate scenarios.

You can easily perform a precise calculation by using Excel or an online loan payment calculator, such as the one at *www.fanniemae.com*. Ultimately, the interest rate on your loan will depend on your credit his-

---

[4] See following sections on "Purchasing a Home" and "Completing the Loan Transaction."

[5] This depends on how you would invest the money; for example, if you invested in an S&P 500 index fund, you might use the average annual return on the fund, approximately 12%. If you invested in a savings account, the return would be about 3.5% (see chapter 10).

TABLE 5-3
INTEREST RATE SCENARIOS FOR A 30-YEAR FIXED RATE MORTGAGE

Home Price	10% Down payment	Closing Costs	Amount Financed	Monthly Payment at 5% Interest	Monthly Payment at 7% Interest
$150,000	$15,000	$7,500	$135,000	$725	$898
$250,000	$25,000	$12,500	$225,000	$1,208	$1,497
$350,000	$35,000	$17,500	$315,000	$1,610	$2,096

tory, the type of loan you select, and the amount of your down payment. The following section discusses mortgage options in greater detail.

Your mortgage amount will depend on the size of your down payment, which is generally constrained by the balance of your savings. If you have the capacity to pay a greater down payment, you should weigh the costs (the interest or dividends you will not earn on your savings if you make an additional down payment) versus the benefits of lower monthly mortgage payments. You generally should not pay more than the minimum down payment, because the after-tax cost of your mortgage[6] will generally be less than the after-tax earnings on your investments. You should discuss the advantages and disadvantages of making a higher down payment with your lender and real estate agent before making a final decision.

The next step is to contact your bank, mortgage company, or credit union to get a commitment letter indicating the maximum loan amount for which you qualify. This letter provides assurance to the sellers of your dream home that you will be able to obtain financing. They will more readily accept your offer knowing that you can obtain financing.

The Purchase Process

Deciding which home to buy is an arduous process and largely dependent on your tastes and preferences. Location is a key consideration along with quality of schools, recreation facilities, and potential resale value. Although it is possible to conduct extensive research via the Internet, most buyers consult real estate agents at this point. Many banks

---

[6] After-tax interest rate is the effective interest rate you pay on a loan if you deduct interest expense. For example, if you have an 8% loan and are in the 25% tax bracket, the after-tax interest rate is 8% multiplied by (1 minus 0.25), or 6.00%.

and insurance companies offer relocation assistance, including referrals to real estate agents. By using these services, you may also receive reimbursement of part of the real estate agent's fee (up to $1,000).[7] Agents can provide assistance in evaluating potential neighborhoods and homes. However, you should be aware of the different roles brokers and agents assume as well as their interests and motivations.

A broker has a license to operate a real estate company, while an agent works for a broker. The National Association of Realtors is a trade organization that establishes professional standards for its realtor members. Homeowners typically execute agreements with sellers' agents and pay them a commission to sell their homes (generally 5%). Sellers' agents are obligated to disclose certain information about the homes they list, but their incentive is to sell the homes at the highest possible prices. As a homebuyer, however, you may be better served by choosing your own buyer's agent, whose loyalty is to you, not the seller. You may be asked to sign a buyer's agent agreement, but generally, you should not pay additional fees to your buyer's agent, as he or she will receive a sales commission from the seller of the home you buy.

> *Generally, you should not pay additional fees to the buyer's agent, as he or she will receive a sales commission from the seller of the home you buy.*

Agents can provide you with a market analysis, listings of properties that meet your criteria, and advice on neighborhoods and schools. They will show you potential homes and guide you through the home buying process from offer to closing. It is important to have realistic expectations, stay within your budget, and shop around.

Once you find that ideal home, you should make a purchase offer to the seller. Depending on the local housing market, you may offer less than the seller's asking price and then negotiate to a final bid. Upon acceptance, you must provide a deposit (generally $1,000) to show that you have made a serious offer. That deposit will be applied to the purchase price at closing; however, if you withdraw your bid, for reasons other than those authorized in the contract, you may lose your deposit.

---

[7] USAA is one company that provides this service. Even if you decide not to use a broker referred by the company, the agent you select may agree to return part of the commission to get your business.

Any purchase offer should be subject to a physical inspection by a qualified professional inspector. If at all possible, you should accompany the inspector as you can learn a great deal about any deficiencies in the home. The inspector will provide a report that will serve as a basis for negotiating with the seller to either fix a problem or provide a credit so that you can perform the repairs. If the deficiencies cannot be resolved, you can withdraw your offer and obtain a refund of your deposit.

The final sales contract is executed following a successful negotiation of terms such as final price, expected closing date, expected repairs, and "items that convey" (i.e., appliances, window treatments, and fixtures). Sellers may agree to pay all or part of your closing costs, and agents may be willing to reduce their commissions, depending on the housing market, in order to facilitate an agreement. It pays to negotiate.

Shopping for a Mortgage

Many different types of mortgages are available through banks, credit unions, and mortgage companies. However, mortgages generally fall into two basic categories: fixed-rate and variable-rate. Fixed-rate loans have constant payments and generally mature in fifteen, twenty, or thirty years. You can "lock in" your rate at the time of loan commitment to protect against unexpected rate increases. The interest rate and monthly payments will not increase; they also will not go down if interest rates fall. The fixed interest rate will also be higher than the rate for a comparable variable loan because the lender assumes the risk of interest rate changes. Although fixed-rate loans are popular with many homebuyers, unless you plan to own your home for the duration of the loan, you should consider the benefits of Adjustable Rate Mortgages (ARMs).

An ARM generally starts with a lower rate than a fixed-rate loan of the same maturity. This allows homebuyers to qualify for higher loan amounts. The initial rate is fixed for a period of time (e.g., one, three, five, or ten years). Thereafter, the rate can be adjusted if interest rates rise or fall. The interest rate is based on an index, such as the London Interbank Borrowing Rate (LIBOR) or the rates on U.S. Treasury Bills, plus a margin. Once the initial period ends, the rate can be adjusted based on the prevailing index, subject to the maximum amounts stated in the loan contract (the caps). A sample specification for an ARM might state: "The initial interest rate will be 3% above the index of U.S. Treasury Securities. . . . The rate may be adjusted annually after the initial three-year term. The rate cannot increase by more than 2%

per year, and the maximum increase cannot exceed 6 percent." Table 5-4 provides an illustration.

By estimating the length of time you expect to own your home and selecting a matching ARM adjustment period, you may be able to lower the amount of interest you pay. For example, if you plan to own your home for five years, you can lower your interest payments by selecting a five-year ARM with payments calculated assuming you

---

TABLE 5-4
DETERMINING THE RATE OF AN
ADJUSTABLE RATE MORTGAGE (ARM)

Scenario	Interest Rate
Initial U.S. Treasury (UST) rate	3.1%
Interest rate you pay (3% above UST rate) in years 1 through 3	6.1%
Assumed UST rate in three years	5.5%
Interest rate you pay in year 4 is 8.1%. Although, 3% above current UST rate is 8.5%, your interest rate cannot rise by more than 2% per year, so your interest rate is 6.1% plus 2%.	8.1%
Assume the UST rate in four years	6%
Interest rate you pay in year 5 is 6% + 3%.	9%

---

make payments for thirty years, rather than a fixed-rate loan. If you decide to keep your home beyond the five year adjustment period, your interest rate and payments may rise. But, considering the time value of money, you would generally be better off paying a lower interest rate initially because you can invest the money you saved in an Individual Retirement Account (IRA) or other investment account (see chapters 10 and 12) and potentially earn a higher return.

Completing the Loan Transaction
It can take thirty or sixty days to close on a mortgage loan. The financial institution you select will require the following extensive paperwork to process your loan request:
- A loan application
- Income and employment verification
- A financial statement identifying your assets and liabilities
- Verification of cash for down payment

At the time of application, your financial institution will issue a truth-in-lending statement that indicates the annual percentage rate of interest and estimates settlement costs. The Department of Housing and Urban Development (HUD) provides an excellent guide to settlement costs that can be obtained from your financial institution or via the HUD website at *www.hud.gov*. Banks generally charge an application and an origination fee. They will order an appraisal to ensure the value of the home is greater than the loan amount, a survey of the property, and a title insurance policy.

Engaging a real estate attorney to review your purchase contract and loan documents is generally a wise investment. Loan closings can be stressful and confusing. At closing, you must provide proof of insurance and bring funds for the down payment and your portion of the closing costs. The closing statement will identify costs associated with obtaining your loan and also payments owed to the seller. These are some of the major expense categories:

- Points (as discussed earlier) paid to the lender to obtain a lower interest rate, effectively prepaying interest. (Because a dollar today is worth more than a dollar in the future, unless you plan to own your home for a long time, it is not cost effective to prepay interest.)
- Filing fees to record your mortgage documentation in the county records.
- Lenders' Title Insurance guaranteeing that no one else has an interest in the property. (You should obtain a homeowners' title policy for a small additional charge to protect your interests as well.)
- Mortgage and property taxes.
- Attorney fees.
- Escrow (deposits) for future taxes and insurance payments, generally six months.

Mortgage Guaranty Programs

Most homebuyers obtain conventional mortgage loans, which are not guaranteed by any outside agencies. However, the Federal Housing Agency (FHA) and the Veterans Administration (VA) offer loan guarantee programs that may lower your mortgage costs or down-payment requirements. It is worth the effort to evaluate the benefits of each program, especially if you do not have the savings available to make a large down payment. Each of these options is discussed briefly below.

- *FHA Loans.* Because the Federal Housing Agency insures these mortgages, lenders are more willing to give loans to borrowers with lower qualifying requirements, such as credit problems. FHA loans require only a 3% down payment, thus allowing you to purchase a home with less cash outlay. FHA loans offer competitive interest rates because the loans are insured by the federal government. Specific program terms are identified at *www.fha.org*.

- *VA Loans.* The Veterans Administration offers the VA home loan program to help veterans finance home purchases with favorable loan terms and at competitive interest rate. Because the VA guarantees a portion of the loan amount (the percent guaranteed varies with the loan balance), eligible participants can obtain loans with little or no down payment, interest rates that may be lower than conventional loan rates, and lower closing costs. Lenders currently cap the loan amount at $417,000. Specific requirements and terms are contained in VA Pamphlet 24-6 which can be found at the VA website: *www.va.gov*.

> *If you do not have the funds available to make a large down payment, you should research whether you qualify for an FHA or VA loan guarantee program.*

If you are not able to qualify for an FHA or VA loan and do not have the standard 20% down payment, your bank will require you to purchase Primary Mortgage Insurance. PMI protects the lender against the risk that you will not be able make your loan payments. With this type of insurance, it is possible for you to buy a home with as little as a 3% to 5% down payment. If your loan payment history is favorable, once the loan has been paid down to 80% of the property's value, the PMI requirement will be dropped.

Lowering the Cost of Your Mortgage
Refinancing your home may allow you to lower your cost of borrowing. Refinancing involves obtaining a new loan and paying off the existing mortgage. If interest rates drop after you purchase your home, you may be able to lower your monthly payments or switch from an adjustable to a fixed-rate loan by refinancing. However, your initial out-of-pocket expenses can be quite substantial. Generally, you will be required to pay many of the same closing costs you faced when you

initially bought your home: appraisal, title search, loan application fee, and points.

Even if you do not have adequate cash to pay the closing costs, you still may be able to refinance. Most lenders allow you to add these costs to the new loan amount if the value of your home is more than 20% higher than the loan balance. Although your monthly payment will be a little higher, you may still save money in the long run if the interest rate differential is sufficient.

Before refinancing a mortgage with a new lender, you might ask the holder of your existing mortgage to renegotiate the interest rate. The lender may not go as low as the current market rate, but may be willing to split the difference. This kind of deal is beneficial for both parties: the lender keeps you as a customer at a higher rate than current market rates, and the borrower saves on closing costs. However, your current lender may not be able to renegotiate your interest rate because of financial institution policies, but it never hurts to ask.

A traditional rule of thumb is that if current interest rates are at least two percentage points below your present rate, it may pay to refinance. You should also consider the length of time you plan to own the house. You should have time to recoup the expenses of new closing costs from lower monthly payments. The calculation below estimates the number of months you would need to remain in your current home to break even:

$$\frac{\text{Total closing costs associated with securing a new loan}}{\text{(5\% to 8\% of the outstanding balance of the old mortgage)}}$$
the monthly difference between your old and new loan payments

> *If current interest rates are at least two percentage points below your current mortgage rate, it may pay to refinance.*

Table 5-5 on the following page identifies two other strategies to lower your cost of homeownership.

Selling Your Home
The average length of time most people own their homes is five to seven years. But military members generally move every three years, making the decision to sell or rent your home critical. If you decide to

TABLE 5-5

STRATEGIES TO LOWER YOUR COST OF HOMEOWNERSHIP

Strategy	Benefits
Select a shorter loan term	Switching from a 30-year to a 15-year fixed-rate loan, could save $127,000 in interest (55%) on a $200,000 loan at 6% interest.
Make 26 biweekly payments rather than 12 monthly payments	Even if you take a 30-year loan, paying every two weeks, rather than monthly, can save $50,000 in interest payments on a 6%, 30-year loan. Your loan would be repaid five years earlier.
Switch from a fixed-rate to an ARM	If interest rates have fallen, you can save money by switching from a fixed to an adjustable-rate loan.

sell, you also have to determine your asking price and whether to use a broker.

You may choose to sell the home yourself or use a real estate agent. The ultimate concern is which choice will give you a larger net amount: selling the house yourself and avoiding the commission, or using the professional marketing expertise of a real estate agent. For a commission (generally 5–6% of the sales price), agents provide the following services: determine the fair value of your home, schedule appointments and screen buyers, and suggest the most cost-effective ways to improve the home's appearance. They also facilitate contract and closing procedures.

Should you decide to use an agent, you should interview potential candidates and ask them to provide you with a marketing plan for your home. You can negotiate the type of listing agreement[8] and commission charged with the agent you select. A higher commission may cause the agent to work harder, but it leaves you with less after the sale. You should consider signing a short-term contract at first, perhaps for two or three months and closely monitor how aggressively the agent markets your home. An agent's skill and resources can result in quick, efficient, and profitable sales, but agents' abilities and helpfulness vary. Do not renew a contract with an agent who is not working hard for you. Be aware that an agent will not want to bend on any of these points, so you must be an able negotiator to get a listing contract that best serves you and not the broker.

---

[8] You should discuss the three basic types of listing agreements (Exclusive Right to Sell, Exclusive Agency Listing, and Open Listing) with your agent.

If market conditions are good and you have the skill and time, you may decide to sell your house without the help of an agent. If you choose this option, ensure you:

1. Screen potential buyers over the telephone to determine how serious they are about buying.
2. Price your house realistically.
3. Present your home in the best possible light as well-presented homes generally sell first and command the best prices.

Renting Your Home

The last housing aspect to be discussed in this chapter is rental property. The scope of this book discuss only single-family homes as rental property. Although not the optimal real estate investment, this is the type of property the typical servicemember will find himself owning. Other forms of investment property, such as duplexes, condos, apartment buildings or even commercial buildings, are beyond the scope of this book and the reach of most servicemembers. If you have an interest in these types of investment properties, there are numerous resources devoted to them on the Internet and in the financial planning section of your local bookstore or library.

As homeowners, military families have the option of turning their homes into income generating rental property when they PCS. Depending on the market (markets are very regional, meaning prices vary by location), this can be a great way to supplement your income and save, but it is not without risks. Although home prices generally appreciate year-to-year, markets fluctuate broadly and even decrease in value. The supply and demand of homes within a region determine the purchase and rental prices in each market, and these prices tend to move in opposite directions of one another.

> *Home purchase and rental prices tend to move in opposite directions of one another.*

Interest rates and taxes are the key factors that affect housing demand directly. The historically low interest rates that the country has been experiencing recently have helped fuel the housing booms because mortgage rates are lower. Therefore, more people can afford to become homeowners with lower rates, or they can afford more home. Consider this, the mortgage payment on a $100,000 loan, with a 30-year mortgage and a rate of 5% is $536.82 per month. If your rate happens to be

8%, your monthly payment is $733.76, a difference of nearly $2,400 per year. So if rates go up, fewer people are willing to buy and more people are willing to rent. This is good news for rental property owners because they can offer rent at a lower cost than a typical mortgage when interest rates are high.

Once you understand the risks involved, owning rental property can be a great addition to your investment portfolio. Owning real estate can help offset the fluctuations in the stock market. Since real estate typically increases in value and prices are not dependent directly on how well stocks are performing, it is a good addition to a portfolio of stocks and bonds. However, before you decide to rent your home, you should carefully analyze your situation to determine if this is your best course of action and that you can afford the risks involved.

There are several reasons why you may wish to hold onto your home as a rental. First, you may be unable to sell your home. If your local housing market has cooled, you will want to consider renting your home since most servicemembers cannot afford to maintain two households, and the mortgage has to be paid whether you are living in the house or not. While your current BAH covers housing costs at your new duty station, there typically is not enough BAH to cover both housing payments. Renting the home you vacated at your previous duty station may be a short-term solution to cover the second mortgage while you wait for the market for home sales to improve.

The second reason to rent is that you have plans to return to this duty station later in your career or possibly upon retirement. When you bought your home you obviously chose it for a good reason, either for location or aesthetics or feel. Because this is the place you wanted to live and would probably not mind living there again, renting it may be an excellent source of secondary income until you are ready to reoccupy it. Additionally, having a home where you can return reduces the stress of moving as well as searching for and buying a home again.

The final reason you may want to hold on to your home is solely for financial reasons. If the rental market is hot, the idea of supplementing your income with monthly rent checks may be appealing. To take full advantage of this situation, the rent you receive must cover not only the mortgage, but also taxes, insurance, and repairs[9] (see Table 5-6 for

---

[9] There are tools on the internet that can calculate the Capitalization Rate of renting your home. If that rate you calculate is less than long-term Treasury yields, then you should probably sell. You can find one such calculator at *www.forbes.com*.

TABLE 5-6
EXAMPLE OF MONTHLY RENTAL INCOME
AND COST ANALYSIS

Income	
Rent Received	$1,500.00
Costs	
Property Manager Fees[1]	$150.00
Mortgage[2]	$825.00
Taxes	$250.00
Private Mortgage Insurance (PMI)	$100.00
Repairs[3]	$75.00
Total Monthly Gain or Loss	$100.00

[1] Normally property managers take 10% of current rents. If you manage the property yourself, then this expense goes away. However, reputable property managing firms provide one of the most crucial aspects of renting: getting the right person in the home who will pay always and on time.
[2] Mortgage includes principle and interest.
[3] Repairs is the monthly estimate, i.e., replacing air conditioner or furnace, calking the tub, etc.

rental income example). If rental income you will receive exceeds these costs for you to maintain your home, then renting will be profitable under normal market conditions. Obviously, having someone else pay all costs to live in your home is a winning situation. Depending on the type of mortgage you have on the home, your renter is also paying down your principal—a profitable situation that becomes very clear when you sell the house and you realize all the appreciation and equity the house has accrued using someone else's money.

When making the right decision on whether to rent your home when you PCS you must carefully weigh the advantages and disadvantages for your unique situation. You cannot forget that as a landlord you are operating your own business; therefore, any money that you receive from renting your home is taxable. However, there are many ways in which to reduce your tax bill. TurboTax has an excellent article that will cover the tax implication on rental property. The article can be found at *www.turbotax.com/articles/FAQonTaxesandRentalProperty.html.*

ALTERNATIVE REAL ESTATE INVESTMENT OPTION

If you have determined that home ownership is not an option for you but you would still like to include real estate in your investment portfolio, Real Estate Investment Trusts (REITs) may be an alternative to pursue. REITs resemble mutual funds and invest in properties that generate income or appreciate in value. The benefit of REITs is that your

---

Typical Advantages and Disadvantages
of Renting Your Home

Advantages
1. Provides additional income every month if rental fee exceeds your costs to keep your home.
2. Pays down the mortgage debt on the home at someone else's expense.
3. Can deduct expenses and improvements from your income taxes up to the amount of the rent you collect.
4. Gives you the ability to ride out unfavorable selling markets.
5. Hedges against inflation.
6. Diversifies investor portfolios.

Disadvantages
1. Becoming a landlord can consume much of your time.
2. Risk of rental rates dropping below your costs to maintain and pay for your home.
3. Risk of periods when home is not rented.
4. Depending on how long the home is rented, you may no longer be able to take advantage of the capital gains exemption when you sell (as mentioned earlier in the chapter as one of the advantages of owning a home).

---

money is pooled with a large group of investors and someone else is making the investment decisions across a broad range of real estate opportunities. This allows the average investor to diversify across a number of real estate holdings. For more information of REITs visit *www.investinreits.com.*

6

Purchasing an Automobile

Most people in the United States consider an automobile a necessity. Your automobile is most likely one of the largest purchases you will ever make. Transportation is second only to housing in most household budgets; therefore, making wise decisions when buying a car is critical to sound financial planning. The Internet has revolutionized the car buying experience. Never before have consumers had access to so much information. Consider these sites when researching your next automobile purchase: *www.kbb.com*, *www.usaa.com*, *www.edmunds.com*, *www.autobytel.com*, and *www.beatcar.com*.

This chapter offers practical advice and identifies helpful references in your quest for an automobile, whether new, used, or leased. It will help you negotiate the maze of automobile decisions and devise a systematic plan to guide you through your automobile purchase choices. If you use the information in this chapter, you will be an informed consumer with the ability to get a good deal on an automobile that meets your transportation requirements and does not interfere with your financial goals.

Almost every decision you make in buying a new car will affect the amount you ultimately pay. Selecting options, negotiating the purchase price, determining the trade-in value, and financing and insuring your new car are all decisions you must make and understand in order to get the best deal for your circumstances. Therefore, take the time to systematically identify what is important to you; do some homework and prepare yourself with this information before you visit car dealerships.

DETERMINING HOW MUCH CAR YOU CAN AFFORD
It is very important to begin your car-buying process with a solid idea of how much you are willing to spend each month for transportation. Your

monthly car payments are only a portion of the total monthly cost of driving a car. Insurance, operating expenses, and maintenance add to the total bill. A good rule of thumb is to spend no more than 15% of your pretax income for transportation. To estimate your monthly transportation expenses, you must make estimates for the various expenses associated with automobile ownership. The first step is to determine the amount of your monthly budget that must be alloted to transportation expenses. Your household budget (see chapter 1) is a useful tool to assess how spending on transportation affects your budget and savings plan.

> ***Spend no more than 15% of your pretax income for transportation.***

Gathering Cost Information

Payments. Automobile payments are usually the largest outlay in most transportation budgets. Table 6-1 shows the monthly payments per $1,000 financed at various interest rates for twenty-four, thirty-six, forty-eight, and sixty months. To use these tables: (1) determine the amount you plan to finance after making your down payment; (2) select a payment period shorter than the time you expect to own the automobile; and (3) select the interest rate corresponding to what banks or credit unions offer for car loans. In each column, the amount below the interest rate will be very close to your monthly payments per $1,000 financed. Multiply this number by the amount, in thousands of dollars, you plan to finance. This will give you a close estimate of your monthly automobile payment. For example, financing a $15,000 automobile purchase for four years at a 10% interest rate (assuming no down payment)

TABLE 6-1
MONTHLY PAYMENTS (PER $1,000)

Rate (Length of Loan)	4%	5%	6%	7%	8%	9%	10%	11%	12%
24 mos	$43.42	$43.87	$44.32	$44.77	$45.22	$45.68	$46.14	$46.61	$47.07
36 mos	29.52	29.97	30.42	30.88	31.34	31.80	32.27	32.74	33.21
48 mos	22.58	23.03	23.49	23.95	24.41	24.89	25.36	25.85	26.33
60 mos	18.42	18.87	19.33	19.80	20.28	20.76	21.25	21.74	22.24

would result in a monthly payment of approximately $380 (15 × 25.36 = $380.40).

Your monthly payment consists of two components: principal and interest. The principal portion of the payment is really paying for the car; the interest portion is paying for the loan. This process of repaying the loan is known as amortizing the loan. Most banks offer amortization tables (charts or calculators allowing you to see the manner in which your loan is repaid). Table 6-2 illustrates the monthly principal and interest payments for a four-year, $15,000 loan at 10%. A loan calculator, spreadsheet program, and some financial software packages can also create a loan payment table that reflects principal and interest payments for each month to help you better understand your payments.

Insurance. Insurance costs vary significantly depending on several factors. You must consider these costs when deciding which car to buy. Your insurance company will gladly give you quotes on the two or three models that you are considering so that you can accurately estimate your total monthly transportation expenses. The USAA Foundation publishes (at no charge) *The Car Guide* at *www.usaa.com*, which compares the safety features of most models, as do other companies. This guide helps identify automobiles that have desirable insurance characteristics such as passenger safety in accidents, less damage in accidents, and lower theft rates. *Consumer Reports* at *www.consumerreports.org* also publishes in April two annual buying guides, the *New Car Buying Guide* and the *Used Car Buying Guide*, that review reliability records and safety test reports. You should be aware that most lenders require

---

TABLE 6-2
MONTHLY PAYMENTS (INTEREST VS. PRINCIPAL)
FOR A FOUR YEAR $15,000 LOAN
AT A 10% ANNUAL INTEREST RATE

Month	Payment	Interest	Principal	Remaining Principal
First	$380	$125.00	$255.00	$14,745.00
Second	380	122.87	257.13	14,487.87
Third	380	120.73	259.27	14,228.60
Fourth	380	118.57	261.43	13,967.17
Twelfth (1 year)	380	100.62	279.38	11,795.73

full coverage (collision and liability) on cars that you have financed. Chapter 14 explains in more detail the various types of automobile insurance available and coverage guidelines.

> *Your insurance company will gladly give you quotes on the two or three models you are considering so that you can accurately estimate your total monthly transportation expenses.*

Operation. Operating expenses consist primarily of fuel charges. Annual operating expenses will vary significantly depending on the gas mileage of the car you choose. The typical automobile owner in the United States drives 1,000 miles each month. Calculate your operating expenses by dividing the number of miles you expect to drive by the miles per gallon (MPG) rating of your automobile. This gives you the number of gallons of fuel you will use each month. Multiply the number of gallons you expect to use monthly by the price you expect to pay per gallon in order to get an estimate of your monthly operating expenses. For example, if you plan to drive 1,000 miles per month, get twenty-five MPG, and expect to pay $2.50 per gallon for gas, monthly operating expenses would be $100 ([1,000 miles ÷ 25 MPG] × $2.50 = $100). New cars include an estimated annual fuel expenditure that can serve as a general basis for comparison.

Other annual costs for most car owners are the annual vehicle registration and inspection fees. Many states require an annual automobile emissions inspection in order to have a valid vehicle registration for that year. Costs vary widely within the United States from $50 to over $100, depending on where you live.

Maintenance. Maintenance expenses include the cost of scheduled maintenance, such as fluid changes, as well as replacing worn-out and damaged parts. Maintenance costs vary depending on the items covered under warranty or coverage bought under a separate maintenance contract. For the first several years, monthly maintenance costs for a new car should be low. Annual maintenance costs during the fifth year, however, may triple those in the first year. The average maintenance costs over a five-year period are likely to be about $20 per month or more. Actual repair costs, of course, will vary with the specific model and your use of the car. The *Consumer Reports Annual Buying Guide* makes current estimates for average maintenance expenses and provides useful information concerning specific problems with various models.

Depreciation. Depreciation is how much resale value a car loses each year. In other words, it is the decrease in the value of an automobile due to time and use. It is an implicit cost of automobile ownership. Many automobile owners ignore depreciation because they do not write a monthly check to pay for it, yet it is one of the largest expenses of automobile ownership. Table 6-3 provides one example of a typical depreciation schedule. It shows that a $15,000 automobile depreciates more than 60% in five years. For example, the owner could sell the car for $8,128 after three years, but after four years he could sell it for only $6,909. In essence, the owner has paid $1,219 to use the car during that year. Notice that with depreciation a one-year-old car is worth $11,250; however, according to Table 6-2, you would still owe approximately $11,796 principal on your loan. If you were to have an accident or decide to trade in your car for a new one, you would owe more to your bank than the insurance payoff or trade-in value.

Depreciation varies considerably across makes and models. New automobiles depreciate much faster than used automobiles; thus, depreciation expenses decrease as automobiles get older. Generally, automobiles lose 25% of their purchase value in the first year and 15% of the remaining value each following year. Models with excellent maintenance and resale records will generally hold their value better than average cars. *Kelley's Blue Book* at *www.kbb.com* and the *NADA Official*

TABLE 6-3
DEPRECIATION SCHEDULE/RESALE VALUE

Automobile Age	Value	% Change	Annual Depreciation
New	$15,000		
One year old	11,250	25	$3,750
Two years old	9,562	15	1,688
Three years old	8,128	15	1,434
Four years old	6,909	15	1,219
Five years old	5,872	15	1,037
Total depreciation (years 0–5)			9,128
Remaining depreciation (years 6–?)			5,872

Used Car Guide at *www.nadaguides.com* are good sources for determining depreciation—providing average resale values by model, make, condition of the vehicle, year, and location. *Kelley's Blue Book* is more liberal in its quotes; therefore, most dealers will utilize the *NADA Official Used Car Guide* when determining the value of a trade-in vehicle.

An often overlooked aspect of depreciation concerns the time during the model year when consumers buy their new car. An automobile bought late in a model year depreciates much more rapidly than the same automobile bought early in that model year. Dealers will typically offer sizable discounts on "old" models to make room for the new models on their lots. Keep this point in mind, especially if you are considering the purchase of last year's model after new car models have been introduced. If you plan to own the car for the entire length of the loan, then buying at the end of the model year may be a wise decision. However, if you plan to sell or trade in the car within a couple of years, then you should be aware of the effects of depreciation on your next car purchase.

Total Expenses

Having allocated your transportation budget and gathered the cost data for owning an automobile, you can now calculate (or estimate) the price of a car that you can afford. For example, assume your monthly transportation budget is $450, based on 15% of a $3,000 pretax income ($0.15 \times \$3,000 = \$450$), you have about $2,500 for initial costs, and you can finance your car at a 10% interest rate for forty-eight months. You have made the following expense estimates for the model you are considering:

Transportation budget	$ 450
Less insurance	– $ 100
Less operation	– $ 60
Less maintenance	– $ 10
Maximum payment	$ 280

This leaves you $280 per month for automobile payments. From Table 6-1, you see that it will cost $25.36 for each $1,000 financed over a forty-eight-month period. You can thus afford to finance $11,041 ([$280 ÷ $25.36] × $1,000 = $11,041).

Initial costs include down payment and tax, title, and registration (which average about $1,000). You can estimate these costs more accurately by calling your local vehicle registration/tax assessor office and asking for a quote. Be sure to ask if military members receive relief form any fees or taxes, as is the case in many locales.

Thus, subtracting $1,000 from your available $2,500, leaves you $1,500 to make a down payment. You could afford a car that retails for about $12,541 ($11,041 + $1,500). Your actual expenses will obviously vary from this example, but as you can see, a $450-a-month transportation budget will not finance a new $30,000 car. Be realistic about how far your limited transportation budget will take you.

DETERMINING WHETHER OR NOT TO BUY A USED CAR

In most cases new cars are much more expensive to own and operate than used cars (when accounting for all costs discussed above). Buying a used car may be more affordable or allow you to set aside more money for your savings plan. If you are unwilling to make a large down payment or a large monthly payment, a used car may be for you. Often a good bet is to buy a used car that is one or two years old. In this case the bulk of the depreciation has already occurred, yet the car mileage (and subsequent wear and tear on the car) is relatively low. Previously leased cars with low mileage may be good candidates for purchase. These cars may also be attractive to buyers who prefer up-to-date models and styling, but otherwise cannot afford the latest models.

There are basic expense trade-offs between new and used cars. Depreciation and insurance are more expensive for newer cars; maintenance is more expensive for older, higher-mileage cars. Consider your maintenance aptitude and your tolerance for car trouble when making this decision. Table 6-4 illustrates these trade-offs, but it does not

---

TABLE 6-4
TYPICAL AUTOMOBILE OPERATING COSTS*

	1st Year	2nd Year	3rd Year	4th Year	5th Year
Depreciation	$3,750	$1,688	$1,434	$1,219	$1,037
Insurance	1,200	1,100	1,000	900	800
Interest costs	1,500	1,125	956	813	691
Operation	720	720	720	720	720
Maintenance	80	110	190	240	280
Total costs	$7,250	$4,743	$4,300	$3,892	$3,528

* Based on a new purchase price of $15,000 and borrowing at 10%.

account for the inconvenience or major repairs that a used car may entail.

If you consider buying a used car, you should compare the costs of new and used cars by constructing a table similar to Table 6-4. Estimate the depreciation and operating costs using the techniques previously described in this chapter. Insurance costs (see chapter 9) will decline as the appraised value of the automobile declines. For these comparisons, annual interest costs should be based on the amount you will owe each year, assuming that you are financing your purchase. The car's market value multiplied by the interest rate is a good proxy for your annual interest cost. For example, if you borrow at 10%, the interest cost for the first year is $1,500 (0.10 × $15,000). The interest cost for the second year is $1,125 (0.10 × $11,250 [$15,000 less $3,750, or 25% depreciation the first year]). To get a more accurate interest cost for each year, you can use a spreadsheet or financial calculator, or contact a bank or other lender.

To estimate the cost of a used car, simply use the column that represents the age of the used car. For the example shown in the table, a three-year-old car would have annual costs of about $4,300. The annual operating expenses for a three-year-old car are 59% ($4,300 ÷ $7,250 = 0.59, or 59%) of those for a similar new car. Differences of this magnitude between the costs of owning new and used cars are typical.

Once you have made calculations to compare the cost of a new versus a used car, you will probably find that on a financial basis, a used car will be less expensive. Consider your budget, preferences, lifestyle, and uses for your car to determine whether the added expense of a new car is worthwhile.

SELECTING THE RIGHT METHOD TO FINANCE YOUR VEHICLE

Once you have decided how much you can afford and whether to purchase a new or used car, the next decision is how to finance your purchase. Most servicemembers have three choices: self-financing (paying cash), borrowing (getting a loan), or leasing. Your choice will depend primarily on your personal financial situation.

You should research financing arrangements before you begin to car shop. Arranging your financing in advance serves three purposes. First, you know the price range that fits your transportation budget. Second, it gives you more control over your purchase decision. You will have a financing alternative rather than being dependent on the financing arrangements offered by the automobile dealer. And third, you will be able to recognize a good deal if the dealer offers one.

Self-Financing

Congratulations if you have saved enough to pay cash for your new car. Even if you plan to pay cash for your car, there is still a financing cost. This financing cost is the opportunity cost of foregone interest. By purchasing the car you are giving up any interest your money would have earned by having the money deposited in a bank. For example, if your money was in an account earning 7.5% interest and your marginal tax rate is 15%, your opportunity cost (financing cost) is 6.375% (0.075 × [1 − 0.15]). Self-financing is an excellent method of buying an automobile; it is very difficult to get a consumer loan at a lower rate of interest than the opportunity cost of your investments. Self-financing is an even better method if you have the discipline to pay yourself back. To do this, you should calculate payments that include both principal and interest. Select a reasonable "loan period" and make monthly payments directly to your savings. With self-financing, it is hard to go wrong.

Car Loans

Many Americans borrow money to pay for their cars. As discussed in chapter 3, car loans are a good use of credit since you repay the debt as you use the asset. Having estimated the amount you will borrow, you must decide the source and duration of the loan. Your decisions in each of these areas will affect your credit costs, both the total interest you will pay and the amount of your monthly payments. Careful evaluation of various sources of auto loans will help you reduce credit costs while making monthly payments that fit your budget. Financing sources often have loan terms that obscure the actual cost of borrowing money. By law, all lenders must provide you with a rate of interest based on a standardized calculation. This rate of interest is the annual percentage rate (APR). The APR is the most useful method of comparing the cost of different loans.

The two primary sources for borrowing money are dealer financing or a third-party loan. Dealer financing is when the car manufacturer lends you money to buy its car. Car dealers often advertise below-market-interest-rate loans or cash-back rebates to attract customers to their products. Timing is often a factor in these promotions. At the end of a model year, dealerships must move the old inventory to make room for the new models. Some American automobile manufacturers have even offered 0% financing and $0 down payment in recent years. Dealer financing can be a good deal, but check with banks or credit unions to see if you can get the same interest rate. If this is possible, you can choose the cash-back rebate from the dealer and finance through a third party for the same low interest rate.

> *Be aware that dealers often are less willing to negotiate prices when they offer attractive financing.*

A third-party loan is when you borrow money from a bank or credit union to buy your car. These institutions are potentially excellent sources from which to secure automobile financing. First, your credit institution should treat you well. Car loans are one of their primary businesses, and they want to maintain good relationships with their customers. Second, it is convenient to have your car loan directly paid from your allotment or direct deposit. Some banks and credit unions offer a discounted loan rate if you have your car payment automatically deducted from your military pay. Third, they are more likely to explain your credit options in detail. Finally, they can provide you with detailed value estimates (wholesale and retail) for both a used car and a new car that you plan to buy. You should apply to your bank or credit union for a loan at least seven days before you begin to shop for your automobile. This allows adequate time to process your loan application and will ensure that the money is ready when you need it.

Loans are also available online. While these often provide attractive options, they can sometimes have hidden costs. For example, an online loan service may distribute your credit information to as many lending institutions as possible and then provide you with the best loans, but this may lower your credit score and put you at greater risk of identity theft. The internet is a good option, but be sure to use reputable sites. Some suggestions are *www.capitalone.com*, *www.eloan.com*, and *www.lendingtree.com*.

Another alternative for homeowners is using a home equity line of credit. Homeowners who have enough equity in their homes can borrow against their equity rather than taking out third-party loans or using dealer financing. The advantage of this financing option is that the interest on this loan may be tax deductible when filing your federal income taxes.

Having decided the source of financing, the next major decision is the term, or duration, of the loan. Most lending institutions finance new cars for up to seventy-two months. Most lenders finance used cars for thirty-six months and occasionally for forty-eight or more months. The trade-off is clear. Longer-term loans have lower monthly payments, but you will *ultimately pay more in interest.* Shorter-term loans have higher monthly payments, but you repay the loan faster, thus paying less in interest.

Consider the following example. You want to borrow $10,000 of your new-car purchase. After shopping around, the best deal you can find is a bank that offers the following loan schedule: thirty-six months at 8%, forty-eight months at 10%, or sixty months at 12%. Your payments under the various terms are shown in Table 6-5.

As you can see, the longer the duration of the loan, the smaller your monthly payments are; but the result is that you pay the bank additional interest for the privilege of stretching out the payments from thirty-six to sixty months.

Another consideration when deciding the loan duration is the value of the car in relationship to the amount owed on the loan. The longer the loan period, the slower the loan is amortized (repaid). Because automobiles depreciate very rapidly when they are new, cars may depreciate faster than a long-term loan is amortized. As a result, it is possible for you to receive less on a trade-in (or from insurance if your car is stolen or destroyed) than the outstanding balance on your loan. In the automobile business this is called being "upside down" or "financially inverted."

For example, assume you borrow $10,000 for forty-eight months at 10% interest to buy an automobile, but you have a wreck after one year

---

TABLE 6-5
FINANCING UNDER VARIOUS LOAN TERMS

Loan Duration

	36 Mo. 8%	48 Mo. 10%	60 Mo. 12%
Monthly payments	$ 313	$ 254	$ 222
Total principal payments	10,000	10,000	10,000
Total interest payments	1,281	2,174	3,347
Total payment to bank	11,281	12,174	13,347

and the car is totaled. On average, the car would have been worth $7,500 after one year, and you could expect the insurance company to pay you that amount. However, the principal balance on the loan would be $7,830.18, so you would have to write the bank a check for $330.18 to clear the loan. If you had financed the car for thirty-six months, the remaining principal would be only $6,992.57. In this case the check from the insurance company would allow you to fully repay the loan and still apply $507.43 toward a new car. The lesson here is that besides costing you less in interest over the period, loans of shorter duration reduce the risk of having the value of your asset fall below the loan principal. You should shop for automobile financing as diligently as you shop for your automobile. If you ignore financing alternatives, you can easily squander the money you saved through careful research of dealer cost information and skillful negotiations.

LEASING

In recent years, leasing an automobile has become an increasingly popular way to meet transportation needs. Leasing can be an attractive option because it allows you to "drive more car for your money." Leasing is similar to renting a car on a long-term basis. Monthly payments are lower than they would be for buying the same car because you are not paying for any equity (the amount of "value" the car has, determined by its selling price minus what is owed on it) in the car. You are paying only for the depreciation you use—since you do not pay the entire depreciation up front—and for the interest on the "loan." Although monthly payments are lower, the disadvantage of leasing is that at the end of the contract you own nothing.

Car manufacturers have been aggressively marketing leases for the last several years. You often see advertisements for "$299 a month with no money down." This is not necessarily the case. The actual check you write to cover a "$299 a month" payment may be more than $450. You will normally pay a security deposit equal to the first and last monthly payments. There could be an additional "acquisition fee" ranging from $250 to $700. You must also pay taxes and title and registration fees either up front or as an addition to your monthly payments. Protect yourself by reading the fine print. Be careful to understand all expenses, *including additional insurance requirements*, before signing a leasing agreement.

Leasing an automobile can be a sound financial choice for some people. Whether or not you are a good lease candidate depends on your car preferences, personal driving habits, and financial situation. A lease candidate is someone who fits the following profile:

- Wants to drive a new car every two to four years.
- Drives less than 12,000 miles per year.
- Wants a smaller monthly payment.
- Takes good care of his or her car.
- Wants to drive a more expensive car than he or she could afford to buy.
- Does not want the hassle of selling or trading in a used car.

Today, lease contracts are closed-ended. Closed-ended leases are those for which you have no financial responsibilities other than scheduled maintenance and monthly payments. At the end of the lease, you return the automobile to the leasing company. Normal wear and tear is acceptable; however, excess mileage and/or wear and tear on the vehicle may be an additional expense to the consumer

Depending on the terms of the lease, you are responsible for all scheduled maintenance during the lease period. Most leases have a stipulation stating the maximum number of miles the lessor allows during the lease period. If you exceed the limit, you must pay a penalty of perhaps 15 cents per mile. When leasing be sure to ask what happens if you are deployed. Leases that offer a "deployment clause," allowing you to terminate the lease prematurely, are more valuable to military members than those that do not have this safeguard.

GETTING THE BEST DEAL
Buying from a Dealer
Do your homework if you plan to buy from an automobile dealer. Know exactly what model and options you want. Research the dealer cost for both the base price of the model and the options you want. Have a financing plan. Shop several dealers so that you are more likely to get a fair deal. Keep in mind that the dealer's price is listed online and that even if you pay the invoice (or what the dealer pays) the dealer will still make money through kickbacks from the manufacturer. These kickbacks are also listed online and the astute buyer will find out what they are and use them while negotiating. Manufacturers' sites sometimes list the kickback; otherwise check *www.smartcarprices.com* or *www.auto.consumerguide.com*.

There are several advantages to buying from a dealer rather than ordering the car from the factory. First, there is very little time delay in getting the car you want. If it is not on their lot, most dealers can locate the car you want and execute a dealer trade within a few days. Second, you can see and thoroughly inspect the actual vehicle that you will be getting. Third, the dealer from whom you buy your automobile is likely to be more responsive to maintenance problems after the sale.

There are a couple of disadvantages to buying from a dealer, however. First, it is very possible that the available car that most closely meets your needs will have undesired, costly options. Second, you need to know which car you want and how much you are willing to pay for it before you start negotiating with a dealer whose goal is to sell his or her existing inventory and make a profit.

You can also factory order a new car from a dealer. Dealers would much rather sell you a car off their lot because they get the profit immediately. An advantage of ordering your new car from a dealer is that you get and pay only for the options you want. A disadvantage is that you will have to wait from four to six weeks for delivery. Also, you cannot inspect the car before you sign a purchase contract.

Negotiation with a Dealer
If you decide to buy your car from a dealer, there are several things of which you must be aware before you see the dealer. From the moment you set foot on the lot or in the showroom, you will undergo a battle of wits and several stages of negotiations with the dealer.

Negotiating with a dealer will be a matter of your personality type. There are any number of books and guides that will help you in developing your negotiating plan. Additionally, there are some things you can do to enhance your position before the negotiations begin. Timing, for example, is a significant indirect negotiating tool.

There are times when dealers are more favorable to making good deals than others. Dealers typically have monthly and quarterly sales targets and frequently have bonuses tied to these targets, making them more likely to negotiate near the end of the period. Dealers are also more likely to make a good deal when business is slow. More customers shop for cars on weekends than during the week; therefore, midweek may be a better time to shop than on weekends. Also, some dealers have a bonus for the first sale made on a weekend, so Saturday morning may be a good time to deal as well. Weather also affects the number of customers. You are more likely to get a good deal when rain or snow keeps most shoppers away, making it an ideal time for the bargain hunter. Automobile dealers are more likely to offer deals during and after the Christmas season for several reasons. There are fewer automobile customers during the holiday season because people are spending money for other things and dealerships are trying to cut year-end inventory for tax purposes. Also, as previously mentioned, summer may be a good time because dealers are trying to clear their inventory of last year's models to make room for the new models that arrive in the fall.

To maximize the best deal for you, consider using a pricing or buying service (discussed below) to determine the actual dealer cost of the car you want and to get a price quote. If a dealer cannot beat the buying service price, you may not be getting the best deal.

Many car dealerships are honest businesses with an ethical sales force. You must watch for the ones that are not. Understand that you are dealing with experienced professionals who are adept at turning your money into dealer profit. Some dealerships train their sales representatives to "pass you off" to another representative or the sales manager if they cannot sell you a car. You will usually negotiate your deal with a salesperson, and then he or she will try to get you into the closing room. There, the closer, whose specialty is writing sales contracts, will write up the deal. Sometimes the closer will intentionally manipulate the cost, trade-in, down payment, and financing numbers to confuse the customer. Customer confusion can equal dealer profit. Once the purchase order is written, the closer will try to add unnecessary, high-profit options—fabric protection, rust proofing, floor mats, dealer warranties, and even insurance. The closer must then present the purchase order to the sales manager for his approval and signature. Passing you off from person to person reduces your resistance to buying and creates confusion. Each person in the process tries to sell you additional options you do not want, change the terms of the deal, and get more money from you. Remember, these professionals have closed hundreds of sales transactions.

The following are some general guidelines that will be helpful if you decide to negotiate your new-car purchase with a dealer:

- Know what model automobile and what options you want, and have your financing prearranged, before you go to a dealer's lot with the intention of buying.
- Let the dealer know you are a serious buyer. You should be ready to buy a car if you get the deal you want. Say to him, "I will buy a car today if you have the car and deal I want."
- If necessary, let the dealer know that you have done your homework. Tell him, "I know your cost for this car." When you confront a dealer with this information, he will often try to tell you that your information is outdated or incorrect. Do not allow him

> *Keep the four major parts of the automobile purchase transaction separate. It is too confusing to discuss your trade-in, down payment, and financing while you are trying to negotiate the purchase price of a new car. Make each an independent transaction: First, negotiate price, then trade-in, and finally the down payment and financing. Tell the salesman, "We can discuss my trade-in and financing when we have agreed on the total sale price."*

to convince you that you are wrong. Your cost estimate will be very close. Besides, you can always buy your new car from the buying service that provided you with the price quote.

- If you do not get the deal you want, tell the dealer that you think you can get a better deal by shopping around. Dealers hate to hear those words. Record the terms of the deal offered on the back of the dealer's business card.
- After you have negotiated a satisfactory deal, do not allow your dealer or another dealer representative to reopen negotiations.
- Make sure that the purchase contract or sales order lists exactly the car and options you want and that it stipulates that no dealer-installed equipment will be substituted for factory-installed options.
- If you order your car from the factory, make sure that the sales contract states in writing that the order is contingent on timely delivery within four to six weeks.
- Do not sign a purchase order or sales contract that has blank spaces. Write "n/a" in blank spaces before signing.
- Do not sign a sales contract or purchase agreement unless you have read every word. Question the dealer on any point that you do not fully understand. Remember, confusion on your part almost certainly means more dealer profit.
- Make sure that the sales manager or an officer of the dealership signs the purchase order or sales contract. Many dealerships will not honor a contract signed only by a sales representative.
- Domestic cars include dealer preparation charges in the basic list price. Dealer preparation charges for imported cars are separate from the list price. Make sure that the purchase order or sales contract is clear if there is a separate charge for dealer

preparation. Watch out for extra dealer preparation charges and for unwanted dealer-installed options. Dealers sometimes charge customers for dealer preparations that they did not perform and attempt to add high-profit, dealer-installed options to purchase orders or sales contracts.

- Make sure your purchase order or sales contract records your deposit. The contract should have a stipulation that the deposit is refundable if the dealership does not meet the terms of the contract.
- If you have a trade-in, be sure that the purchase order or sales contract records its value.
- Any verbal promise from the sales representative must be explicitly written on the purchase order or sales contract if you expect the dealership to honor it.

Using an Automobile Pricing or Buying Service

If, like many Americans, you find the process of buying a new car difficult, expensive, and frustrating, a buying s ervice will reduce the time and energy you spend searching for a car, and perhaps save you a considerable amount of money. Buying services allow you to order exactly the car you want, equipped with only the options you want. You will pay the service a predetermined fee above dealer cost; with some models the fee is a fixed dollar amount, and with others it is a percentage above the dealer cost. There are many buying services such USAA at *www.usaa.com*, Edmunds at *www.Edmunds.com*, or Autobytel at *www.autobytel.com*. In our example we will use a predetermined fee of 1.5% above dealer cost on the base car and options. The result is that you save over $2,000, as calculated below:

If you do not mind negotiating with dealers, then you might investigate an auto pricing service. Most auto pricing services will provide

Dealer cost of base car	$10,646
Dealer cost of options	$1,650
Total wholesale cost	$12,296
1.5% of wholesale cost	$184
Gas, oil, advertising	$100
Freight	$375
Your cost	$12,955

you with detailed cost information on particular models, usually for less than \$10 per model. Normally it takes two to four weeks to process your specific request. Also, they may offer to buy your car for you and to have it delivered to a local participating dealer. The USAA Auto Pricing/Buying Service provides both services, and regional services are available in many areas. Other services are available through the Internet, in which you can "surf" your way through various cars and options. Pricing services are worthwhile if only to estimate accurately the wholesale cost of an automobile to the dealer. This information will help you determine how much you should pay a dealer for a particular car.

7

Paying for College

This chapter is written for parents who are saving for their children's education, but the advice is just as applicable for children who are saving for their own education. Even adults saving for their own education can make use of the advice in this chapter.

Providing for children's college education is one of the greatest financial concerns of American families today. Financial experts debate over who should bear the financial burden for college tuition and the associated costs. Some advocate that children should pay for part or all of their own college expenses to give them a sense of ownership of their education. Others believe that parents should accept responsibility for college expenses in order to prevent their children from starting off their independent lives in debt. Whether or not to pay for college or what percentage of college expenses to cover is a decision that families have to make on their own; however, they should keep a few things in mind when making that decision. First, college expenses are formidable, and there are significant benefits of starting to save for college early in a child's life regardless of whether the parents save money or the child saves his or her own money. Second, the parents' financial assets and income will affect the child's qualification for financial aid even if the parents are not willing to pay tuition. Therefore, it is critical for all parents to have a basic understanding of financial aid qualification calculations.

College planning should consider any means to maximize the use of financial incentives provided by college financial aid programs and government tax laws. As in all investment decisions, parents have to understand the trade-off between the return necessary to finance a college education and the risks necessary to get higher returns. A sound college savings program should therefore consider three crucial factors:

the portfolio risk-return profile (refer to chapter 10), the program's impact on the financial aid process, and the tax structure of the college portfolio. One of the most important lessons of this chapter is that the earlier you start with your plan to provide for college, then the more financially prepared you and your children will be. Even two or three years of failing to contribute to your college savings plan can mean a difference of thousands of dollars for your children's education.

Several factors determine how much you need to save for college. First, college savings should be viewed in the context of your family's other financial goals, such as saving for a house or your own retirement. College is important, but it is a much less significant expense than providing for decades of your own retirement. Second, you should take your current and future financial situation into account. Can you afford to save now, or will you have more significant income in the future? Finally, though the cost of a four-year college education is high and getting higher, you do not have to pay the entire amount yourself. How much will you really need to contribute after taking financial aid into account?

The last two factors will be discussed in this chapter. First, you will learn how to determine how much you really need to save. You will then look at the total cost of a college education and compare it to the financial aid opportunities available. That will serve as the basis for calculating your monthly contributions to your child's college savings plan.

THE COST OF A COLLEGE EDUCATION

The bad news first: College is expensive, and costs continue to rise at about twice the rate of inflation. The components of college costs include tuition and fees, books and supplies, room and board, transportation, and other personal expenses. The College Board, a nonprofit organization that connects students to college opportunities, conducts annual trend analysis of college pricing and tuition inflation rates and posts them on the Web at *www.collegeboard.com/prof/index.html*. For the 2005–6 school year the College Board calculated a total cost of $31,916 for a typical private college and $15,566 for an in-state public college ($23,239 out of state). Using data collected over the last few years, the College Board has identified an average increase in college expenses of 5.5% per year. If costs continue to increase at this rate, a typical four-year private college education will cost over $363,000 dollars in 2023. A typical public college with in-state tuition will cost over $177,000.

To figure the cost of colleges to which your child might apply, find the current annual cost at that college's web page; then use a college cost calculator such as the one found at *www.finaid.org/calculators/costprojector.phtml*. For example, a Harvard education cost $39,880 annually in 2005. Compounded at 5.5% (estimated tuition inflation rate from the College Board research), that same education will cost a total of $418,176 for four years starting in 2023. Using the lump sum and monthly payment calculations in chapter 1, you can estimate your required monthly contributions to meet your college savings plan goals. For instance, if you want to send your newborn to Harvard in eighteen years, but have not yet begun your college savings, you will need to put away $1,175 per month and earn 8% on your savings to cover that cost. Multiply that number by how many children you have, and the figures can become terrifyingly large. A more realistic goal is to be able to pay for half of total college costs. As we will discuss below, government assistance, assistance from the college itself, and private scholarships will assist you in covering some of the college costs.

Financial Aid Opportunities
Now, the good news: Financial aid is defined as economic assistance based on need and is available to most families. It can be provided by the federal or state government or by the college itself. There are two main categories of financial aid: grants and loans. Grants carry no obligation to repay the grantor, while loans must be repaid. Detailed information on federal student aid is found in the annual *Funding Education beyond High School: The Guide to Federal Student Aid* published by the U.S. Department of Education and posted on the Web at *studentaid.ed.gov/students/publications/student_guide/index.html*.

Many states offer grants and subsidized loans to complement federal programs, and parents should be sure to fully explore this option. Contact information for state funded financial aid is available through the National Association of State Student Grant & Aid Programs at *www.nassgap.org/membershipdirectory.aspx*.

Additional financial aid opportunities are provided by many of the colleges which your child might choose. These schools offer financial aid to help alleviate the financial stress on their students and enhance the student college experience. Most colleges will have a financial aid office accessible through their websites. A growing portion of tuition and other expenses is now being covered by financial aid at most universities.

Bottom line: The high cost of college is subsidized by financial aid for most students. At some private institutions, financial aid alleviates up to two thirds of the typical student's college bill.

Determining Financial Aid Needs

Based on your family's financial situation and other variables, colleges will expect you to contribute a certain amount to your child's education. Imagine that your child gets accepted to three different colleges . . .

	College A	College B	College C
Total Annual Cost	$10,000	$25,000	$40,000
Parental Contribution	$10,000	$10,000	$10,000
Student Contribution	$ 1,800	$ 1,800	$ 1,800
*Self Help (loan/job)	$ 3,000	$ 3,000	$ 3,000
*Total Need (College View)	$ 0	$10,200	$15,200

* Some colleges will expect students to take out loans and/or work during their years at college, to cover some of the costs, when considering total need.

The amount of financial aid you might be offered is based on your total need. Federal and state financial aid agencies will take into account parent and student contribution capabilities to determine need. If your child is able to get into each of these three colleges, then you would receive no financial aid at College A, but $15,200 at College C. Notice that the costs of College B and C are identical after financial aid is considered, $14,800. Thus, though total college expenses are important to know, the relevant figure for planning a college savings program is the Expected Family Contribution (EFC). That is the best estimate of the amount a family needs to save for college costs.

The EFC is determined in one of two ways: the *Federal Methodology*, used by federal processors and school financial aid administrators, or the *Institutional Methodology*, used by many private colleges and universities. While the two methods use similar factors to determine eligibility, you should find out the exact rules (such as the expectation for students to work to pay for a portion of college expenses) used by the schools you are considering at least one year before your child will enter college.

You can calculate your Expected Family Contribution given your family's particular situation at a number of different Internet sites. Good examples are *apps.collegeboard.com/fincalc/efc_welcome.jsp* provided by the College Board and FinAid's *www.finaid.org/calculators/finaidestimate.phtml*. Even if your children are younger, the calculator will give you some idea of how much you should expect to pay for college. To do so, answer the calculator's questions as if your child was starting college next year and describe what you think your financial situation will be when your child starts college. This means you will have to estimate future income, savings, value of assets, and income tax information in order to enter this data in the calculator. Do not forget to factor in the effects of inflation. After you complete the calculator, be sure to multiply the annual result by four years. The result is the amount you will be expected to pay for your child's college education in the future.

If you do not have the patience to work through an online EFC calculator, consider some of the key factors upon which these calculators are built and on which colleges base their aid decisions. Both methodologies consider the parents' after-tax income and readily available savings. Approximately one third of parental income is added to the EFC per year and up to 5.5% of parental assets. Parental assets under the *Federal Methodology* do not include such items as insurance policies, individual retirement accounts and 401(k)s, or home equity; however, the Institutional Methodology will include home equity. EFC calculations also consider any after-tax income that the child generates as well as readily available savings which are titled in the child's name, such as trust accounts. Plan to add half of the child's taxable income and up to 35% of his or her assets per year. Family size and number of children enrolled in college in a given year along with demographic information, such as the family structure (single- or dual-parent home) or special expenses such as a family's obligation to care for handicapped children are considered. Bottom line: Current income has a greater influence over EFC than saving, and students are expected to furnish a much larger amount of their income and savings toward the cost of college than their parents. Of course individual colleges can modify their formulas for calculating EFC.

As mentioned at the beginning of this chapter, even if parents do not pay for their children to go to college, the parents' financial assets and income are taken into consideration when calculating a student's financial aid qualifications. Simply not claiming a child as a dependent on tax forms is no longer compelling enough to allow students to claim to be independent of their parents' support when applying for financial aid. The current qualifications to be considered independent are as follows:

- The student must be twenty-four years or older by the end of the year financial aid is awarded; or
- The student is an orphan or ward of the court until age eighteen; or
- The student is a graduate student or U.S. military veteran; or
- The student is married or has legal dependants other than a spouse.

Financial Aid Mistakes

While financial aid is an important consideration in meeting the funding challenge, parents should caution themselves against some common financial aid mistakes.

- *The Expected Family Contribution (EFC) rules will vary.* Do not assume that the EFC is the exact amount you will be expected to pay. Often you will be asked to pay more or less depending on the school's financial condition or admissions policies.
- *Focusing too much on the financial aid rules.* As with any system, the rules governing financial aid may change. Parents should guard against trying to arrange their finances to maximize financial aid at the cost of sound financial decisions. Financial aid eligibility is an important consideration, but not a central one. Furthermore, many colleges are more willing to accept full-paying students than students they will have to support with financial aid.
- *Focusing on the zero tuition option, while failing to shop for value.* Parents and students should remember that college is a once-in-a-lifetime value decision. The lower-cost college, whose tuition drops to zero after financial aid, is not necessarily a better value than the higher cost college whose tuition is reduced to an affordable (though still costly) level. Parents and students should shop around to compare and select the school that offers the best value for the price, yet still accommodates the preferences and ability of the student.
- *Remember: "No" is not final.* Parents with college-age children likely have many friends who can tell tales of negotiating with schools for better aid packages than the initial estimates indicated. Parents and students should actively seek out opportunities to maximize their financial aid package.

Applying for Financial Aid

When your child applies to colleges, pay close attention to the financial aid information provided with the admissions packet, and be sure to submit the appropriate documents required by each school, even if you do not think you qualify. You may be pleasantly surprised to discover that you meet the criteria for a variety of subsidized loan programs. Often, schools will require you to submit both the Free Application for Federal Student Aid (FAFSA) with the Department of Education and the PROFILE Application with the College Scholarship Service. The FAFSA can be submitted between January 1 of the year prior to entering college up until June 30 of the year entering college. The PROFILE Application should be submitted between January 1 and February 1 of the year your child plans to enter college. Both forms should be available from your child's high school counselor, financial aid offices at the colleges to which your child is applying, and online. The FAFSA can be found at *www.fafsa.ed.gov/*, and the PROFILE Application is at *profileonline.cbreston.org/*. Much of the information needed for the FAFSA is found on the family's income tax forms so you must have them available.

DEVELOPING A COLLEGE SAVINGS PLAN

Earlier this chapter we explained the costs of attending college and how financial aid can reduce college expenses. The first step to developing a college savings plan is to estimate the cost of college for each of your children. Then, calculate your Expected Family Contribution toward that cost for each child. Your college savings goal should be whichever is less: your Expected Family Contribution or your estimate of the cost of college. If the cost of college is greater that the Expected Family Contribution, you can reasonably expect to receive financial aid to cover the difference, whether in the form of direct grants or subsidized loans. Once you have determined a college-savings goal, you must decide how to invest those college-savings dollars.

Does it matter how old my children are?

Chapters 10 and 11 explain general investment strategies that apply to all types of short-, medium-, and long-term goals. Saving for college tuition is just another financial goal. Your investment decisions will be based on your risk tolerance; the longer your time horizon the greater risk you can afford. Therefore if you start saving for college shortly after your child's birth, the eighteen-year time horizon allows you to take greater risk and create a portfolio heavily focused in equities (stocks), which historically have provided a greater rate of return. As time nears for your child to enter college, you will want to adjust the asset allocation for your child's savings plan to more of a fixed-income (bonds) portfolio to provide greater security for your savings. Once your child is in college you will want to move investments to more liquid and risk-free assets such as money market accounts and cash in order to have the flexibility to quickly withdraw money for necessary expenditure.

The Effects of a College Savings Plan on Financial Aid

If you completed the Expected Family Contribution calculations discussed in the first part of this chapter, you realize that anything you manage to save for college will increase your EFC per year by 5.5% of your savings and 35% of your child's savings. In other words, every $100,000 you save in your name for college will increase your EFC by almost $22,000 over four years. If you save that $100,000 in your child's name, your EFC will increase by $140,000 over four years. To compensate for this effect, you should rerun the EFC calculator, but be sure to include your—and your child's—expected college savings. Doing this might cause you to increase your college savings goal because your EFC has increased. There are three additional points you should bear in mind when developing your college savings plan.

First, parents should exercise care in the amount of assets they place in their child's name. Student-owned assets more rapidly lower eligibility for financial aid than assets placed in the parents' names.

Second, family savings in the form of Thrift Savings Plan (TSP) and Individual Retirement Accounts (IRAs), employer sponsored retirement savings plans (such as 401(k) accounts), and home equity (using the *Federal Methodology*) are not part of the financial aid consideration and therefore do not increase your EFC. These sources can themselves be important vehicles against which families may borrow to finance college tuition. Consequently, families should place the priority on funding these savings vehicles above all others, as their limited impact on the financial aid calculation makes these already attractive savings vehicles even better.

Third, if a child has significant expenses during the year before he or she applies to college (such as summer camps, orthodontic work, or a cross-country trip to visit colleges), parents should carefully consider how they fund those expenses. If the parents have a choice to take money from their own savings or from the child's trust account (other types of accounts are discussed later in this chapter), they should choose to spend the child's money to reduce the expected family contribution to college. This expense shifting is legal since the parent is the trustee of the account until the child is twenty-one and the expenditure is clearly for the benefit of the child.

Taking Advantage of the Tax Laws to Accelerate College Savings

UGMA/UTMA Accounts. The federal government has established two types of tax-favored trust accounts in which parents may accumulate funds designated for their child's college education. These accounts are commonly referred to as UGMA (Uniform Gifts to Minors Account) and UTMA (Uniform Transfers to Minors Account). Both of these vehicles represent a low-cost, tax-advantaged means of saving for a child's college education.

UGMA/UTMA accounts offer the same tax treatment and differ only in the type of asset that can be in the account. UTMA accounts allow parents to deposit any assets for the benefit of minors; UGMA may hold only cash or securities. Parents may establish these accounts through a bank or mutual fund, and they usually designate themselves as the trustee.

The advantage of either account is that a portion of the account's unearned income (interest and dividends) is taxed at a lower rate than the parents' income. For accounts of children under fourteen during tax year 2005, the first $800 unearned income generated by the assets in an UGMA/UTMA is tax-free, while the next $800 of unearned income is taxed at the child's marginal tax rate (usually 10%). All unearned income in excess of $1,600 is taxed at the parent's marginal tax rate. UGMA/UTMA accounts belonging to children over fourteen are taxed at the child's marginal tax rate, with an $800 standard deduction. These thresholds are adjusted for inflation annually. For the most current limits see IRS Publication 929 at *www.irs.gov/formspubs/ lists/0,,id=97819,00.html.*

The UGMA/UTMA provisions represent rather sizable tax savings for parents in higher tax brackets. For instance, a parent in the 25% tax bracket would pay a 25% tax of $350 on $1,400 of dividends and interest generated in an ordinary account. Assuming the child was under 14 and in the 10% tax bracket, the same $1400 in dividends in a UGMA would be assessed a tax of $60 ($1,400 minus the $800 deduction taxed at the 10% tax rate), a savings of $290. While this may not sound like a large amount, if the $290 is invested each year and earns just 7%, after taxes, it will provide an additional $10,840 in eighteen years. That will come in handy at tuition time.

Obviously, the tax advantages of UGMA/UTMA accounts come early in the child's life, so parents wishing to receive the full benefits of the account must establish them. Also, the greatest tax savings come for parents in higher tax brackets. Parents in lower tax brackets will receive less benefit from UGMA/UTMA accounts. However, these accounts are important tools, especially for dual-career couples who might find themselves in higher tax brackets.

The major disadvantage of the UGMA/UTMA is that assets transferred to these accounts are an irrevocable gift which can be spent only for the benefit of the child before age twenty-one and belongs completely to the child at age twenty-one. Parents having any doubts about their child's financial discipline should consider carefully the wisdom of establishing UGMA/UTMA accounts. Also, parents might find themselves irrevocably giving assets to a child who might be able to secure financial aid or scholarships on his or her own. Parents could find that they have transferred assets to one of their children that they more urgently need for another child's college fund or that they could have invested in their retirement portfolio. The Coverdell Education Savings Account (CESA), covered later in this chapter, allows for transfer of assets from one child's savings account to the other and may be a better option than the UGMA/UTMA because of its additional flexibility. CESAs and State sponsored Qualified Tuition Plans (QTPs), covered below, receive tax benefits and are considered parents' assets and therefore do not increase EFC as severely.

U.S. Savings Bonds. Some parents use series EE Savings Bonds as a partial way to fund their children's college education. The good news is that interest earned when redeeming Series EE bonds bought after 1989 is tax exempt if higher-education costs in the redemption year exceed principal and interest received. U.S. Savings Bonds are a safe form of investment offering a predictable rate of return further enhanced by the tax free provision. EE bonds are guaranteed to double in value from their issue price no later than twenty years after their issue dates. If the fixed rate on the bond does not double the value by twenty years the Treasury will make a one-time adjustment. This means that EE bonds will guarantee at least a 3.5% average return over the twenty years. However, parents might find that the 3.5% average rate of return on these bonds is lower than that desired to build a sufficient college fund. (The details of purchase, redemption, and interest payments on bonds are discussed in chapter 11.) Savings bonds are available in electronic and paper form. Electronic EE bonds can be purchased directly from the Treasury Department by opening a TreasuryDirect online account at *www.treasurydirect.gov*. Paper savings bonds can be purchased through a financial institution.

It is important to note the restrictions on the use of these bonds to ensure that the interest is tax free. The bonds must be registered in the name of someone at least twenty-four when the original purchase is made. This person is considered the owner of the bond. College costs must be for the bond owner or the owner's spouse or dependent. (Note: These bonds can be bought by anyone, but must be registered as explained above.) Tuition and fees, but not room and board, are considered eligible costs. Costs offset by scholarships and financial aid are not eligible either. Also, if married, the owner will have to file a joint tax return in the redemption year, and the tax benefit is only available to people who meet certain income restrictions in the year the bond is redeemed. In 2005 the tax benefits for these bonds were phased out for married couples with a combined taxable income greater than $91,750 or single head-of-household taxable income greater than $60,750. Refer to IRS Publication 550, IRS Form 8815, and IRS Form 8818 to find the most up-to-date information on tax exemption for college tuition and fees.

What is more important is that you must decide whether the safe, conservative investment in savings bonds will yield enough return to provide the income you will need to finance your children's college education. Military families may put some of their college fund into tax advantaged savings bonds, but most families will have a sizable portion of their children's college fund in stocks or mutual funds that invest in stocks.

Coverdell Education Savings Account. The Coverdell ESA (CESA) allows you to save for tuition expenses in a nondeductible account, and then withdraw your earnings tax-free when used on qualified education expenses (QEEs) at an eligible education institution. Qualified expenses include tuition, fees, books, supplies, equipment required for enrollment or attendance, and certain room and board costs. CESAs can also be used to pay for public, private, and religious—elementary and secondary—school expenses (see publication 970, Tax Benefits for Education found on the Web at *www.irs.gov/publications/p970/index.html* for specifics on QEEs). The limit on contributions to education CESAs is

$2,000 per year per child until the child is eighteen. This limit is reduced for joint tax filers with over $190,000 in adjusted gross income, and those filers with over $220,000 in income may not contribute at all—not an issue for most servicemembers. CESAs can be opened by anyone for your child, but combined contributions cannot exceed the $2,000 cap per year per child. In January 2004 there were several significant changes to treatment of the CESA that will benefit parents and children using the CESA for college savings. First you can now fund both a CESA and a 529 plan (see below) in the same year. A child can also use the CESA distributions to pay for college expenses tax free at the same time that the parent is claiming education tax credits (which will be addressed at the end of this chapter) as long as they are not used for the same expenses. A very important change is that assets from one child's CESA can be rolled over into another child's CESA. This is beneficial for parents who would like to keep balances equitable for their children because it gives parents the flexibility to move assets from one child's account to another child who may have less access to financial aid. Situations where this could occur are when there are differences in the cost of the college education expenses for your children and differences in parents' income or assets at the time each child is applying for financial aid. Finally, if the CESA is owned by a parent, it is considered a parental asset. As you remember from the previous discussion on determining expected family contributions (EFC) for financial assistance calculations, families are expected to contribute only 5.5% of parental assets—but 35% of the child's assets. These changes to the rules of the CESA make it one of the most attractive option for saving for college expenses.

　　Roth IRAs. Roth IRAs allow you to save for retirement expenses in a nondeductible account, then withdraw your earnings tax-free. Contributions are capped at $4,000 in 2006 and 2007, and $5,000 in 2008. These contributions may be withdrawn tax- and penalty-free to fund education expenses. Furthermore, such contributions are not considered in the EFC calculations, so they do not reduce your eligibility for financial aid. However, once retirement assets are withdrawn to fund education, they cannot be returned to the Roth IRA. This method of funding college expenses would make sense only if you had substantially met your retirement savings goals in another type of tax-advantaged retirement account, such as the TSP or 401(k). Remember, it is better for your child to have some student loans than to have to support you financially in your retirement years. A child who has earned income can also start an IRA, but these IRA contributions can be funded with gifts or inheritance instead of actually using the child's earned income. Withdrawals from the child's IRA could also be used one time, tax- and penalty-free, to fund education expenses; however, an IRA will count as the child's asset for EFC calculations.

State-Sponsored Qualified Tuition Plans (529 Plans). There are two types of QTP 529 plans (so called after section 529 of the Internal Revenue Code): prepaid programs and savings programs. Every state offers at least one of the two types. Eligible educational institutions also offer QTPs. The benefit of QTPs is that distributions used to fund qualified education expenses (QEEs) at accredited colleges and universities nationwide (which are not limited to the state that sponsors the plan) are nontaxable. State program information can be found at *www.collegesavings.org* and at *www.savingforcollege.com.*

States and educational institutions will limit either your total contributions to their 529 plans or the balances held in those accounts. The general rule is that QTP contributions are limited to the amount necessary to provide for QEEs. Once you establish a QTP, the state and educational institution-hired securities firms will manage the QTP; although they will offer a variety of investment options, this means that there will be limitations to the control you as the beneficiary or contributor have over the investment of the funds within their QTP. Many state plans are exempt from state taxes for their residents, so it pays to investigate your own state's offering before shopping for plans in other states. Many plans automatically adjust your 529's asset mix as your child approaches college age, which may cost a bit more in fees but relieves you from worrying about reallocating the risk of your child's college savings. The 529 plans are not limited by the gift tax, which generally permits tax-free gifts of up to $12,000 per year in 2006. Instead, the unique feature of the 529 plan is that in 2006 you can contribute a maximum of $60,000, or $120,000 per couple, per beneficiary in a single year without incurring a federal gift-tax impact. That is five times the annual gift-tax exclusion. This large contribution is possible because you are allowed to prorate the gift over five years to avoid triggering the gift tax.

There are several other unique attributes of a QTP that may make it more attractive as a college savings choice. QTPs have no adjusted gross income phaseout so even high-income taxpayers can take advantage of QTP benefits. A single beneficiary can have both a QTP and CESA (though the tax benefits on distributions are still restricted to those that pay for qualifying educations expenses). QTPs, like CESAs, also allow for rollover of distributions from one beneficiary to another related family member. As discussed earlier, this allows parents to provide equity in their children's savings plans or to move assets from one child to another based on EFC. Finally, there are thousands of companies that support 529 college savings plans by offering kickbacks to your 529 account on a portion of your purchases from them. This is done through a nonprofit organization, Upromise at *www.lty.s.upromise.com/8299.0.do*. There are tens of thousands of stores, thousands of restaurants, and hundreds of online retailers participating in the Upromise program, with more joining all the time. It may be worthwhile to fill out the free application in order to accelerate your 529 savings.

ADDITIONAL OPTIONS TO FUND A GAP IN COLLEGE SAVINGS

The goal of your college savings program is to pay for the expected costs of sending your children to college. You should maximize your return commensurate with risk while considering tax implications and any adverse impacts on the financial aid decision. In the end, even the most carefully planned savings program may not yield enough funds to cover your college costs. This is the case for most families who must then face the fact that they will have to bear a large share of college funding themselves. This final section will touch on some vehicles which families may use to help finance college costs.

Gifts. Grandparents and relatives are important sources of funding, especially in the early years of a child's life. Often, it is the grandparents who have the most to gain from the tax advantages of UGMA/UTMA provisions, as they may be in higher tax brackets during the early years of their grandchild's life. *Recognize, however, that gifts to the student will reduce the level of financial aid available much more than gifts to the parents.*

Merit Scholarships. Parents should not overlook the scholarship opportunities that their child's inherent talents might bring them. Scholarships range from partial- to full-tuition awards for scholastic, athletic, or artistic merit. Often, schools will not include scholarship awards in their financial aid calculations. Scholarship search services are available through the College Board website at *www.collegeboard .com/pay*. The Princeton Review also offers free scholarship search at *www.princetonreview.com/college/finance/*. Parents should be cautious when using the services that search for scholarships for a fee. There are many scams out there; check with the Better Business Bureau to verify the legitimacy of such agencies.

Military Scholarships. A unique opportunity for children of parents in the armed forces is that they are eligible for many military specific scholarships. Scholarship information is available online at

- *www.moaa.org/mygroup/mygroup_gr/serv_education/serv_education_new_students/serv_education_scholarships_application_letter.htm*
- *edu.military.com/education/scholarship/ScholashipSearch.jsp*

Financing College with Current Income (Working). In addition, parents should not overlook the option of financing a part of college tuition from family monthly income, as many parents will find themselves still working during their child's college years. The financial burden of paying college costs with current income can be alleviated by claiming various tax credits and deductions. The Hope and Life-Long Learning Credit and the tuition and fees deductions can be almost as beneficial as a grant since they can provide a great savings on tax "costs." Information on these tax considerations can be found on the Internet at *www.nysscpa.org/cpajournal/2004/604/images/p44.pdf*.

Parents should also consider the option of having their children bear some expenses with student jobs while in college. Many universities will expect students to work when they calculate your Expected Family Contribution, including their forecast of your student's future wages in your EFC.

Financing College with Future Income (Borrowing). Tuition costs, either full or partial, may be financed through loans against their family's net worth. Subsidized student loans such as those mentioned earlier are one important source of funding. Parents may also find that years of mortgage payments have built an important source of equity against which banks will provide loans at very favorable rates. The interest on these home equity loans will be tax deductible. Many employers will also allow employees to borrow against the assets of their 401(k)s or employer-sponsored savings plans.

However, families should be careful about sacrificing the benefits of tax-deferred accounts to fund college costs if alternatives exist. Liquidation of traditional IRA and tax-deferred retirement accounts can trigger tax penalties of 10% over normal income taxes. There is a possibility that withdrawals may be exempt from the 10% additional penalties if the withdrawals are not greater than qualified educational expenses (QEEs). See IRS publication 590 for specific information on

QEEs at *www.irs.ustreas.gov/pub/irs-pdf/p590.pdf*. To avoid the possible tax penalties, a better option for parents, particularly older ones, may be to finance college tuition through loans; this will defer the final loan repayment until age 59.5, when they can begin drawing from IRA accounts and avoid early distribution penalties. Parents will also find that their retirement accounts hold significantly more assets, having been afforded the opportunity to allow longer tax-deferred growth.

There are also potential tax savings from children taking out student loans. A person with a student loan may deduct the interest that is paid (up to $2,500 a year) if modified adjusted gross income is less that $65,000 for a single person or $130,000 for married couples filing jointly. The deduction can be taken for the life of the loan. Those with student loans can also save on interest payments after they start repaying student loans. Many lenders will reward on-time payments with a 2% point reduction in interest rates after forty-eight consecutive on-time payments.

The Military Alternative. Students should consider the merits of military service as a source of college funds. All military services offer Reserve Officer Training Corps (ROTC) scholarships, which may pay for one or more years of schooling. These scholarships are available at hundreds of colleges and provide money based on merit to pay for tuition, books, and fees. A monthly stipend, currently $500 for seniors, helps defray other costs. Service obligations vary in length, with longer service required for more generous scholarship awards. Service may be performed in either the active, reserve, or National Guard components. See *www.goarmy.com/rotc/* for more information.

Students should also consider the merits of a military academy education, which is tuition free to the student, but carries a five-year active-duty service obligation. To explore this option, contact the admissions offices at the various academies: *www.usma.edu* (The United States Military Academy), *www.usna.edu* (The United States Naval Academy), *www.usafa.af.mil* (The United States Air Force Academy), *www.cga.edu* (The United States Coast Guard Academy), and *www.usmma.edu* (The United States Merchant Marine Academy).

Finally, some students might wish to consider enlisting in the armed services. Enlisted servicemembers can participate in the Montgomery GI Bill program that provides up to thirty-six months of educational benefits for college. See *www.gibill.com/gibill.cfm* for more details. In addition to earning money for college after your term of enlistment expires, servicemembers can also go to college while serving, and the armed services will pay 75% of the tuition for approved courses. Furthermore, many states now offer free in-state tuition to those who enlist in their National Guard or reserve units.

The Army also runs a new education portal on the Internet called Army University Access Online (*www.eARMYu.com*). At no cost, the enlisted soldier can work toward a degree online from a network of over twenty-eight participating universities offering over 148 degrees or certificate programs. The soldier receives a technology package to support his or her studies as well, also free of charge. This package includes a laptop computer, printer, and Internet access. The Navy and the Air Force also offer distance learning capabilities for sailors, marines, and their dependents. Information on Navy and Air Force sponsored education opportunities can be found at *www.navyadvancement.com/navy-store/navy-college-education.php* and *www.nu.edu/Admissions/Military Admissions/USAirForce.html* respectively.

8

Meeting Medical Expenses

Every year American families incur medical expenses. These expenses range in price and predictability from low-cost, health-maintenance office visits to high-cost, major medical procedures that require exotic equipment and highly skilled medical professionals. Somehow, of course, the bills for these medical services must be paid. If the only medical services used were the routine, low-cost office visits, families would budget for these as they do their grocery or telephone bills, and this chapter would not be necessary. If the rare, high-cost major medical procedures were not life-threatening, families could postpone the purchase of the service or save for it as they do for a home or college expenses. It is the urgent nature of the high-cost, life-threatening medical procedures that necessitates a chapter on the issue of medical expenses.

There is a possibility that a family will face a significant life-threatening medical procedure in any given year. The high-cost nature of this expense typically cannot be paid out of pocket by any but the wealthiest Americans. Since this type of unfortunate event will happen unexpectedly, it is very difficult to budget for it. When families face the risk of large unexpected medical expenses, they will often choose to purchase an insurance policy to protect themselves. This chapter will discuss the basics of health insurance and then examine the particulars of TRICARE, the health insurance program available to military families.

HEALTH INSURANCE

Almost all health insurance plans purchased by American families have two parts to them. The first part is a health-maintenance contract. This is like a service contract you would buy for your car or any complicated piece of equipment; it covers the expenses associated with routine health maintenance office visits like checkups, immunizations, and common ailment treatments. The second part is an insurance policy, comparable to the accident insurance you would have on your car or the fire insurance you would have on your house. This insurance policy covers the risk of rare life-threatening major medical procedures.

A typical health insurance plan would cost an American family between $7,000 and $15,000 a year in premiums, based on the extent of the policy's coverage. However, the American family will often have a large portion of that health insurance premium covered by an employer as part of an overall employment compensation package. As a general rule, employer-provided health insurance is paid only partially by the employer. For example, the employer pays a certain amount, say $6,000 of the employee's health insurance plan premium. The employee then pays a monthly enrollment fee (for instance, $250 each month) for a particular plan. In this example, the employer is giving the employee a chance to buy a $9,000 health insurance plan for $3,000. Since there is no way for the employee to recover the $6,000 benefit offered by the employer except through participation in the company's health plan, the employee will usually enroll in the health plan.

As a general rule, health insurance plans do not pay all of an enrollee's medical bills. There are certain medical treatments that are not included in the health insurance coverage, called *exclusions*. For these treatments, the enrollee must pay the whole bill. Elective cosmetic surgery usually fits into this category.

Even if a medical treatment is not excluded, you will find certain payments that you are required to make. The first of these required payments is called the *deductible*. Most insurance policies do not start paying until you have paid some set amount. For example, if you have a deductible of $1,000, then your insurance company will not start paying your medical expenses until you have paid for the first $1,000 of your covered medical expenses.

The second of these required payments is called *co-insurance*. After the deductible is paid, the health insurance company may pay only a portion of the bill for a medical procedure. For example, they may only pay 80% of the bill leaving you responsible for the remaining 20%.

The third of these required payments is called *co-payment*. The co-payment is a flat fee that the insurance company requires you to pay for a medical service provided. An example of this is a required $10 payment for each doctor's office visit you make.

Most health insurance plans place an annual limit on the combined totals of your deductibles, co-insurance costs, and co-payments. This limit is called your *out-of-pocket maximum*. If you have paid a $10,000 annual out-of-pocket maximum, your health insurance plan will cover 100% of all other non-excluded medical treatments that year.

Your health insurance plan protects itself as well with a *maximum dollar limit*. The maximum dollar limit is the most a health insurance plan will pay per covered person in a prescribed time period. For example, the health insurance plan will not pay more than $10,000,000 for any covered person in his or her lifetime. The maximum dollar limit may be for a particular medical procedure. For example, the health insurance plan may not pay more than $1,000 per year for chiropractic treatments.

Types of Health Insurance Plans

There are three basic types of health insurance plans in which you can enroll. They differ in the flexibility and ease with which an enrollee can determine his or her health care treatment. The basic health insurance plans are defined below from most to least flexible:

1. Preferred Provider Organization Plans or PPOs. A PPO is a group of health care providers such as physicians, clinics, hospitals, and labs that are organized by the health insurance company. This group agrees to provide medical services to those insured by the company as outlined by the PPO's medical practice policy and for the PPO's fee schedule. This group of health care providers is called the network.

   The PPO encourages enrollees to use the network of health-care providers by charging smaller co-insurance costs for medical procedures performed by network health care providers than for medical procedures provided by out-of-network providers. It is important to stress that an enrollee in a PPO does have access to out-of-network health-care providers if the enrollee is willing to pay higher out-of-pocket expenses.

2. Point-of-Service Plans or POSs. A POS is similar to a PPO in that there is a network of health care providers that agree to provide medical services according to the POS's medical practice policy and fee schedule. In a POS plan you choose a primary caregiver who acts as a gatekeeper for all specialized medical

treatments you need. If you need a specialized medical treatment, you first go to your primary caregiver. Your primary caregiver evaluates your need for the specialized medical treatment and then writes a permission slip (a referral) for you to seek out the specialized treatment. Your primary caregiver usually selects a specialist from within your POS network.

If you want to have an out-of-network specialist, you can do so, but like the PPO, it comes at a price, usually in the form of higher co-insurance. Often you are responsible for the initial payment of the out-of-network bill, and you then will be reimbursed after you file a claim.

3. Health Maintenance Organization Plans or HMOs. An HMO is a health insurance company that owns clinics and labs, and also hires physicians and health-care providers to cover the needs of their enrollees. The enrollee selects a physician as a primary caregiver (as done in the POS plan) who then refers the enrollee to HMO specialists as the need arises. Only in rare occasions does an enrollee get medical treatment outside the HMO system. An HMO can be inconvenient for frequent travelers or those living great distances from the HMO's facilities.

As a general rule, a health insurance plan, whether it is a PPO, a POS or an HMO will have a prescription drug plan as well. These plans work in two ways. First a prescription drug plan may have preferred drugs. These are drugs that your health insurance provider can get at a discount through volume purchases, and these discounts are passed on to the enrollee. In addition your premium entitles you to a subsidy on the prescription drugs you purchase. You may only pay 50% of the price the pharmacy charges, while your insurance provider pays the rest.

Health Savings Accounts
Remember that health insurance plans provide essentially two services. The first is a health maintenance contract. This contract covers routine, very predictable, and low-price medical services. For the most part, American families can anticipate and budget for these medical expenses. In addition, most are not urgent and can be postponed if the family budget does not allow the expense at a particular point in time. The routine nature of these medical expenditures allows the health insurance provider to anticipate the amount an average insured family

will spend on these medical procedures. Health insurance premiums will directly reflect these average expenditures. For example, if the average insured family spends $6,000 a year on health-maintenance procedures, your health insurance premiums will include this $6,000 to cover the expected health-maintenance contract costs.

The second amount of the premium that you pay is for your insurance against the risk of unexpected medical procedures. If you have a health insurance plan whose premium is $9,000 annually, and $6,000 of that premium is for the health maintenance contract portion of your plan, then only $3,000 is being spent to cover the risk of unexpected, costly medical procedures.

A way to make a health insurance plan more affordable is to reduce or remove the health maintenance contract portion of the plan, leaving only the medical insurance portion of the plan. This is usually achieved by increasing the deductible and co-payments that the enrollee is required to pay. Since the increased out-of-pocket expenses are routine and predictable, the enrollee can budget and pay for these expenses in the same way as they would any other recurring bill.

To make paying routine medical expenses easier and to capture the tax advantages that employer-provided health-care plans have, the congress introduced Health Saving Accounts or HSAs. These HSAs are tax savings accounts dedicated solely to paying medical expenses. The money deposited into these accounts is tax deductible and the interest earned in these accounts is tax free. An HSA must be paired with a high deductible health insurance plan with a minimum deductible of $1,000 for single coverage and $2,000 for family coverage. In addition, the health insurance policy's out-of-pocket expenses cannot be more than $5,000 for individuals and $10,000 for families. After the age of sixty-five, money from the HSA can be withdrawn for any reason.

If your family has routine health care expenses that are lower than the average insured family's routine health care expenses, then reducing your contribution to the health-maintenance portion of your medical insurance plan, putting money into an HSA, and paying your routine health-care expenses out-of-pocket can save you money. These savings can accrue in your HSA until retirement at age sixty-five, where they become available for any use.

MILITARY HEALTH-CARE BENEFITS: TRICARE
The TRICARE system is a Department of Defense–wide program combining the assets of military treatment facilities (MTFs), and supplemented by civilian health-care providers from the surrounding com-

munities. The DoD, in an attempt to reduce medical costs and improve the quality of and access to care, adopted the same philosophy as many large companies—provide health care to servicemembers and their dependents through an HMO.

> ***TRICARE is similar in many aspects to a civilian HMO.***

TRICARE is a regionally managed health care program for active-duty servicemembers and their families, as well as retired members and their families. To ensure that there are enough health-care providers for all of its beneficiaries, the military has created four health-care networks based on geographic regions to supplement the care provided by military treatment facilities. Additionally, all military hospitals have been realigned into these four geographic regions (see Figure 8-1), with each TRICARE region having a major medical center for major surgeries as well as several regional hospitals providing specialized medical care. This means that both servicemembers and their families may have to travel to receive certain medical treatments.

TRICARE is not one large network. It is actually several separate networks that are independent of one another. You are authorized to enroll your family in the regional network where you are stationed.

The TRICARE program offers three options for all beneficiaries except active-duty servicemembers. Active-duty servicemembers are automatically enrolled in the TRICARE Prime option during in-processing, and other beneficiaries are considered to be in TRICARE Standard and Extra, unless voluntarily enrolled in TRICARE Prime.

Figure 8-1
TRICARE Regions

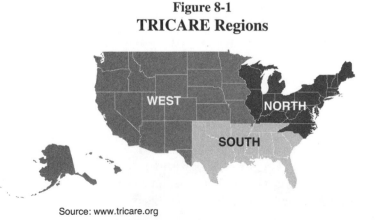

Source: www.tricare.org

1. *Option 1: TRICARE Prime.* This is the managed-care network option. If you enroll in this option, you will receive the majority of your care in the MTFs. In return for giving up your choice of doctors, the cost of receiving medical treatment is reduced.
2. *Option 2: TRICARE Standard.* This is the traditional fee-for-service option. You can choose any health care provider you want, but the costs to you will be greater than with TRICARE Prime. Additionally, TRICARE will reimburse you only for fees that it deems reasonable. If TRICARE Prime is not available where you are stationed, your only option is to enroll your family members in TRICARE Standard.
3. *Option 3: TRICARE Extra.* This option is similar to TRICARE Standard except that if you use providers who are on the TRICARE-approved list, you will receive a discount on the costs you would have had to pay under TRICARE Standard. This option should be used by those who do not live near a TRICARE Prime network and wish to reduce their medical expenses.

TABLE 8-1
TRICARE OPTION COMPARISONS
Source: www.tricare.org

	TRICARE Prime	TRICARE Extra	TRICARE Standard
Type of Program	TRICARE Prime is a health maintenance organization (HMO).	TRICARE Extra is a preferred provider option (PPO).	TRICARE Standard is a fee-for-service option.
Enrollment & Fees	• You must enroll in TRICARE Prime. • This option offers fewer out-of-pocket costs than any other TRICARE option. • Retirees, their families, survivors, and eligible former spouses must pay an annual enrollment fee. • There is no enrollment fee for active duty servicemembers and active-duty family members.	• There is no enrollment required for TRICARE Extra. • There is no annual enrollment fee. • You are responsible for annual deductibles and co-insurance.	• There is no enrollment required for TRICARE Standard. • There is no annual enrollment. • You are responsible for annual deductibles and co-insurance.

TABLE 8-1 (*continued*)

	TRICARE Prime	TRICARE Extra	TRICARE Standard
Medical Provider Choice	You receive care from military treatment facilities or the TRICARE network of civilian providers.	You can elect to receive care or services from a medical provider within the TRICARE provider network.	You may seek care from any TRICARE-authorized provider.
Additional Details	• You must select a primary care manager, or one will be assigned. • Your PCM will provide and coordinate care, maintain patient health records, and refer patients to specialists when necessary. • Specialty care must be arranged and approved by the PCM to be covered. • You must live in a service area where TRICARE Prime is offered. • Those who do not live in a TRICARE Prime service area may be eligible for TRICARE Prime Remote. • TRICARE Prime beneficiaries are also given priority appointment status at MTFs.	• Co-insurance is lower from a network provider and you will not have to file your own medical claims. • This program is available for all TRICARE-eligibles who choose not to enroll in TRICARE Prime. • It is not available overseas or to active-duty Servicemembers. • The TRICARE network provider list is online at www.healthnetfederal services.com or call Health Net at 1-877-TRICARE (1-877-874-2273).	• You pay higher co-insurance for the flexibility of seeing an authorized TRICARE provider of your choice. • Out-of-pocket expenses vary for different categories of eligible persons. • The provider or the beneficiary must file a medical claim. • If you file the claim, the the payment will be mailed to you. You must pay the provider. If the provider files the claim, he or she will be paid by TRICARE.

TABLE 8-2
ACTIVE DUTY FAMILY MEMBER COSTS
Source: www.tricare.org

	TRICARE Prime	TRICARE Extra	TRICARE Standard
Annual Enrollment Fee	None	None	None
Annual Deductible	$0/individual $0/family Unless point-of-service option is used	For E1-E4: $50/individual or $100/family For E5 and above: $150/individual or $300/family	For E1-E4: $50/individual or $100/family For E5 and above: $150/individual or $300/family
Civilian Outpatient Visit Co-payment	$0 co-payment per visit	15% of negotiated rate after the deductible is met	20% of allowed charges for covered service after the deductible is met
Clinical Preventive Services	$0 co-payment per service	Applicable deductible and cost-shares apply per service	Applicable deductible and cost-shares apply per service
Civilian Inpatient Co-insurance	$0 per day	$13.32 per day ($25 minimum charge per admission)	$13.32 per day ($25 minimum charge per admission)
Emergency Services	$0 co-payment per visit	15% of negotiated rate	20% of allowed charges
Civilian Outpatient Behavioral Health	$0 co-payment per visit	15% of negotiated rate after the deductible is met	20% of allowed charges for covered service after the deductible is met
Civilian Inpatient Behavioral Health	$0 per day	$25 per admission or $20 per day, whichever is more	$25 per admission or $20 per day, whichever is more
Civilian Inpatient Skilled Nursing Facility Care	$0 per day	$25 per admission or $13.32 per day, whichever is more	$25 per admission or $13.32 per day, whichever is more

[1] ADSMs must enroll in TRICARE Prime. ADFMs have the option to enroll in TRICARE Prime, TRICARE Prime Remote for Active Duty Family Members or use TRICARE Extra or TRICARE Standard. TPR and TPRADFM offer the same benefits and costs as TRICARE Prime.

[2] Co-Payments that are reported as a dollar amount are subject to change (i.e., $13.32 per day).

TABLE 8-3
RETIRED SERVICEMEMBERS, THEIR FAMILIES, AND SURVIVORS COSTS
Source: www.tricare.org

	TRICARE Prime	TRICARE Extra	TRICARE Standard
Annual Enrollment Fee	$230/individual $460/family	None	None
Annual Deductible	$0/individual $0/family Unless point-of-service option is used	$150/individual or $300/family	$150/individual or $300/family
Civilian Outpatient Visit Co-payment	$12 co-payment per visit	20% of negotiated rate after the deductible is met	25% of allowed charges for covered service after the deductible is met
Clinical Preventive Services	$0 co-payment per service	Applicable deductible and cost-shares apply per service[1]	Applicable deductible and cost-shares apply per service
Civilian Inpatient Co-insurance	$11 per day ($25 minimum charge per admission)	$250 per day or 25% of the negotiated rate for institutional services, whichever is less, plus 20% of separately allowed professional charges	$459 per day or 25% of the negotiated rate for admission) institutional services, whichever is less, plus 25% of separately allowed professional charges
Emergency Services	$30 co-payment per visit	20% of negotiated rate	25% of allowed charges
Civilian Outpatient Behavioral Health	$25 (individual visit) $17 (group visit)	20% of negotiated rate after the deductible is met	25% of allowed charges after the deductible is met
Civilian Inpatient Behavioral Health	$40 per day	20% of the negotiated rate for institutional services, plus 20% of separately allowed professional charges	Low-volume hospitals: the lesser of $164 per day or 25% of hospital-specific per diem High-volume hospitals: 25% of hospital-specific per diem

[1] Cost-shares reflecting a dollar amount are subject to change (i.e., $13.32 per day).

TABLE 8-3 (*continued*)

	TRICARE Prime	TRICARE Extra	TRICARE Standard
Civilian Inpatient Skilled Nursing Facility Care	$11 per day ($25 minimum charge per admission) (No separate co-payment for separately billed pro-professional charges, catastrophic cap protec-limits apply.)	Lesser of $250 per day or 20% of the negotiated fee for institutional services, plus 20% of the negotiated professional fee	25% of allowed charges for institutional services, plus 25% of separately allowed professional charges

TRICARE Prescription Drug Plan

TRICARE offers several convenient ways for you to have prescriptions filled based on your family's specific needs:

1. You may have prescriptions filled (up to a ninety-day supply for most medications) at a military treatment facility pharmacy free of charge. Be aware that not all medications are available at MTF pharmacies.
2. TRICARE Mail-Order Pharmacy is available for prescriptions you take on a regular basis. You can receive up to a ninety-day supply.
3. Prescription medications that your doctor requires you to start taking immediately can be obtained though a retail network pharmacy.
4. Non-network retail pharmacies are the most costly option to obtain your medications. Eligible beneficiaries usually receive reimbursement of 80% of the full retail price for medications, after they have met the TRICARE annual deductible amount ($150 per individual, $300 per family or $50 individual/$100 family for lower-grade enlisted families) which applies to services obtained from non-network pharmacies. TRICARE Prime beneficiaries who use non-network pharmacy services will continue to pay the 50% point-of-service co-payment as well as a deductible of $300 per individual or $600 per family.

It is DoD's policy to substitute generic medications for brand-name medications when available. Brand-name drugs that have a generic equivalent may be dispensed only if the prescribing physician is able to justify medical necessity for use of the brand-name drug in place of the generic equivalent. If a generic equivalent drug does not exist, the brand-name drug will be dispensed at the brand-name co-payment.

Benefits are available to:

1. Active duty beneficiaries worldwide, including Reserve/National Guard personnel and their family members on Title 10 or Title 32 (federal) active-duty orders for more than thirty days.

TABLE 8-4
TRICARE PHARMACY CO-PAYMENTS/COST SHARES
IN THE UNITED STATES
Source: www.tricare.org

	Formulary		
Place of Service	**Generic (Tier 1)**	**Brand Name (Tier 2)**	**Non-formulary* (Tier 3)**
Military Treatment Facility (MTF) pharmacy (up to a 90-day supply)	$0	$0	Not Applicable**
TRICARE Mail Order Pharmacy (TMOP) (up to a 90-day supply)	$3	$9	$22***
TRICARE Retail Pharmacy Network (TRRx) (up to a 30-day supply)	$3	$9	$22***
Non-network retail pharmacy (up to a 30-day supply) *Note:* Beneficiaries using non-network pharmacies may have to pay the total amount of theirprescription first and then file a claim to receive partial reimbursement.	For those who are *not* enrolled in TRICARE Prime: $9 or 20% of total cost, whichever is greater, after deductible is met (E1-E4: $50/ person; $100/family; all others, including retirees, $150/person, $300/family) TRICARE Prime: 50% cost share after point-of-service deductibles ($300 per person/$600 per family deductible)		For those who are *not* enrolled in TRICARE Prime: $22 or 20% of total cost, whichever is greater, after deductible is met (E1-E4: $50/ person; $100/family; all others, including retirees, $150/person, $300/family)

* For more information on non-formulary medications, beneficiaries can use the TRICARE
** MTFs are prohibited under the Code of Federal Regulations from carrying non formulary medications.
*** If medical necessity is established for a non-formulary drug, patients may qualify for the $9 co-payment for up to a 30-day supply in the TRRx or a 90-day supply in the TMOP program.

TABLE 8-5
BENEFICIARY COPAYMENT/COST SHARE
AT ALL OTHER OVERSEAS LOCATIONS
Source: www.tricare.org

	Active duty servicemembers	Active Duty family members (ADFMs) enrolled in Prime	ADFMs not enrolled in Prime	Retirees and family members
Co-payment/ Cost-Share	No co-payment/ cost share	No co-payment/ cost share*	20% cost share after deductible of $50/100 for E1-E4 ADFMs; $150/300 for E5 and above ADFMs is met	25% cost share after deductible of $150/300 is met

* ADFMs enrolled in TRICARE Overseas Program Prime (at an MTF) who use host nation pharmacies are subject to Prime point of service deductibles of $300/600 and 50% cost-shares.

2. TRICARE-eligible beneficiaries, all ages. (Note: Retired reservists, guardsmen, and former members and their family members do not obtain TRICARE eligibility until age sixty.)
3. Continued Health Care Benefit Program Enrollees.
4. If you turned sixty-five before April 1, 2001, you may participate in the program without being enrolled in Medicare Part B; beneficiaries who turn sixty-five on or after April 1, 2001, must be enrolled in Medicare Part B and must ensure their DEERS profile is updated to participate.

Who is eligible for enrollment in TRICARE?

In order to receive care at military medical facilities, all must be enrolled in DEERS, including newborns after 120 days. The following groups are eligible for TRICARE medical coverage:
1. Active-duty servicemembers.
2. Spouses and unmarried children (under twenty-one years old) of active-duty servicemembers.
   - Children (twenty-one years and older) if handicapped prior to twenty-first birthday.
   - Children (under twenty-three years old) if in school full time (but may not be eligible for TRICARE Prime if they live in a different region).
   - Divorced spouses are not covered except as in number 8, below.

- Children (including stepchildren who are adopted by the sponsor) are covered even if the divorced spouse remarries (but not eligible for TRICARE Prime if they live in a different region).

3. Servicemembers who separate before they are eligible for retirement and their eligible family members may receive TRICARE benefits for a period of 60 to 120 days after the separation date under the Continued Health Care Benefit Program.

4. Retirees (under sixty-five years old), their spouses, and their unmarried children.
   - Children have the same restrictions as above.
   - Retirees who are Medicare eligible are not covered at the current time. However, on October 1, 2001, retirees enrolled in Medicare Part B had their Part A eligibility restored if they lost it because of age.

5. Unremarried spouses and children of servicemembers who died. (Children have same restrictions as above.)

6. Spouses and children of reservists who are ordered to active duty for more than thirty consecutive days. (They are covered only during the reservists' tours. Children have the same restrictions as above.)

7. Spouses and unmarried children of reservists who are injured or aggravate an injury, illness, or disease during active-duty training and die as a result of the injury, illness, or disease.

8. Former spouses of active or retired servicemembers who served for at least twenty creditable years. There are other restrictions for this category. Contact your TRICARE Service Center for complete eligibility rules.

9. Dependent parents and parents-in-law do not qualify for TRICARE benefits. However, they may use military medical facilities on a space-available basis.

10. Other categories of persons may be eligible for TRICARE benefits. Visit the TRICARE website or contact your TRICARE Service Center for the current information.

Supplemental Health Insurance

Obviously, it makes little sense to buy additional insurance for needs that will be met through programs to which your family is entitled. But there are gaps in the medical care provided by TRICARE, and supplemental insurance is designed to provide coverage for these gaps. Since the cost of prolonged medical care for a dependent can substantially reduce your family's standard of living, it is wise to consider additional medical coverage, particularly if there is a family history of illness or disease that may require expensive care. In deciding whether to purchase supplemental insurance, you should consider the coverage provided by TRICARE, the cost of the supplemental insurance premium, the likelihood of future illness in your family, the type of care covered, your ability to pay both expected and unexpected medical expenses, and the age of your dependents. Remember, each TRICARE option exposes you to different risks. Financially, you have more exposure to large medical expenses under TRICARE Standard than TRICARE Prime. Therefore, the TRICARE option you choose will have a large impact on whether you need a supplemental policy. It is possible that certain family conditions may require someone who is enrolled in TRICARE Prime to purchase a supplemental policy.

> *Certain family conditions may require some servicemembers who are enrolled in TRICARE Prime to purchase a supplemental medical insurance policy.*

Supplemental TRICARE insurance pays only after TRICARE pays its portion. Coverage varies widely among supplemental insurance plans, as do annual premiums. The annual premiums for inpatient and outpatient care can range from $75 to $250 for an active-duty spouse and $20 to $90 for each child. These plans are provided through various commercial firms and typically have a period, normally six months or one year, for which the cost of care for a preexisting condition is not reimbursed. Rules on preexisting conditions vary depending upon your state and whether you had a previous insurance policy. You should ask each company specifically about its policy.

For many active-duty servicemembers with a working spouse, health insurance may be provided for the spouse by the civilian employer. In this case, TRICARE is required by law to pay only after the private insurance plan pays its share. For your family members, this includes their stay in a military hospital. If you do not have additional civilian health-care insurance, you may want to consider a CHAMPUS supplemental policy.

In evaluating the options offered in supplemental CHAMPUS insurance plans, you should first determine the specific coverage you need. As you compare policies, try to use the same criteria for each one, and do not be discouraged when you find that there are many different "packages" offered. The program that costs more may or may not offer additional coverage for your premium dollar.

As with any service or product you buy, read the terms carefully, and do not hesitate to ask questions about specific provisions that you do not understand. The long-term commitment you make to a health insurance program can easily add up to many thousands of dollars over your lifetime. It is worth your time to make the best decision you can when you buy such coverage, to review that coverage periodically, and to keep informed about new programs.

9

Deployment

Deployments have become a routine occurrence in military life, especially since the beginning of the Global War on Terror. For those getting ready to deploy for the first time, or those who will deploy away from a spouse and children for the first time, the challenges that deployments present are anything but routine. When most people think of deploying, they think of risk: risk of injury, risk of separation, possible career risk, etc. What is important to remember is that with risk, comes reward. The trade-off between risk and reward is one of the fundamental principles of finance.

Firms, banks, and public entities pay higher rates of return to investors that are willing to finance riskier projects. In a similar fashion, employers provide extra compensation to workers who assume additional risk in the workplace. In the military, this compensation for risk, discomfort, and family separation comes in the form of tax-free military pay and special entitlements. Military deployments present a unique opportunity to take stock of your financial situation in order to develop a refined financial plan. By using the principles of financial planning outlined in the previous chapters, you can capitalize on the many financial rewards associated with going overseas to fight and win our nation's wars.

The checklist that follows this section is a comprehensive, but not exhaustive, list of steps you should take before, during and after deployment. Because deployments often come on short notice, you should not wait until receipt of orders to begin a review of your financial plan. If you are already up to date with your financial planning, then these steps will be relatively simple to execute in addition to all of the other pre-deployment tasks that you will be completing. Some of these tasks may require the assistance of your local finance office or, when third parties are involved such as spouses or next of kin, you will need assistance from the local Judge Advocate General (JAG). There are also countless lessons that may be gleaned from the experiences of other servicemembers or from information available at military websites. Several useful military websites are listed at the end of this chapter.

The remainder of this chapter is a "checklist" interspersed with boxes highlighting key information regarding benefits or programs. This format is designed to help servicemembers prepare for deployment under tight time restrictions.

DEPLOYMENT CHECKLIST
Before Deployment
☐ Review your financial plan (see chapter 1).
  • Update your budget based on the expected financial costs and benefits associated with your deployment.
  • Reevaluate your financial goals.
  • Assess the performance of your current investments.
  • Reevaluate your personal property and life insurance needs (see chapters 13 and 15) .

☐ Familiarize yourself with benefits extended to servicemembers in combat zones
  • Combat zone tax exclusion.
  • Entitlements upon arrival in a combat zone.

Combat Zone Tax Exclusion: IRS Publication 3 specifies that service members serving in a combat zone may exclude the following pay from their taxable income:
• Active Duty pay.
• Imminent danger/hostile fire pay.
• Reenlistment bonuses when the reenlistment occurs in a month you served in a combat zone.
• Monetary awards for suggestions made while serving in a combat zone.
In addition, the IRS grants combat zone income tax filing extensions as well as extensions for contributing to Individual Retirement Accounts (IRAs).

Note: For 2006, officers are tax-exempt up to the following monthly amounts: $6,724.50 with dependents and $6,499.50 without dependents This amount is equal to the base pay of the highest ranking enlisted military servicemember.

Combat Zone Tax Entitlements. The following entitlements will start upon arrival in a designated combat zone. Upon departure from the combat zone, contact your finance office to confirm that they have stopped so that you do not incur a debt that will have to be repaid to the government.

Entitlement	Amount Remarks	Remarks
Hardship Duty Pay	$50, $100, **or** $150/month (based on the location)	Prorated over 30 days. Does not start until you are in a combat zone for 30 days.
Hostile Fire Pay	$225/month	Full Month entitlement, regardless of time spent in the zone.
Family Separation Pay (married servicemembers only)	$250/month	Prorated over 30 days. Begins on first day of separation, but will not appear on you LES until you have been deployed for 30 consecutive days.

- Combat zone leave. Servicemembers earn 2.5 days of leave per month (partial or full) while serving in a combat zone. Upon departure of the combat zone, any leave that is taken (that was earned in the designated combat zone) is free of federal and state tax when the leave is paid. Combat zone leave will be used prior to any other previous leave days accrued. The combat zone leave must be used within three years.
- Savings Deposit Program (SDP).[1]
- Reduced interest rates on credit cards and loans (select banks).[2]
- Deferred or reduced minimum payments on credit cards and loans.

---

[1] SDP = 10% guaranteed rate of return on savings up to $10,000 during your deployment

[2] Ask your preferred lender about special discounted APRs on credit cards and consumer loans during the course of your deployment. The Servicemembers Civil Relief Act of 2004 (SCRA) caps interest payments on pre-service debt at 6% APR.

- Tax filing extensions (for details read Publication 3, *The Armed Forces Tax Guide*, or visit the IRS website at *www.irs.gov*).
- Servicemembers who are deployed for a year and, thus, have no taxable income can still make Roth IRA contributions up to the annual limit thanks to the 2006 Heroes Earned Retirement Opportunities (HERO) Act (see chapter 12).
- Increased contribution limits to Thrift Savings Plan (TSP).[3]

Thrift Savings Plan Tax Advantages. There are two tax benefits to making tax-deferred contributions to the TSP (see chapter 12):
- Your TSP contributions are taken out of your pay before taxes are withheld, so you pay less tax now and
- Taxes on contributions and attributable earnings are deferred until you withdraw your money.

Additionally, when you serve in a *combat zone or qualified hazardous duty area*, most compensation you receive for active service is *excluded from your gross income* on your IRS Form W-2, regardless of whether you contribute any of it to the TSP. You receive no direct tax benefit from contributing pay to the TSP, which has been excluded from gross income; however, the earnings on those contributions are tax-deferred. When you make a withdrawal, money is taken from your total account balance proportionally from your taxable funds and your tax-exempt funds. The amount attributable to tax-exempt contributions will *not* be taxable. Your service will notify the TSP whenever your contributions are from tax-exempt money. The TSP will then account for your tax-exempt contributions and, as indicated above, will ensure that these amounts are not reported to the IRS as taxable income. Consequently, those contributions will not be subject to taxation when you withdraw them. Your quarterly participant statement will show your tax-exempt balance separately.
Source: *www.tsp.gov*

---

[3] When deployed to a combat zone, you get additional benefits associated with TSP contributions. For instance, in 2006 the elective deferral limit (the amount of your pay that can be contributed to your TSP account) is $15,000. If you are in a combat zone, there is no elective deferral limit, but there is an IRS provision that limits contributions to $44,000.

☐ Familiarize yourself with opportunities to decrease your expenses while in a combat zone.

- Suspend your cell phone usage plan.
- Consider storing your vehicle and suspending your vehicular insurance (except for comprehensive coverage, see chapter 14).
- Ensure you complete proper pre-storage maintenance if you do decide to store a vehicle. Check with your local service center or dealer for the appropriate procedures for your vehicle.
- Consider putting household goods in storage (especially single soldiers or soldiers whose spouses decide to move closer to home).
- Consider subletting a room or entire apartment if your lease permits it or consider breaking your lease altogether.[4]
- Maintain absolute minimal levels of heat and electricity. You may even cancel your utilities outright, but make sure that you do not run the risk of freezing pipes if your residence is in a cold climate.
- Terminate or suspend subscriptions to magazines and newspapers (most companies will not ship your correspondence to APO addresses).

☐ Make a new financial plan based on increased income and reduced expenses while in a combat zone (see chapter 1). Do not forget to budget some spending money for yourself. Most Forward Operating Bases in Iraq and Afghanistan come fully equipped with Burger King, Taco Bell, Subway, and gourmet coffee shops in addition to the usual BX/PX. Be sure to review this plan with your family members BEFORE you deploy.

☐ Consult your local JAG to update or create a will (consider a living will as well).

☐ Consult your local JAG to update or create a Power of Attorney (POA) so that your designated representative can legally handle your financial affairs in your absence.[5]

---

[4] SCRA also allows military personnel to break the terms of a lease or rental agreement upon receipt of PCS orders (greater than 90 days) or deployment orders.

[5] Consider a specific power of attorney if you do not want this representative to have unlimited powers over your assets.

☐ Review your SGLI to ensure the beneficiaries listed are consistent with your will.

☐ Wherever possible, establish online accounts for checking, savings, insurance, investment, and regular bills.
  • Make use of automatic bill payment functions for recurring bills (It is recommended that you become familiar with these sites several months in advance) to ensure that they are set up properly. You might have less access to NIPR (unclassified) computers than you expect.
  • If your spouse or designated POA holder will be in charge of the finances in your absence, make a list of usernames and passwords for each account and keep them in a secure place.
  • Notify companies that someone else will be managing your accounts. Ensure that they set up joint accounts if you want your spouse to have full authority to make necessary transactions on your account.

☐ Review TRICARE and DEERS status, benefits, and procedures with dependents to avoid costly medical expenses in your absence (see chapter 8).

☐ Review your Veteran's Affairs and Survivor Benefits (see chapters 16 and 17).
  • Make these benefits known to your beneficiary.
  • Identify a point of contact to assist with these benefits in case of a tragedy.

During Deployment:
☐ Check your LES online at *https://mypay.dfas.mil/mypay.aspx* to ensure you are receiving your combat zone benefits.
  • Check to see that your hostile fire, family separation, and hardship duty entitlements have commenced. (Note: Family separation and hardship duty entitlement will not begin until you have been in theater for thirty days.)
  • Check to see if your federal income tax withholding has ceased.
  • Check to see if your combat zone leave days are accumulating.

☐ Check to see if your new allotments have taken effect. These can be verified through the MyPay website as well.
  - Increased TSP contributions.
  - Increased contributions to other retirement portfolios (Roth or Traditional IRA).

☐ Check your azimuth.
  - Are you (and your spouse) staying on budget?
  - Are the bills getting paid on time?
  - Are you taking advantage of every possible deployment benefit?
  - Are the goals you set realistic? Are they too high? Too low?

☐ Focus on your financial goals.
  - If your azimuth is true, stick to your budget.
  - Pay off debt with the additional income.
  - Eat at the dining facility as much as possible.
  - Be conscious of special discounts offered to deployed service-members on certain big-ticket items (Military Car Sales, watches, rugs, etc.), but do not buy it if you do not need it.
  - Keep your long-term goals (such as a comfortable retirement) in mind.

After Deployment:

☐ Check your LES online at *https://mypay.dfas.mil/mypay.aspx* to ensure your combat zone benefits have stopped.
  - This should occur automatically when you swipe your ID card prior to boarding your redeployment aircraft. If it does not, your personnel representative should submit the redeployment orders immediately upon return to your home station.
  - SOMETIMES these benefits do not automatically stop. If you continue to receive these benefits for a period of time after you redeploy, you may encounter serious financial hardship when you are forced to repay the money to the government.

☐ Notify your creditors that you have redeployed.

☐ Reinitiate automobile coverage if you suspended it.

☐ Reevaluate your predeployment financial plan at your current level of income and expenses.

☐ Readjust your budget based on your normal (non-combat zone) pay and allowances.

☐ Resist the urge to splurge.

☐ Take a vacation.
  • Use your combat zone leave days after you redeploy so that you enjoy additional tax-free days (that do not count against your regular leave days accrued).
  • Research discounted vacation packages that are offered to military veterans through your local MWR office or at the following travel websites:
    • *www.armymwr.com*
    • *www.mwr.navy.mil*
    • *www.offdutytravel.com*
    • *www.afvc.com* (Armed Forces Vacation Club)
    • *www.shadesofgreen.org*
    • *www.rockymountainblue.com*
    • *www.halekoahotel.com*
    • *www.dragonhilllodge.com*
    • *www.edelweisslodgeandresort.com*
    • *www.interliner.com*

USEFUL WEBSITES WHEN PLANNING FOR DEPLOYMENT
General Military Information:
  • *www.militaryonesource.com*
  • *www.military.com*
  • *www.deploymentguide.com*

Financial Planning:
  • *www.usaa.com*
  • *www.usaaedfoundation.org*
  • *www.aafmaa.com*

Military Sites:
- *www.army.mil; www.armyonesource.com*
- *www.navy.mil; www.navyonesource.com*
- *www.af.mil; www.airforceonesourc.com*
- *www.usmc.mil; www.mccsonesourc.com*
- *www.uscg.mil*

Relief Sites:
- *www.redcross.org*
- *www.nmfa.org*
- *www.nmcrs.org*
- *www.aerhq.org*
- *www.afas.org*

PART III

INVESTING FOR YOUR FUTURE

10

A Basic Investment Strategy— Mutual Funds and ETFs

Any investor, regardless of financial knowledge, must have an investment strategy in order to reach his or her financial goals. Investors must determine where they are, where they want to be, and how they will use their available resources to get from here to there. Here are six steps to develop a comprehensive investment strategy:

1. Determine how much you can afford to invest.
2. Set your investment horizon.
3. Assess your risk tolerance.
4. Identify investment instruments.
5. Evaluate investment performance.
6. Adjust/rebalance your investment portfolio periodically.

DETERMINE HOW MUCH YOU CAN AFFORD TO INVEST
Chapter 1 discussed the development of financial goals as well as a personal budget. There is no need to have an investment strategy if your monthly budget requires consumption of all your income for bare necessities. However, in most cases, the budget supports some amount left over for investment. Once that amount is determined, investors (especially beginners) should set up automatic monthly allotments to ensure that they "pay themselves first" by having those investments transferred from their checking accounts at the beginning of each month. In addition to "paying themselves first," investing the same amount each month will automatically ensure investors the benefits from "dollar cost averaging," a concept worth explaining now before proceeding further.

Dollar cost averaging simply involves investing a constant dollar amount at specific intervals, usually each month, into a mutual fund. Over time, this method enables you to pay less per share than the actual average share price. The key to dollar cost averaging is that by purchasing the same dollar amount each period, you buy more when the market is low (since shares cost less) and buy less when the market is high (since shares cost more). Consequently, you will earn a positive return even if you sell your shares at a price per share equal to the average price per share you paid. Table 10-1 illustrates the mechanics of dollar cost averaging using $100 per month for three months in three different market scenarios.

Dollar cost averaging is the most common tool for investing in mutual funds. Once you have selected the mutual fund(s) that match your investment strategy, it is time to get the most out of your money. Dollar cost averaging is most frequently mentioned in financial news articles because it is the easiest investment method and requires little or no "active" participation by investors. If you have not accumulated a sizable amount of money to invest yet or feel uncomfortable taking an investment plunge with all your money at one time, then dollar cost averaging is for you.

Most mutual funds make it simple and convenient to dollar cost average by offering systematic investment plans. The fund will take a constant amount out of your checking or savings account once every month. Many will also reduce or waive the minimum initial investment if you start a systematic investment plan, so if you do not meet that

TABLE 10-1 DOLLAR COST AVERAGING

	Amount Invested	Rising Market		Declining Market		Fluctuating Market	
		Price Paid for Each Share	Number of Shares Bought	Price Paid for Each Share	Number of Shares Bought	Price Paid for Each Share	Number of Shares Bought
Jan	$100	$10.00	10.00	$10.00	10.00	$10.00	10.00
Feb	100	10.45	9.57	9.55	10.47	9.25	10.81
Mar	100	10.90	9.17	9.10	10.99	10.25	9.76
Total	$300		28.74		31.46		30.57
Average Share Cost to you[1]			$10.43		$9.54		$9.81
Average Share Price[2]			$10.45		$9.55		$9.83

[1] Average share cost = total dollars invested ÷ total shares purchased
[2] Average share price = sum of price paid per share column ÷ 3

minimum initial investment, check to see if you can avoid the minimum amount by initiating a systematic investment plan.

Once investors determine the systematic investment amount, they (especially beginners) should set up automatic monthly allotments to ensure that they "pay themselves first." The easiest way to do this is to have money transferred on a set date from their checking accounts to their investments of choice.

SET YOUR INVESTMENT HORIZON, ASSESS YOUR RISK TOLERANCE, AND IDENTIFY INVESTMENT INSTRUMENTS

Based upon the financial objectives that you set in chapter 1, you must also consider how long you will invest funds to meet a particular financial objective. Investments with greater risk (volatility) provide the greatest potential for higher returns in the long term but also the greatest potential for losses in the short term. Your tolerance for risk is driven by your investment horizon and your personality. If you need the funds for a financial objective that is only a short time away (short investment horizon), then you should not be willing to accept as much risk. If you cannot sleep at night due to the volatility of your portfolio, then you are not willing to accept as much risk. The length of the investment period, along with your risk tolerance will dictate your investment selections.

Typically, you should select nearly risk-free investments such as money market funds as a vehicle to invest funds earmarked for financial objectives less than one year away; an example might be an emergency fund that could be needed at any time. For financial goals that are one to five years away, you might consider fixed-income mutual funds (corporate and/or government bond funds).

For financial objectives that are more than five years away, such as retirement, you should invest in a combination of fixed-income and equity mutual funds (those funds that buy and sell the stocks of publicly traded U.S. and foreign companies) with more emphasis on equity funds the further away retirement and your other long-term financial goals are. For example, one guideline recommended to fairly conservative investors is that 100 minus your age is the percentage of your retirement investments that should be invested in equity-stock mutual funds. You can increase this percentage if you can tolerate the added risk, and should decrease this percentage if you have a risk-averse personality.

EVALUATE INVESTMENT PERFORMANCE AND ADJUST/REBALANCE YOUR INVESTMENT PORTFOLIO PERIODICALLY

Later this chapter will discuss how to select mutual funds, which are the cornerstone for any beginning investor. At least annually, you should compare the performance of your selected funds to the benchmarks against which they compete. If the funds consistently are not performing well against the benchmarks, you might consider moving to a different fund or investing in the benchmark index itself. Continue to monitor your financial objectives as you approach them, and adjust the funding needed to support those objectives into a more conservative investment option as the time nears when you will need to withdraw the money. These topics will be covered in further detail later in this chapter.

Websites for Evaluating Investment Performance

www.morningstar.com
finance.yahoo.com
www.marketwatch.com
moneycentral.msn.com
www.investopedia.com

EXPLAINING MUTUAL FUNDS

Mutual funds provide a means of virtually hassle-free investing. With more than 10,000 different mutual funds, there is a vast spectrum of investment opportunities ranging from a country or industry sector, to a diversified market portfolio.

Investment companies develop mutual funds by pooling money from different individual investors. Mutual fund companies sell shares in a particular fund to raise money to invest in different securities. When you buy shares, the fund uses the money, as well as the investments of other fund shareholders, to purchase stocks, bonds, and other financial instruments according to the fund's objectives. Some funds buy only one type of security—such as stocks of large blue-chip companies or stock from companies in one specific industry. Others have greater diversification. A typical fund portfolio may include from thirty to several hundred different investment instruments.

Professional money managers direct the mutual fund by continually buying and selling securities. Investors (mutual fund shareholders) gain profits or losses in proportion to the number of mutual fund shares they own. Shareholders can track the status of a mutual fund by checking the fund's price in the newspaper, by phone, via the Internet, and through monthly, quarterly, or annual statements.

By law, mutual fund companies must provide a prospectus for every fund they offer. The prospectus is a valuable tool for analyzing the fund's objectives, learning about the management team, and receiving a summary of investments and fees. Typically, the prospectus will also include quarterly and annual reports and discuss recent performance trends. Most mutual funds require an initial investment of $500 to $3,000. Fund companies often waive this minimum if you enter into an automatic monthly investment plan of $100 (some funds even go as low as $50) or more monthly. Once you have an account, you can usually make additional contributions whenever you like. The minimum additional investment is usually $50 to $200.

The Advantages of Mutual Funds
Diversification. The primary benefit of mutual funds for most investors is the diversification of risk at a small cost. Mutual funds allow you to achieve a diversified portfolio by investing only a few hundred dollars. Since most mutual funds invest in more than thirty different stocks or bonds, even a small investor can have a diversified portfolio—particularly if the manager invests in a number of different asset classes.

Convenience. Mutual funds permit small investors to have their money professionally managed. Professional managers have access to a wide range of information and can perform more extensive research than the small investor when selecting securities for a portfolio. Mutual funds are convenient to buy and sell as all major funds have telephone and online exchange and redemption options. Finally, the ease at which an investor can open an account online without having to go through a broker makes this option very hassle-free.

Flexibility. Mutual funds allow the investor to reinvest capital gains distributions and dividends in the fund or receive them directly. Also, investors have the ability to conduct simple online transactions to move in and out of mutual funds in order to rebalance their portfolio.

Mutual Fund Family of Funds
Most mutual fund companies offer several different funds, typically called a family of funds. There are hundreds of mutual fund families that offer funds to everyday investors. The largest mutual fund families are: Vanguard, American, and Fidelity. Other popular fund families

include T. Rowe Price, Putnam, Janus, and American Century. These firms allow average investors to move money back and forth among the different funds in the family at little or no cost (except what might become taxable short-term capital gains if you move the funds fairly often). The different funds within the family usually offer a broad mix of mutual fund types to appeal to a full spectrum of investor objectives. Consolidated account statements also make personal financial planning a less daunting task for the beginning investor. Fund families provide you the ability to respond quickly to changes in market conditions, investment strategy or risk tolerance, and to balance your portfolio by quickly transferring your money from one fund to another.

Remember that profits and losses have tax implications. This is true even if you are redeeming shares to transfer from one fund to another within the same family of funds. Your mutual fund company will usually provide you with the information you must report to the IRS. Also, some families do charge a fee for transfers between different funds. Before you decide to invest within a particular mutual fund family, you should first consider whether the fund family offers you the flexibility to transfer funds (at little or no cost) and the variety of funds available within the family.

Mutual Fund Categories

Mutual funds are usually classified by their investment strategy. Table 10-2 lists the common fund categories and a general measure of their risk. Certain types of mutual funds may be better suited for you than others based on your financial goals, retirement horizon, and willingness to accept risk.

Over 90% of all mutual funds are open-end. The remainder are called closed-end funds which means they are limited to a predetermined size (or dollar amount). In contrast to closed-end funds, the more you or other investors put into open-end funds, the larger the fund grows. Therefore, you can buy or sell shares in open-end funds from the mutual fund itself, through a financial advisor, or through a broker. Open-end fund shares are not traded on the stock market (whereas closed-end funds are). An open-end fund will sell as many shares as investors demand and must redeem (buy back) investors' shares whenever investors want to sell them. The share price of an open-end fund depends on the underlying value of the securities in its portfolio and are generally favored by small investors over both closed-end funds and direct investment in individual stocks because of the relative ease of investing. However, some closed-end funds, such as ETFs (Exchange-

TABLE 10-2
MUTUAL FUND TYPES

Type of Fund	Primary Objective	Volatility/Risk
Aggressive growth	Capital appreciation[1]	Very high
Growth	Capital appreciation	High
Growth and income	Capital appreciation and current income	Moderate to high
Balanced	Long-term capital appreciation and current income	Moderate
International stock[2]	Capital appreciation from foreign securities	Moderate to high
Sector	Invests in companies in a particular industry or commodity	Moderate to high
Income stock	Increasing dividend income, current income, and long term capital appreciation	Moderate
Index	Invests in companies to replicate a specific index such as the S&P 500	Moderate
Income	Current income	Moderate
Bond[3]	Current income	Low to moderate
International bond[2]	Current income from foreign bonds	Moderate
Money market	Current income	Low

[1] Capital appreciation refers to the rise in the market price of a particular asset; in this case, a mutual fund.
[2] For international funds, the risk of currency exchange rate changes must be considered.
[3] Bond funds will typically specialize as corporate, government, or tax-exempt (municipal). Each has different risk structures and tax benefits.

Traded Funds), are becoming increasingly popular even though they are currently less common. The end of this chapter will address the emergence of ETFs as an attractive option to everyday investors.

Common Types of Mutual Funds

Index Funds. Since there are over 10,000 open-end mutual funds from which to select, the task of selecting representative investments for each asset class may seem daunting. A simple technique that has gained popularity in recent years is the use of index or "passive" funds.

The intent of an index fund is to replicate the return of a particular index such as the Standard & Poor's 500 (largest 500 U.S. companies) or the Russell 2000 (smallest 2000 U.S. companies). There are index funds for most asset classes. Index funds have low management and expense fees since they require less management. The fund manager is simply replicating an already determined portfolio of stocks or bonds based on defined characteristics. In a sense, the investor "owns the market" that the index represents. Also, since the index rarely changes, low portfolio turnover results in better tax efficiency for the fund shareholders. Finally, an index fund stays fully invested in the index it represents. Imagine if an individual investor tried to replicate the S&P 500 by buying 500 different stocks—the brokerage fees would be staggering. Mutual fund managers have the ability to do this with relative ease and low cost because of the volume of money available to them.

Index funds offer investors an inexpensive means to own a very diversified portfolio. We recommend beginning investors consider broad index funds, such as S&P 500 funds, as a starting point for their portfolio. As one begins to accumulate wealth, these funds serve as the core of a portfolio of mutual funds. The investor could subsequently diversify and build around this core by adding bond funds, industry funds, and international/regional funds (i.e., Asia, Latin America, and Europe).

Active (Managed) Funds. Funds that are classified as *active* or *managed* usually carry higher fees or a type of load. Often, these funds are classified as Class A, Class B, or even Class C funds. These funds have either a front-end load (sales charge as a percentage when you put the money in the fund), back-end load (charges when you remove money), or a constant load (a fee paid annually as a percentage simply for owning the fund). Additionally, these funds might be solely invested in a specific industry such as life science, technology, or energy. The justification for this "fee" is usually that the fund will "beat" index funds on average because "more qualified" management is taking more of a hands-on approach to the stocks that make up the fund. In other words, the fee is simply the cost of being in a fund that requires more involvement by a fund manager (s) and a fund that must buy and sell securities more often. Some stockbrokers buy and sell these funds exclusively because the commission on them can be significant over the long term. Many investors are led to believe that the return on load funds will more than compensate for the sales charge; but in reality, there has been no statistical proof that this occurs.

Life-cycle funds. Life-cycle funds are the newest type of investment that allow individual investors to diversify their entire portfolio easily and with the least amount of time and effort by investing in just one fund. Life-cycle funds blend together multiple mutual funds (usually within the same fund family) with the desired aim at broad-based diversification. These funds allocate a percentage of your investments among different mutual funds based on your age and risk profile (i.e., 60% U.S. stocks, 30% foreign stocks, 10% bonds) and then automatically adjust these percentages as you get older, thus requiring very little management intervention. An investor simply picks one of these funds based on his or her desired retirement date (usually sixty-five years old for planning purposes), and the percentage of stock funds within the portfolio will decrease as the individual nears retirement. This way, an investor can be appropriately diversified with the desired blend of mutual funds without ever having to switch funds over time.

Mutual Fund Fees

Fees will lower your return. Though mutual funds are one of the least expensive ways to invest, you still pay three basic types of fees: loads, management fees, and 12B-1 fees. You will find these fees disclosed in the mutual fund's prospectus. The largest hidden fee is that the average managed fund spends 0.44% of its average annual balance on trading expenses that are not listed in any of the three fees listed above. This is one of the main reasons why it is wise to consider investing in passive funds such as index funds.

Annual Management and 12B-1 Fees. Management fees range from 0.25 to 1.5% of your investment. The fund collects these fees out of the fund's assets. Thus, the greater the fees, the less your net return. Most larger funds charge less than 1% of the principal. 12B-1 fees cover marketing and advertising costs. About 50% of all funds charge this fee and it will reduce your total return, so it is wise to do the research on all associated fees. While management and 12B-1 fees (even in no load funds) will degrade an investor's return, it is a relatively minor cost for the benefit of having the ability to invest in a fund. Every mutual has a management fee, and most have 12B-1 fees as well.

Load Versus No-Load Funds. If you buy a mutual fund through a broker, then the fund is typically loaded. As mentioned before, there are three types of load funds: front-end, back-end, and normal (annual) load. By law, mutual funds can charge a sales commission of up to 8.5% of your investment. The typical range is 2 to 8.5%. Obviously, a large front-end load will significantly affect the amount of your investment actually used to purchase shares.

Back-end loads, often called redemption fees, charge a commission (usually 2 to 6%) to sell your fund shares. Funds commonly impose redemption fees to discourage short-term investing or market timing (switching in and out of a fund to make short-term profits). Redemption fees are not prominently advertised, so you must read the fund's prospectus carefully to see if the fund has any. Some funds have declining redemption fees that start out high and then decline to a very low fee or no fee after you have held the shares for some time period. Five years is typical.

No-load funds, when purchased directly from the mutual fund company, do not charge commissions.

> *Most financial experts strongly encourage beginning and intermediate investors to choose only no-load funds.*

Cautionary Note on Contractual Mutual Funds. The most expensive type of front-end load fund that you can buy is a contractual mutual fund. Insurance agents, commissioned financial planners, and other mutual fund peddlers prefer to sell you this kind of fund because the salesman's compensation is much more lucrative than with other loaded funds. As a result of a 2004 *New York Times* article, the firms selling these products came under great scrutiny because they tended to target service members, used "high-pressure" tactics, and used former military officers and noncommissioned officers to sell their products.[1]

Contractual mutual funds obligate you to invest a set number of dollars every month over a ten- to twenty-year time frame. This "contract" is generally not considered a legal obligation, and you can cancel it whenever you wish. A significant drawback to contractual plans is that they take the majority of your total (8.5%) commission for your expected investments over the full life of the plan and charge it "up front" in the first year. This means that up to 50% of your first year's investments goes into the salesman's pocket, not into your account! Also, if you cancel your "contract," you may lose up to 50 % of your initial investment because the up-front commissions are nonrefundable after your grace period (usually eighteen months) expires. Fortunately, many recent laws have been implemented that require the sellers of these funds to be much more explicit in their explanation of the contract.

Should You Ever Buy a Load Fund?
Considering the fact that loads buy you nothing and simply reduce your return, should you ever buy a load fund? Looking at all the available evidence, no study has shown that load funds consistently outperform

---

[1] Diana B. Henriques, "Company Settles Charges on Funds Sold to Soldiers," *New York Times*, 16 December 2004, C2.

no-load funds. Remember that the load fee does not pay for superior research or better management; it simply compensates the salesman for selling you the shares. Based on the evidence, you should buy only a load fund if you are willing to pay someone to pick a mutual fund for you. The simple example in Table 10-3 shows the difference a load can have on your return. In summary, although you will have to invest a little time to pick your own fund, no-load mutual funds provide a better return than load funds with similar characteristics.

Researching Mutual Fund Prices

Financial publications regularly review and rank mutual fund performances. You can also get a daily snapshot of your fund's performance by checking the mutual fund quotations section in some major newspapers or using an online service. Since there are so many mutual funds, it is nearly impossible to print all of the fund prices daily. Therefore, finding a fund's share price online using the fund's ticker symbol (usually a four to five letter symbol for the fund) is the easiest way. Most online news websites have a quick lookup for share prices at the top of the home page or the money section. Similarly, the mutual fund company's website is usually the best place to get the most comprehensive information on particular funds.

At a minimum, you are likely to find basic information on the fund, such as the share price (or Net Asset Value [NAV]), the change from the day prior, and the year-to-date total return on the fund. An example is shown in the Table 10-4 on the next page.

Selecting a Mutual Fund

Almost all information about a fund can be found in the fund's prospectus. However, before you order a prospectus, you should (1) formulate

---

TABLE 10-3 COMPARISON OF NET RETURNS IN LOAD AND NO-LOAD FUNDS(ASSUMING A STEADY 12% RATE OF RETURN)

MONTHLY TOTAL VALUE OF INVESTMENT

Fund	Investment	Net of Load	After 5 Years
No-load	$100.00	$100.00	$8,167
8.5% load	100.00	91.50	7,473
Contractual	100.00	50.00 (1 year)	6,992
		97.50 (2–5 years)	

TABLE 10-4
TYPICAL MUTUAL FUND PRICE QUOTE

NAME	NAV[C]	NET CHG.[D]	YTD % RET.[E]
American Century Inv[A]			
Bond[B]	9.35	−0.02	+3.5
Real	14.83	+0.04	+5.1
Ultra	29.93	+0.12	−7.5

[A] Funds are categorized by "family name" first. The first listing is from the American Century family of funds.
[B] Funds within the family appear in alphabetical order. Usually the name relates to the funds' objectives by category.
[C] NAV is the daily price of one of the shares.
[D] The net change is the change in NAV from the previous day's close.
[E] YTD percentage change assumes reinvestment of all distributions, after subtracting annual expenses. None of the figures include sales charges (loads).

your financial goals and financial objectives as discussed in chapter 1; and (2) select a fund category that matches your investment strategy as discussed in the six steps at the beginning of this chapter.

In general, the fund category you choose will depend on your own risk preference and time horizon. The longer your horizon, the more attractive riskier funds become. You may also have to consider your tax situation and need for steady income.

As a basic guideline, you should invest savings for short-term goals (less than one year) in money market or low-risk bond mutual funds. For medium-term goals (one to five years), you should consider short-term government or corporate bond funds. To satisfy long-term goals, you should have a diversified mix of stock, balanced, international, and perhaps sector funds.

Once you decide on the category of fund, you should read the fund's prospectus so that you can gain a better understanding of the fund's objectives, main asset holdings, and fees and expenses. Investors can request a prospectus from any mutual fund company by telephone, in writing, or by submitting a request online at the company's website. Company websites frequently allow investors to download the prospectus immediately.

The second step in selecting a mutual fund is to assess the fund's performance relative to similar funds or industry benchmarks. There are many resources available for this type of research. There is no shortage of Internet sites that provide insightful, professional, and objective analyses. A sample list of these websites can be found in the chart at the beginning of this chapter. In addition, these sites provide rankings relative to other funds in the same category and also give an "outsider's" opinion or commentary on the fund. Other sources of information include financial magazines such as *Money* magazine and *Kiplinger's Personal Finance* magazine as well as financial newspapers such as the *Wall Street Journal*.

The purpose of reading the prospectus and researching mutual funds is to determine whether a particular fund is consistent with your investment objective, time horizon, and risk tolerance and to assess your individual fund's performance against benchmarks. In particular, a funds prospectus should, at a minimum, include the following information:

- state the fund's investment strategy.
- list the fund's expenses.
- recap the fund's past performance as well as comparing this performance to more common benchmarks, such as the S&P 500.
- identify the manager (or managers) and discuss the manager's philosophy.
- provide information on opening a fund account and/or provide an application to start one.
- discuss how and when distributions are made and taxed.
- cover any other important administrative data about the fund, such as contact information, changes to the fund (if relevant), etc.

Selling Your Mutual Fund Shares

The time to sell your fund shares is when you need the money to meet your financial goals. Another reason to sell your fund may be if the fund changes portfolio managers and the star manager leaves. However, you may want to follow the fund's performance over the next year to evaluate how the new manager's performance.

The performance of your fund may be another reason to sell. If the return does not match your expectations or is consistently below returns of funds with similar objectives, then you may want to sell your shares and invest elsewhere. You will need patience and discipline; avoid the temptation to sell in disgust just because your fund or the market has a bad quarter or year, as even the best funds have periods of subpar performance. Always focus on the long-term record. Many inexperienced and undisciplined investors sell out at market bottoms, missing the ride back up to the top, and then buy back at the market peak when it is too late. This behavior directly contradicts the old Wall Street adage of "buy low, sell high."

Should an investor try to time the market by attempting to follow the economic cycle and adjusting instruments in mutual funds accordingly? Probably not. Our economy is affected to a large extent by random, unpredictable events. Experts who spend their whole lives analyzing the economy have trouble accurately forecasting what will happen next or to what degree. Studies of experts that claim the ability to time the market show that few, no more than would be expected by random chance, are able to beat the return of those that buy and hold on to their mutual funds over the long-term. The major results of attempting to time the market are more taxes, higher transaction costs, and lower average returns.

Mutual Fund Returns

Mutual fund returns come from three sources: dividends, capital gains distributions, and changes in the share price of the fund. When a mutual fund earns dividends or interest on its securities, the fund passes those along to you, the shareholder, in the form of dividends. If a mutual fund sells some of its securities for more than it paid for them, it must pass that profit along to the shareholder in the form of capital gains distributions. Finally, if you sell your fund shares for more than you paid for them, you will earn a profit, or capital gain, on those shares. However, you could have a loss on the shares by selling them for less than you paid. Your total return on the mutual fund includes profits or losses from all three sources. Of course, if you paid a load, this will also reduce your return. Most fund companies send annual summaries of your investment. You should keep these statements as part of your financial record keeping.

Record Keeping

One of the biggest problems for investors in mutual fund shares is that of good record keeping. Many investors pay too much in taxes when they later sell mutual fund shares because they did not keep all the records of purchase that their fund sent them. You should keep records of purchases, reinvestments, dividends, capital gains distributions, and sales proceeds received for as long as you own any shares in that fund and then a few more years to satisfy the IRS. At a minimum, keep the annual summary statements as well as all tax documents.

EXCHANGE-TRADED FUNDS (ETFs)

An Exchange-Traded Fund, or ETF, is an index fund that trades on the market similar to how a stock trades. ETFs are relatively new and have become popular in the last few years because they are very practical and allow investors to follow major stock indexes, such as the Dow Jones Industrial Average, the Standard & Poor's 500 Index, and the Nasdaq Composite. Almost every major index, from gold to real estate to international trusts, has an ETF. Investors should understand that this form of investing is simply another method of diversifying assets. Instead of picking stocks, investors are literally buying a particular market of similar stocks; much like a mutual fund operates. ETFs are a class of mutual fund as they fall under the same SEC rules for mutual funds. Their main difference lies in how they are purchased, which is similar to how stocks are purchased.

ETFs blend the benefits of stock trading together with the benefits of traditional index fund investing. The annual fees for ETFs are lower than the annual fees for mutual funds. This is due mainly to the fact that mutual funds are actively managed, while ETFs are not. However, ETFs must be bought through brokerage firms just like a stock is purchased, so there is a transaction cost, although this is negated with sizable trades. ETFs can be traded intra-day at a price set by the market, whereas mutual funds are priced at the end of the day after all trading has ceased. In other words, you cannot quickly sell a mutual fund during a daily market rally or downturn, while you can sell or buy an ETF during the day just as you would a stock. This "flexibility" in purchasing and selling shares is seen as a benefit to some investors. Finally, ETFs tend to generate fewer capital gains than mutual funds because of the low turnover of the securities that comprise them. On the other hand, you can generate sizable capital gains or losses if you sell ETF shares just as you would with stocks.

The biggest ETF group is Barclay's Global Investors iShares family, which offers over 80 ETF options. As of 2005, iShares began listing on the New York Stock Exchange. More information about ETFs and information on families of ETFs can be found at the following websites: *www.Shares.com*, *www.Powershares.com*, *www.SPDRindex.com*, *www.StreetTracks.com*, and *www.FrescoShares.com*.

Mutual funds and ETFs allow individual investors a convenient opportunity to invest in a broad mix of securities (stocks and bonds). They both achieve the same goal of diversification, although they operate and are classified differently. In response to the introduction of

ETFs, many major mutual fund companies have lowered the management fees of their index funds. For example, Fidelity lowered fees on its major index funds in 2005 in order to rival the low ETF management fees.[2] Needless to say, the introduction of ETFs is great for individual investors, as more competition among funds will inevitably result in downward pressure on management fees for traditional open-end funds over the long term. Additionally, ETFs provide yet another reliable method for investors to diversify assets at little cost.

ETFs Versus Mutual Funds

Since ETFs and mutual funds are identical in concept, you may wonder in which one you should invest first. Perhaps the biggest consideration in deciding in which one to invest rests on how much you will be investing initially. If at any given time you are making large purchases of an amount over $1,000–$2,000, it might make sense to invest in an ETF because one-time brokerage fees and ETF maintenance fees will be lower when compared to mutual fund maintenance fees. Alternatively, if you plan to make monthly systematic investments over time, then you should consider a mutual fund rather than an ETF so that you avoid brokerage fees for the multiple-share purchases. In summary, mutual funds are best for more frequent purchases of shares, while ETFs are best for large dollar-amount purchases.

Although there are no guarantees of profit, mutual funds and ETFs offer the investor a convenient and low-cost method of achieving diversification. You should consider both of these types of investments as part of your overall financial strategy.

ADDITIONAL SUGGESTED INVESTING GUIDES

Bernstein, William J. *The Four Pillars of Investing: Lessons for Building a Winning Portfolio*. New York: McGraw-Hill Companies, 2002.

Edleson, Michael E. *Value Averaging: The Safe and Easy Strategy for Higher Investment Returns*. Chicago: International Publishing, 1991.

Morris, Kenneth M. *Wall Street Journal Guide to Understanding Money and Investing*. New York: Lightbulb Press, 2004.

---

[2] Dan Cullton, "The ETF Year in Review," *Morningstar.com*, 10 January 2006.

11

Advanced Investment Strategy

As discussed in chapter 10, there are six steps that one must take in order to develop a comprehensive investment strategy. (1) determine how much you can afford to invest; (2) set your investment horizon; (3) assess your risk tolerance; (4) identify investment instruments; (5) evaluate investment performance; and (6) adjust/rebalance your investment portfolio periodically.

This chapter uses those same six steps to introduce some advanced investment concepts and theories for those servicemembers wanting to take a more hands-on approach with their family's financial assets and have a full understanding of the topics introduced in the previous chapter. Some readers may not find this chapter "advanced" enough for their interests. Others who are looking to gain insights into technical financial analysis, sophisticated investing techniques, or into the trading of derivatives, currencies, and other alternative assets, may want to seek advice from one of the many guides found in the personal finance section of a local bookstore, as those topics are beyond the scope of this book and the needs of most servicemembers. However, most readers should find this chapter extremely beneficial when putting together personal investment strategies.

DETERMINE HOW MUCH YOU CAN AFFORD TO INVEST
Chapter 1 discussed the development of financial goals as well as a personal budget. There is no need to have an investment strategy if your monthly budget requires consumption of all your income for necessary goods and services. However, in most cases, the budget supports some means for investment. Advanced investors normally have performed this basic budget analysis and already have determined the amount available for investment.

SET YOUR INVESTMENT HORIZON

Based upon the financial objectives that you determined in chapter 1, you know how long you will invest funds to meet a particular financial objective. Investments with greater risk (volatility) provide the greatest potential for higher returns in the long term but also the greatest potential for losses in the short term. How do you determine what combination of assets might be right for you? Part of the answer lies in understanding your time horizon to understand which risks are more relevant to you. Table 11-1 illustrates the impact of an investor's time horizon and which type of asset he or she should choose.

Most investment managers equate the risk of a financial asset (e.g., stocks or bonds) to the volatility of its expected return. Historically, the financial markets have been very good at rewarding investors with higher returns for their more volatile assets. That is to say, if you are willing to accept the risk of having a few bad years with negative returns, the good years will reward you with higher returns. Looking at Table 11-1, the wide range in annual returns for stocks versus the relatively low variation in returns for Treasury bills demonstrates the past volatility of these financial assets. Therefore, the decline in volatility shown as you view the table from left to right is directly related to the decline in risk you assume as you invest in each asset category.

> *The risk of a financial asset equates to the volatility of its returns.*

Examine the one-year holding period returns at the top of the table. Note that either small or large company stocks had the highest return in forty-nine of the seventy-five one-year holding periods. However, they both had a negative return nearly a third of the time. Thus, if the time horizon for a particular goal is only a year away, stocks would not be a prudent selection for meeting it. Treasury bills would be a better choice since there was only one instance in which they had a negative return in a one-year time horizon.

Moving a little further out on the investment time horizon, look at the five-year holding periods. Notice that small company stocks had nine five-year periods with a negative return and large company stocks had seven. That means that if you had randomly chosen five consecutive years in this time period and invested in small company stocks, you would have lost money about 12% of the time. By contrast, government bonds were negative in only six periods—less than 9% of the time.

TABLE 11-1
COMPOUNDED ANNUAL RETURNS FOR VARIOUS TIME PERIODS (1926–2000)

	Small Company Stocks	Large Company Stocks	Long-Term Corporate Bonds	Long-Term Government Bonds	T-Bills	Inflation
	High		RISK		Low	
One-Year Holding Periods (75)						
Highest annual return	142.9%	54.0%	42.6%	40.4%	14.7%	18.2%
Lowest annual return	−58.0%	−43.3%	−8.1%	−9.2%	0.0%	−10.3%
Negative periods	23	21	17	21	1	10
Periods outpacing inflation	52	51	48	45	50	n/a
Periods with best return	32	17	0	14	12	n/a
Five-Year Holding Periods (71)						
Highest annual return	45.90%	28.55%	22.51%	21.62%	11.12%	10.06%
Lowest annual return	−27.54%	−12.47%	−2.22%	−2.14%	0.07%	−5.42%
Negative periods	9	7	3	6	0	7
Periods outpacing inflation	59	57	43	40	45	n/a
Periods with best return	37	23	0	9	2	n/a
Ten-Year Holding Periods (66)						
Highest annual return	30.38%	20.06%	16.32%	15.56%	9.17%	8.67%
Lowest annual return	−5.70%	−0.89%	0.99%	−0.07%	0.14%	−2.57%
Negative periods	2	2	0	1	0	6
Periods outpacing inflation	60	59	37	33	39	n/a
Periods with best return	37	22	0	3	4	n/a
Twenty-Year Holding Periods (56)						
Highest annual return	21.13%	17.87%	11.49%	11.99%	7.72%	6.36%
Lowest annual return	5.74%	3.11%	1.34%	0.69%	0.42%	0.07%
Negative periods	0	0	0	0	0	0
Periods outpacing inflation	56	56	32	22	36	n/a
Periods with best return	50	6	0	0	0	n/a

Source: Computations from Ibbotsons, 2001.

Now look at the twenty-year holding periods. Stocks not only had no periods with a negative return, but they also had the best return in each of the different twenty-year periods. Of those periods, small company stocks had the superior return fifty times and large company stocks six times. The important implication for developing an investment strategy is that the longer the investment time horizon, the more risk you can take in a portfolio to gain a better return. That is because over time, the good years have an opportunity to offset the bad years. On the other hand, the shorter the time horizons, the more important it is to invest in Treasury bills or bonds to reduce the impact of negative returns.

Considering the previous discussion, what should you conclude about risk? The greatest risk to a portfolio in the short term is the volatility of the stock and bond markets. Thus, you should place funds designated for short-term goals in an investment that provides lower volatility—and, correspondingly, a lower return. On the other hand, the greatest risk to your portfolio over the long term is the negative impact of inflation and taxes. Thus, you should invest funds with longer-term objectives in assets that provide the greater return over time to outpace inflation and taxes. Though there is greater risk with such investments, over time the good years can offset the bad years, thereby creating a positive return and increasing wealth.

> *Funds designated to meet your short-term goals should be placed in investments that provide the lowest volatility.*

ASSESS YOUR RISK TOLERANCE

The rate of return of stocks and other asset classes with high returns cannot properly be evaluated without also discussing risk. As already shown, the way to make your portfolio grow most quickly would be to choose the investment that provides the highest expected return. Clearly, the return associated with stocks would enable the quickest growth. So why shouldn't everyone invest his or her entire portfolio in stocks? Your tolerance for risk is driven by your investment horizon as well as your personality. If you need the funds for a financial objective that is a short time away, then you should not be willing to accept as much risk. If you cannot sleep at night due to the volatility of your portfolio, then you have not been honest with yourself regarding risk tolerance.

Risk is the extent to which an asset's returns vary from the expected rate of return. Stocks provide the greatest return, but stocks also provide the greatest risk, as reflected in their greater variation. If not for the trade-off between risk and return, most investors would choose the investment that provides the highest rate of return.

Standard deviation, a mathematical measure of variability, serves as a convenient measure for risk. Figure 11-1 depicts the range of returns that are within one standard deviation of the average return for four investments. You can see that the greater return corresponds to

Figure 11-1
Range of Expected Returns

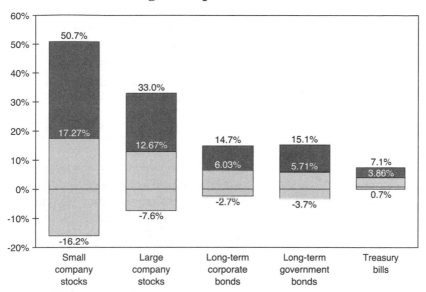

greater fluctuations in return, as measured by the standard deviation. Clearly, the distribution of likely returns is smaller for lower-risk investments, such as Treasury bills. It is possible for the returns to fall outside these ranges. In fact, a range of one standard deviation provides only a 68% level of confidence that a particular year's return will fall inside the range.

IDENTIFY INVESTMENT INSTRUMENTS
The investment horizon, along with your risk tolerance will dictate your investment selections. Diversification is an important technique to mitigate some of the risk mentioned in the previous section, and you probably have heard the cautionary expression about not putting all your eggs in one basket. Figure 11-2 below demonstrates why. Assume that you have a choice of two investments, depicted by curves A and B. Both have a positive return, and both fluctuate with the economy, stock market, technological progress, and other conditions. Over time, the upswings cancel the downswings and, on average, you will have a positive return. Unfortunately, no one can consistently predict when the swings will occur, and you may need the money from your investment just when it is in a trough instead of at a peak. To minimize that effect, you can buy equal amounts of both investment A and investment B so

that the upswings of one can counter the downswings of the other. Line C represents this portfolio, in which half of your investment is placed in A and the other half in B. Portfolio C has less volatility than either A or B, without sacrificing any of the return. Because investments react differently to the same economic conditions, it is possible to put together a portfolio with reduced volatility. This is the advantage of diversification.

> ***Diversifying your portfolio will reduce its volatility.***

Chapter 10 explained that mutual funds diversify across companies to eliminate specific company risk, but it is also important to diversify across sectors and asset classes to further protect your long-term investment portfolio. This is accomplished by asset allocation. Each year any asset class might be the best performer, so it is important that you are invested in a combination of asset classes that is consistent with your risk tolerance and investment horizon.

It is important to be an investor not a speculator. An investor has a consistent, long-term strategy, whereas a speculator responds to the market and attempts to time the market. Chasing the market trying to find the hot sector or asset class rather than simply rebalancing periodically can lead to poor portfolio performance. For instance, in the past thirty years, two thirds of all gains in the S&P 500 index occurred in only ten of the 360 monthly periods. If you were trying to time the market and were only invested in the S&P for the other 350 months during

Figure 11-2
Benefits of Diversification

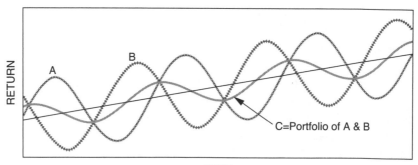

this period, your portfolio would have barely outperformed Treasury bills during the same time period. Unless you are lucky, a rebalanced portfolio will consistently outperform a speculator's portfolio in the long term.

Establishing an asset allocation is the process of determining the proportion of funds allotted to different asset classes within a portfolio. An asset class is a grouping of investments with similar characteristics or features. Figure 11-3 shows an asset allocation using three broad asset classes: stocks, bonds, and cash. While this figure shows a specific allocation to each of the asset classes, you should adjust these proportions to fit your own time horizon and risk preference.

How important is the asset allocation decision in relation to the returns of a portfolio? According to a study by Brinson, Hood, and Beebower,[1] 91.5% of the return associated with a portfolio can be explained by the asset allocation. Market timing and security selection explain only 1.8% and 4.6% of the returns associated with a portfolio, respectively.

Clearly, the most important decision is not which securities or funds to select, or when to get in or out of the market, but how to allocate holdings among asset classes. Most popular investment publications have countless articles on security and mutual fund selection and

Figure 11-3
Broad Asset Classes

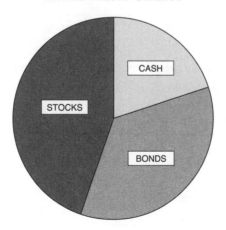

---

[1] "Determinants of Portfolio Performance," Brinson, Hood and Beebower, 1986.

market timing strategies, yet very few on asset allocation (although fortunately, this is changing). As a result, many believe that investment selection and market timing are the most important aspects of their investment decisions. In truth, they are only minor issues. Even the *Wall Street Journal* trivializes the ability of portfolio managers to pick individual securities by pitting these managers' selections against a dartboard selection of stocks; more often than not, the dartboard wins!

Within the three broad asset classes depicted in Figure 11-3, we now provide a more detailed and comprehensive listing of investment vehicles, which can be used to divide your investment portfolio, as shown in Table 11-2.

You must keep some portion of your portfolio readily accessible for everyday life and current spending. This portion of your portfolio is represented by cash. In broad terms, there are two other major categories of financial assets, and their features are quite different. The first major category includes all types of debt instruments which allow you the "investor" to loan money to some financial intermediary, such as a bank, the government, or a corporation in return for a specified interest rate over a fixed period of time, at which point the principal (the amount

TABLE 11-2
ASSET CLASSES

Cash	Debt Instruments (Bonds)	Equity Instruments (Stocks)	Other
Checking Account	Savings Bonds	Small Company Growth Stocks	Balanced Funds
Savings Account	Treasury Bills	Small Company Value Stocks	Real estate
Money Market	Treasury Notes	Medium Company Stocks	Precious metals
Certificates of Deposit	Treasury Bonds	Large Company Growth Stocks	Commodities
	Treasury Inflation-Protected Securities	Large Company Value Stocks	
	Municipal Bonds	International Stocks	
	Mortgage-backed Bonds	Emerging Market Stocks	
	Corporate bonds		
	High-yield		
	Corporate Bonds		
	International Bonds		

Note: For a detailed explanation of these instruments, refer to the end of this chapter.

loaned) is returned. We often call debt instruments "fixed-income assets" because the repayment schedule (which is income from your perspective) is fixed. The second major category includes various equity instruments through which the investor buys a stake in a company's profits. In equity investments, no interest rate is specified in advance. The amount you earn (or lose) depends on how the company performs over time. As a general rule, financial assets with higher risk also have higher potential returns, while assets with lower risk have lower potential returns. Review these asset classes and their accompanying characteristics in Table 11-3 below. For a detailed list of these instruments, refer to the end of this chapter.

How do you decide the proportions of funds to allocate to all these different asset classes? To a large extent, the determination of how to divide your portfolio into these different asset classes is based upon the timing of your financial goals and your risk tolerance. Based on when funds might be needed, you would not want to take much risk with money you have saved to achieve short-term goals. After working for several years to save enough for a house down payment, it would be a shame to see those savings lose 30% when you need them because of an unexpected downturn in the stock or bond market. Since few people can predict such downturns correctly (and none can do it consistently), the safe thing to do is to put the money for short-term goals in an investment that will provide a high degree of principal safety. In this case, the extra return that might be earned by leaving it in the stock or bond market over the next year is not worth the risk that the market might take a dip at the very time you want the money. The asset classes listed under "Cash" in Table 11-2 would be suitable for the funds targeted toward short-term goals. In addition, these vehicles are the place to invest your emergency fund, since you do not know when you might need it.

For medium-term goals (one- to four-year time horizon), it is prudent to take some risk to keep pace with the negative effects of taxes and inflation. Still, stock market downturns can be sharp and last for a number of years. It would be sad to think that a well-deserved second honeymoon cruise would be delayed or cost 18% more (typical credit card interest rate) because of a gamble for a slightly higher return. In this case, short-term bonds, longer-term CDs, and Treasury notes make sense as investment alternatives. Once a goal is only a year away, it then becomes a short-term goal, and you should move the funds into a cash equivalent investment.

TABLE 11-3: ASSET CLASSES AND THEIR CHARACTERISTICS

CASH	Returns	Risk	Horizon	Remarks
Checking Account	Low	Low	Short	Daily use funds
Savings Account	Low	Low	Short	Stand-by funds
Money Market Account	Low	Low	Short-Medium	Less liquid than savings
Certificates of Deposit	Low-Moderate	Low	Short-Medium	Early withdrawal penalties
DEBT INSTRUMENTS (Bonds)	**Returns**	**Risk**	**Horizon**	**Remarks**
US Govt Savings Bonds-Series I	Low	Very Low	Medium-Long	Inflation protected, check penalties
US Govt Savings Bonds-Series EE	Low	Low	Medium-Long	Discount buy, doubles in 20 yrs
US Treasury Bills	Low	Low	Short	Zero-coupon bond; all less than 1 yr
US Treasury Notes	Low	Low	Medium-Long	Coupon bond; Federal tax only; liquid
US Treasury Bonds	Low-Moderate	Low	Long	Coupon bond; Federal tax only; liquid
Treasury Inflation-Protected Securities	Low	Very Low	Medium-Long	Coupon bond; adjust w/inflation; liquid
Municipal Bonds	Low-Moderate	Low-Moderate	All horizons	Usually tax free at Fed & State
Mortgage-Backed Securities	Moderate	Moderate	All horizons	Diversifies exposure to real estate
Corporate Bonds	Low-Moderate	Low-Moderate	All horizons	Coupon bond; company pays you
High-Yield Corporate Bonds	High	High	All horizons	Coupon bond; riskier companies
International Bonds	Low-High	Low - High	All horizons	Research host country laws

TABLE 11-3: ASSET CLASSES AND THEIR CHARACTERISTICS

EQUITY INSTRUMENTS (Stocks)	Returns	Risk	Horizon	Remarks
Small Company Growth Stocks	High	Very High	Long	Most earnings growth potential
Small Company Value Stocks	High	Very High	Long	"Bargain" picks selling at discount
Medium Company Stocks	Moderate	Moderate	Medium-Long	Less risky, established stocks
EQUITY INSTRUMENTS (Stocks)	**Returns**	**Risk**	**Horizon**	**Remarks**
Large Company Growth Stocks	Low-Moderate	Low-Moderate	All horizons	Blue chips with growth potential
Large Company Value Stocks	Low-Moderate	Low-Moderate	All horizons	Blue chips selling at discount
International Stocks	Low-High	Low-Very High	All horizons	Numerous unknowns; research
Emerging Market Stocks	Moderate-Very High	Moderate-Very High	All horizons	Diversify your exposure; research
OTHER	**Returns**	**Risk**	**Horizon**	**Remarks**
Balanced Funds	Moderate	Moderate	All horizons	Use to stabilize your portfolio
Real Estate	Low-High	Low-Very High	All horizons	Local conditions rule; tax friendly
Precious Metals	Low-High	Low-Very High	All horizons	Requires speculation; read forecasts
Commodities	Low-High	Low-Very High	Short	Requires speculation; read forecasts

For long-term goals (greater than five years), the greatest risk to increasing wealth and achieving the desired goal is failing to outpace inflation and taxes. Stocks offer the best chance to achieve that purpose. Considering the discussion of diversification previously, you should divide your long-term funds among different investments to take advantage of the fact that different investments react differently to economic conditions.

> *Stocks offer the best chance to outperform inflation and the negative impact of taxes.*

A simple technique for your investments associated with long-term goals is to put 25% of the money into an index fund or exchange-traded fund (introduced in chapter 10) that holds large-company stocks, 25% into small-company stocks, 25% into international stocks, and divide the remaining 25% among the bond or other asset classes shown in Table 11-2. Using this portfolio as a baseline, you can adjust the proportions to accept more risk (by increasing the amount in small-company and international stocks) or less risk (by increasing the amount in bond or large-company stock investments).

As long-term goals become medium-term goals, the cash needed to meet the medium-term goals should be moved into an appropriate medium-term investment. For example, as a daughter enters ninth grade, it is time to shift enough cash out of the investment portfolio to pay for the first year's college costs and put it into one of the medium-term investment vehicles. Similarly, when your daughter enters tenth grade, you should transfer money to pay for the second year's college costs into a medium-term investment. A similar process continues each time a long-term goal becomes a medium-term goal.

Now you can see the importance of starting out with a list of achievable goals. If you fail to list goals and manage your time horizon appropriately, you may find that you will not have enough money accumulated to meet long-term goals because you placed assets necessary for short- and medium-term goals in risky assets. This might force you to raid your long-term goal accounts to pay for short-term needs.

Once you have your asset allocation, it is time to select specific investments for each of the asset classes. As the Brinson study suggests, this decision is much less important than the asset allocation decision. In general, you can either choose the individual securities shown in Table 11-2 or invest in a mutual fund or exchange traded fund that invests in the same type of securities. For most investors, mutual funds are the logical choice because of their professional management, low costs, and diversification. For those investing larger amounts, exchange traded funds might be more appropriate because the commission charges have less impact and capital gains taxes are reduced. Chapter 10 describes both mutual funds and exchange-traded funds in detail.

During the accumulation phase of your investment plan, you may want to reduce the impact of taxes. If you are in the 27% tax bracket (or higher), consider a municipal money market fund for your short-term funds. The dividends of the municipal funds are exempt from federal income tax, and in some cases you can obtain funds that are state tax-exempt if your state has an income tax. For your medium-term funds, consider a municipal short-term bond fund for the same reason. For your long-term portfolio, consider placing investments that generate dividends or capital gains distributions into tax-favored plans such as an IRA or a 401(k) retirement plan. Since you do not need the income to meet your basic expenditures but are only planning to reinvest those profits, you should generally try to defer the taxes as long as possible.

Essentially, there are only three factors that influence the purchasing power of the funds you accumulate: rate of return, inflation, and taxes. Only one of these factors contributes to wealth growth; the other two diminish your ability to buy more goods and services.

> *Rate of return, inflation and taxes influence the ability of your savings to achieve increased purchasing power.*

Rate of Return. Figure 11-4 plots the annual increase of $1 invested in 1926 over seventy years in each of five investments. As you can see, the historical return for small- and large-company stocks is significantly greater than that of government bonds and Treasury bills. You will also notice that while the return of small- and large-company stocks is high, so is the variation from year to year. This annual variation causes the plots of the small- and large-company stocks to be much more jagged than the relatively smooth graphs of bonds and Treasury bills. This graph is not adjusted for inflation or taxes.

Taxes. For most of the assets you choose, taxes will reduce the amount that you earn. Table 11-4 reflects the average annual return rep-

Figure 11-4
Growth of $1 from 1926 to 2000

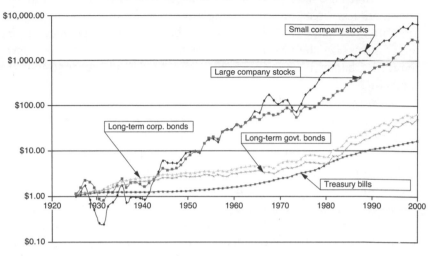

resented by each asset class. The first column shows the annual return. The second column is what is important to most investors: the return you will see after taxes (assuming a 27% marginal tax rate). Paying taxes on your returns reduces the overall return of the portfolio and must be considered as you meet the broad goal of increasing wealth. Though there are some investments that provide tax-favored treatment, such as retirement plans, IRAs, and variable annuities, most only permit deferring taxes. Certainly, the prudent investor takes advantage of these opportunities, but the deferral does not completely negate the impact of taxes; it just delays tax payments until later. *The exceptions to this include the Roth IRA and the Roth 401(k), which is strongly recommended as your first choice in retirement savings options (see chapter 10).*

Inflation. The third column in Table 11-4 shows clearly why you would not want to invest all your money in conservative investments like Treasury bills and certificates of deposit (CDs). Note that a 100% Treasury bill portfolio would actually lose purchasing power. Why? The rate of return associated with Treasury bills is not enough to offset the negative impacts of taxes and inflation over time. This can have a significant impact on your ability to maintain and/or increase your wealth. However, some investors do invest solely in these instruments because it is better than stuffing cash under a mattress. If you retired at age fifty-five and put all of your money in Treasury bills or CDs, the purchasing power of your accumulated wealth would substantially decline during your retirement. That is true even before you withdraw any funds to

TABLE 11-4 ANNUAL RETURN, TAXES, AND INFLATION, 1926–2000

	Average Annual Return 1926–2000	Average Return after 27% Taxes	Average Return after Taxes and Inflation	Standard Deviation
Small-company stocks	17.27%	12.61%	9.44%	33.44%
Large-company stocks	12.67	9.25	6.08	20.32
Long-term corporate bonds	6.03	4.40	1.23	8.69
Long-term government bonds	5.71	4.17	1.00	9.42
T-bills	3.86	2.82	−0.35	3.18
Inflation	3.17	n/a	n/a	4.42

Source: Computations based on Ibbotsons Associates, 2001.

meet living expenses. Since your ability and desire to earn a living will have diminished by the time you reach age seventy-five, you may want to consider an alternative to such a conservative approach.

Note the minimal positive return on long-term government bonds. Returns associated with these investments barely maintain purchasing power for the investor after accounting for taxes and inflation. In contrast, the return for stocks not only outpaces inflation and taxes but permits an increase in wealth. Keep in mind, however, that these returns are historical averages. Year-to-year results can vary significantly, as shown by the standard deviation associated with each of the investments.

One of the best ways to implement your investment strategy is to put as much of your investment program on "autopilot" as possible. You can use allotments, automatic checking-account withdrawals, and mutual fund automatic-investment plans to enforce the savings commitment you made when you developed your budget.

> *Use allotments, automatic account withdrawals, and mutual fund automatic investment plans to enforce your commitment to savings.*

EVALUATE INVESTMENT PERFORMANCE PERIODICALLY

At least annually, you should compare the performance of your selected funds to the benchmarks against which they compete. If the funds consistently are not performing well against the benchmarks, you might consider moving to a different fund or investing in the benchmark index itself. Remember that the fund must beat the index on a continual basis even after considering all fees associated with an actively managed fund—a particularly difficult task to accomplish. Chapter 10 details the advantage of investing in the index itself rather than an actively managed fund.

ADJUST/REBALANCE YOUR INVESTMENT PORTFOLIO PERIODICALLY

Basically, there are two reasons to adjust or rebalance your portfolio. The first has to do with your changing horizon as time passes and the second has to do with asset allocation. First, continue to monitor your financial objectives as they approach. Adjust the funding that supports those that are near-term goals into a more conservative asset allocation.

Second, because asset classes react differently to existing economic conditions, you should periodically check the values of each asset class to see if they are still in line with percentages you have chosen. In all likelihood, some investments will have done so well that their percentage of the long-term portfolio has grown. To achieve the desired asset allocation, you can either add new funds to other assets to bring them back up to the desired percentage or sell some of the investment that has done well to bring it back in line with the desired asset allocation. Keep in mind that if you sell an investment that has performed well, you will incur tax on the capital gain, so adding new funds is the more efficient option. If you choose to sell or buy mutual funds, inquire about the fund's annual or quarterly distribution date for capital gains and dividends. By buying at the "wrong" time, you can trigger an adverse tax event and the result will be that you have bought a capital gains tax liability that you did not earn. If the funds are in an IRA or 401(k), you can move money between accounts without immediate tax implications, provided you never take possession of the funds.

Doing such rebalancing once or twice a year is adequate in most cases. Your portfolio rebalancing should be done at the same time you review your goals; you must then decide whether to move funds either from the long-term to the medium-term portfolio or from the medium-term to the short-term portfolio. Doing so will make for a much more efficient means of achieving the desired asset allocation. The goal would be to minimize the number of selling transactions to defer paying capital gains on the profits. Thus, newly accumulated funds (from your annual military or spouse's income or from having dividends and capital gains sent to a money market fund instead of automatically reinvested) can rebalance your portfolio without incurring additional taxes. The first place to put new funds is into short-term investments that would be subsequently transferred at the next rebalancing; this might be when one of your goals crosses time-frame boundaries, such as from long-term to medium-term or medium-term to short-term. Investing new funds in this way reduces the fund shifting required at the next rebalancing, thereby reducing taxes and transaction costs. If this situation is not applicable, then add the funds to your long-term portfolio by maximizing investments first into pension plans or IRAs, and then into your other long-term investments.

> *Rebalance your portfolio once or twice a year at the same time you review your family's financial goals.*

Once you have made the necessary switches, you can forget about your plan until the next year. The peace of mind of knowing you have a workable plan will make you and your family confident that you will achieve your financial goals.

DETAILED EXPLANATION OF FINANCIAL INSTRUMENTS
The following information was compiled using *www.investopedia.com*. Please visit the website for more information on these topics and a wealth of other financial explanations.

Cash
Checking Account
- DEFINITION: A deposit account for funds intended for frequent use and quick turnover.
- RATE OF RETURN: Checking accounts offer very low interest on unused cash balances. (You are lucky if your checking account earns more than the rate of inflation.) For a good compilation of best checking rates, check *www.bankrate.com*.

Savings Account
- DEFINITION: A deposit account intended for money that you need for unexpected short-term expenses.
- RATE OF RETURN: A savings account offers lower returns than market rates and should be used for emergency funds and

short-term requirements. Writing checks from a savings account generally costs more than from a checking account, so you should limit your amount of withdrawals. For a good compilation of best savings rates, check *www.bankrate.com*.

Money Market Account (MMA)
- DEFINITION: A savings account that offers a competitive rate of interest (real rate) in exchange for larger-than-normal deposits. Many money market accounts place restrictions on the number of transactions you can make in a month (e.g., five or less).
- RATE OF RETURN: You usually have to maintain a certain balance in the account to receive higher rates of interest. Some banks require at least $500 dollars, while others require a much higher balance. As a general rule, the higher the minimum balance (more of your money the bank can lend for profit), the higher the return. For a good compilation of best MMA rates, check *www.bankrate.com*.

Certificates of Deposit (CD)
- DEFINITION: A savings certificate that entitles the bearer to receive interest from money loaned to a financial institution. A CD bears a maturity date, a specified fixed interest rate, and can be issued in any denomination. CDs are generally issued by commercial banks and are insured by the FDIC. The term of a CD generally ranges from one month to five years. A certificate of deposit is a promissory note issued by a bank. It is a time deposit that restricts holders from withdrawing funds on demand. However, it is possible to withdraw the money, but this action will often incur a penalty.
- RATE OF RETURN: A CD's rate of return will vary with the length of maturity and the current interest-rate environment. As a general rule, the longer the maturity (the longer you give up your money), the higher the rate of return. For a good compilation of best CD rates, check *www.Bankrate.com*.

Debt Instruments (Bonds)
U.S. Government Savings Bond—I Bond
- DEFINITION: U.S. government–issued debt security that offers an investor inflationary protection, as its yield is tied to the inflation rate. Available directly from the U.S. Treasury, this debt security is an exceptionally low-risk investment suitable

for the most risk-averse investor; it has virtually zero default and inflationary risk.
- RATE OF RETURN: an I Bond earns a guaranteed real rate of return (inflation adjusted) that compounds interest monthly and is paid out at maturity. It is important to note that the interest earnings from an I Bond may be excluded from federal income tax when used to finance education. Interest on an I Bond is exempt from state and local taxes. If you redeem an I Bond within the first five years, you will forfeit the three most recent months' interest; after five years, you will not be penalized. For more information and current rates on the I Bond, check *www.savingsbonds.gov*.

U.S. Government Savings Bond—EE Bond
- DEFINITION: An interest-bearing U.S. government savings bond issued at a discount from par and sold at half its face value (i.e., you pay $25 for a $50 bond). Available in denominations of $50, $75, $100, $200, $500, $1,000, $5,000, and $10,000. A savings bond must be held a minimum of one year, and there is a three-month interest penalty applied to a bond held less than five years from issue date. At a minimum, Treasury guarantees that a bond's value will double after twenty years (from its original maturity), and it will continue to earn the fixed rate set at the time of issue unless a new rate or rate structure is announced. If a bond does not double in value as the result of applying the fixed rate for twenty years, the Treasury will make a one-time adjustment at original maturity to make up the difference.
- RATE OF RETURN: Rates for new issues will be adjusted each May 1 and November 1, with each new rate effective for all bonds issued through the following six months. Interest accrues monthly and is compounded semiannually. Interest on Series EE Bonds is exempt from state and local taxes. If you redeem EE Bonds within the first five years, you will forfeit the three most-recent months' interest; after five years, you will not be penalized. For more information on the EE Bonds, check *www.savingsbonds.gov*.

U.S. Treasury Bills
- DEFINITION: A short-term debt obligation backed by the U.S. government with a maturity of less than one year. T-bills are sold in denominations of $1,000 up to a maximum purchase of

$5 million and commonly have maturities of one month (four weeks), three months (thirteen weeks) or six months (twenty-six weeks).

- RATE OF RETURN: A T-bill is issued through a competitive bidding process at a discount from par, which means that rather than paying fixed interest payments like conventional bonds, the appreciation of the bond provides the return to the holder. For example, if you buy a thirteen-week T-bill priced at $9,800, essentially, the U.S. government writes you an IOU for $10,000 that it agrees to repay in three months. You will not receive regular payments as you would with a coupon bond, for example. Instead, the appreciation comes from the difference between the discounted value you originally paid and the amount you receive ($10,000) when you redeem it. In this case, the T-bill pays a 2.04 percent interest rate ($200/$9,800 = 2.04 percent) over a three-month period. For more information and current rates on T-bills, check *www.savingsbonds.gov*.

U.S. Treasury Notes
- DEFINITION: A marketable, U.S. government debt security earning a fixed rate of interest every six months until maturity. T-notes are issued in terms of two, three, five, and ten years. T-notes can be bought either directly from the U.S. government or through a bank. When buying from the government, you can either put in a competitive or noncompetitive bid. With a competitive bid, you specify the yield you want; however, this does not mean your bid will be accepted, and you may come away empty handed. A noncompetitive bid is one where you accept whatever yield is determined at auction. T-notes are extremely popular investments as there is a large secondary market that adds to their liquidity.
- RATE OF RETURN: Interest payments on the notes are made every six months until maturity. The income for interest payments is not taxable on a municipal or state level, but it is federally taxed. For more information and current rates on T-notes, check *www.savingsbonds.gov*.

U.S. Treasury Bonds
- DEFINITION: A marketable, fixed-interest U.S. government debt security with a maturity of more than ten years. Treasury bonds are issued with a minimum denomination of $1,000. The

bonds are initially sold through auction in which the maximum purchase amount is $5 million if the bid is noncompetitive or 35% of the offering if the bid is competitive. A competitive bid states the rate that the bidder is willing to accept; it will be accepted based on how it compares to the set rate of the bond. A noncompetitive bid ensures that the bidder will get the bond, but he or she will have to accept the set rate. After the auction, the bonds can be sold in the secondary market.

- RATE OF RETURN: The bonds make interest payments every six months, and the income that holders receive is taxed only at the federal level. For more information and current rates on T-bonds, check *www.savingsbonds.gov*.

Treasury Inflation-Protected Security

- DEFINITION: A special type of Treasury note or bond that offers protection from inflation. Like other Treasuries, an inflation-indexed security pays interest every six months and pays the principal when the security matures. The principal you receive on a TIPS increases with inflation and decreases with deflation (as measured by the Consumer Price Index). When a TIPS reaches maturity, you are paid the adjusted principal or original principal, whichever is greater.
- RATE OF RETURN: If U.S. Treasuries are the world's safest investments, then you might say that TIPS are the safest of the safe. This is because your real rate of return, which represents the growth of your purchasing power, is guaranteed. The downside is that, because of this safety, TIPS offer a lower return. For more information and current rates on TIPS, check *www.savingsbonds.gov*.

Municipal Bonds

- DEFINITION: A debt security issued by a state, municipality, or county, in order to finance its capital expenditures. A municipal bond is exempt from federal taxes and most state and local taxes, especially if you live in the state the bond is issued. Such expenditures might include the construction of highways, bridges, or schools.
- RATE OF RETURN: "Munis" are bought for their favorable tax implications and are popular with people in high-income tax brackets. For more information and current rates on municipal bonds from across the nations, check www.municipalbonds.com.

Mortgage-Backed Securities (MBS)
- DEFINITION: An investment instrument that represents owner-ship of an undivided interest in a group of mortgages. An MBS is a way for a smaller regional bank to lend mortgages to its customers without having to worry if the customers have the assets to cover the loan. Instead, the bank acts as a middleman between the homebuyer and the investment markets.
- RATE OF RETURN: Principal and interest from the individual mortgages are used to pay investors' principal and interest on the MBS (also known as "mortgage pass-through"). When you invest in a mortgage-backed security you are lending money to a homebuyer or business. For more information and current rates, check *www.fanniemae.com/mbs/mbsbasics*.

Corporate Bonds
- DEFINITION: A debt security issued by a corporation, as opposed to those issued by the government. A corporate bond typically has a par value of $1,000, is taxable, has a term matu-rity, and is traded on a major exchange.
- RATE OF RETURN: Every bond issue is given a rating to indi-cate the risk associated with the bond issue. Bonds with lower risk have lower returns and are sometimes called "investment grade" while others with high risk have high returns and are called "high-yield" bonds. For more information on the rating system used for bond issuance, check *www.moodys.com* or *www2.standardandpoors.com*. For a compilation of corporate bond rates, check *www.zionsbank.com/zd_bonds_less.jsp*.

High-Yield Corporate Bonds
- DEFINITION: A bond rated "BB" or lower because of its high default risk (see the Moody's or Standard and Poor's website above for more information on the rating system). You may also hear these bonds referred to as a "junk bond" or "speculative bond." These are usually purchased for speculative purposes, meaning you have some comfortable intuition about the future of the company issuing the bond.
- RATE OF RETURN: Junk bonds typically offer interest rates three to four percentage points higher than safer government issues. For a compilation of high-yield corporate bond rates, check *www.zionsbank.com/zd_bonds_less.jsp*.

International Bonds
- DEFINITION: A bond that is issued in a country by a nondomestic entity. International bonds are issued in a currency other than the currency of the country or market in which the bond is issued. For example, a Eurobond is issued by an international syndicate and categorized according to the currency in which it is denominated. A Eurodollar bond that is denominated in U.S. dollars and issued in Japan by an Australian company would be an example of a Eurobond. The Australian company in this example could issue the Eurodollar bond in any country other than the U.S.
- RATE OR RETURN: A Eurobond is an attractive financing tool as it gives issuers the flexibility to choose the country in which to offer their bond according to the country's regulatory constraints. They may also denominate their Eurobond in their preferred currency. Eurobonds are attractive to investors as they have small par values and high liquidity.

Equity Instruments (Stocks)

Prior to defining an equity asset, it is important to understand how a company's total value is measured in our markets. A company's total value is measured by its market capitalization. Market capitalization is estimated by determining the cost of buying an entire business in its current state. Often referred to as "market cap," it is the total dollar value of all outstanding shares. It is calculated by multiplying the number of shares outstanding by the current market price of one share. For example, if a business has fifty shares, each with a market value of $10, then the business's market capitalization is $500 (50 shares x $10/share).

Brokerages can vary on their exact monetary-amount definitions, but these are the current approximate classes of market capitalization:
- Mega Cap: Market cap of $200 billion and greater
- Big/Large Cap: $10 billion to $200 billion
- Mid Cap: $2 billion to $10 billion
- Small Cap: $300 million to $2 billion
- Micro Cap: $50 million to $300 million
- Nano Cap: Under $50 million

Small-Company Growth Stock
- DEFINITION: Refers to a stock with a relatively small market capitalization. The definition of small cap can vary among bro-

kerages, but generally it is a company with a market capitalization of between $300 million and $2 billion. One of the biggest
advantages of investing in small-cap stocks is the opportunity to
beat institutional investors. Because mutual funds have restrictions that limit them from buying large portions of any one
issuer's outstanding shares, some mutual funds would not be
able to give the small cap a meaningful position in the fund. To
overcome these limitations, the fund would usually have to file
with the SEC, which means tipping its hand and inflating the
previously attractive price. As a growth stock, earnings would be
expected to grow at an above average rate relative to the market.
A growth stock usually does not pay a dividend, as the company
would prefer to reinvest retained earnings in capital projects.
Most technology companies are growth stocks. Note that a
growth company's stock is not always classified as growth stock.
In fact, a growth company's stock can often be overvalued.
- RATE OF RETURN: Most of the growth in our markets is due
  to growth from small companies. Again, you would expect
  above average growth in earnings and you would expect dividends to be reinvested. You can expect that the price of stocks in
  this asset class is higher than its peers because the high growth
  rates will create greater demand with prices being bid up. The
  higher growth rates translate into higher rates of return, but also
  more volatility and the chance of greater losses. You should look
  to invest for the longer term in this asset class.

Small-Company Value Stock
- DEFINITION: Refers to stock with a relatively small market
  capitalization. The definition of small cap can vary among brokerages, but generally it is a company with a market capitalization of between $300 million and $2 billion. One of the biggest
  advantages of investing in small-cap stocks is the opportunity to
  beat institutional investors. Because mutual funds have restrictions that limit them from buying large portions of any one
  issuer's outstanding shares, some mutual funds would not be
  able to give the small cap a meaningful position in the fund. To
  overcome these limitations, the fund would usually have to file
  with the SEC, which means tipping its hand and inflating the
  previously attractive price. As a value stock, this asset tends to
  trade at a lower price relative to its fundamentals (i.e., dividends, earnings, sales, etc.) and thus considered undervalued by

a value investor. Common characteristics of such stocks include a high-dividend yield, low price-to-book ratio, and/or low price-to-earnings ratio. A value investor believes that the market is not always efficient and that it is possible to find companies trading for less than they are worth.

- RATE OF RETURN: Again, you must realize that most of the growth in our markets is due to growth from small companies. As a value stock, you would search for "bargains" within the small cap asset class. This would be small cap stocks that are trading for less than their usual valuation. Obviously, you would be speculating that the "bargain" would create some appreciation in price. There is higher risk in this speculation which incurs greater volatility on the upside and the downside. Again, you should look to invest for the longer term in this asset class.

Medium-Company Stock
- DEFINITION: This asset is the shortened form of "middle cap" or "medium cap." These companies have a market capitalization between $2 billion and $10 billion. As the name implies, mid-cap companies are in the middle of the pack. Mid caps are not too big, but they have a respectably-sized market capitalization.
- RATE OF RETURN: This larger asset class is less risky than small caps and therefore provides lower returns. As you move relatively closer to needing your savings, you may choose to move out of this asset class to an even less risky position (at the cost of lower returns).

Large-Company Growth Stock
- DEFINITION: A company with a market capitalization between $10 billion and $200 billion. These are the largest companies in the financial world. Examples include Wal-Mart, Microsoft and General Electric. However, these stocks are sometimes called "mega caps." As a growth stock, earnings would be expected to grow at an above-average rate relative to the market. A growth stock usually does not pay a dividend, as the company would prefer to reinvest retained earnings in capital projects. Most technology companies are growth stocks. Note that a growth company's stock is not always classified as growth stock. In fact, a growth company's stock can often be overvalued.
- RATE OF RETURN: As a growth stock, above average growth in earnings would be expected, and dividends would be expected

to be reinvested. Also, the price of a stock in this asset class will be higher than its peers because the high growth rates will create greater demand with prices being bid up. The large cap companies are generally well established with lower risk and therefore, lower returns. The large cap companies are the least risky of the individual equity choices. Large cap companies are very stable, with minimal risk, so they traditionally provide the lowest returns.

Large-Company Value Stock
- DEFINITION: A company with a market capitalization between $10 billion and $200 billion. These are the largest companies in the financial world. Examples include Wal-Mart, Microsoft, and General Electric. However, these stocks are sometimes called "mega caps." As a value stock, this asset tends to trade at a lower price relative to its fundamentals (i.e., dividends, earnings, sales, etc.) and thus is considered undervalued by a value investor. Common characteristics of such stocks include a high dividend yield, low price-to-book ratio and/or low price-to-earnings ratio. A value investor believes that the market is not always efficient and that it is possible to find companies trading for less than they are worth.
- RATE OF RETURN: As a value stock, an investor would search for "bargains" within the large cap asset class. This would be large cap stocks that are trading for less than their usual valuation. Obviously, this would be speculation that the "bargain" would create some appreciation in price. The large cap companies are generally well established with lower risk and, therefore, lower returns. The large cap companies are the least risky of the individual equity choices. Large cap companies are very stable, with minimal risk, so they traditionally provide the lowest returns.

International Stock Fund
- DEFINITION: A mutual fund that can invest in companies located anywhere outside of its own country. Many people confuse an international fund with a global fund. The difference is that a global fund includes the entire world, and an international fund includes the entire world excluding its home country. There are many different options to choose when investing outside the United States. If an investor would like exposure to

higher growth rates in different regions or specific countries, then he or she must build some understanding of the social structure, political structure, and government within that area of interest.

- RATE OF RETURN: Depending on the location, the higher risk may be too great—unless the attraction is the higher risks that could generate higher returns. (You should be very cautious when investing outside the United States. Make sure that you diversify your exposure among more than one region.)

Emerging-Market Stock Fund

- DEFINITION: A mutual fund investing a majority of its assets in the financial markets of a developing country, typically a small market with a short operating history. It is in your best interest to diversify emerging-market investments across a few regions of higher growth. Hopefully, a loss in one region could be mitigated by successes in other regions.
- RATE OF RETURN: These funds offer higher potential returns in exchange for greater risk.

Other

Balanced Funds

- DEFINITION: A mutual fund that invests its assets in money market accounts, bonds, preferred stock, and common stock with the intention to provide both growth and income. This asset class is also known as an "asset-allocation fund." A balanced fund is geared towards investors looking for a mixture of safety, income, and capital appreciation. The amount the mutual fund invests into each asset class usually must remain within a set minimum and maximum.
- RATE OF RETURN: The security of a balanced fund may slow upside potential, but it will also slow any downside pressure as well.

Real Estate

- DEFINITION: Land plus anything permanently fixed to it, including buildings, sheds and other items attached to the structure. Unlike other investments, real estate is dramatically affected by the condition of the immediate area where the property is located. With the exception of a global recession, real estate is affected primarily by local factors.

- RATE OF RETURN: Since real estate is affected by local conditions, it may be better to diversify holdings in the same fashion mentioned within the emerging-markets asset class (discussed above in this chapter). An investor who would like to gain some real estate exposure while minimizing local area risks can invest in Mortgage Backed Securities (MBS) or REITs (see chapter 5). Before buying a single property, an individual investor should research forecast about future real estate appreciation (or depreciation) within its local area. The risk and reward of any real estate investment will be governed by the conditions within its local area. For more information on MBS, check *www.fanniemae.com*.

Precious Metals
- DEFINITION: Valuable metal such as gold, iridium, palladium, platinum, or silver. A precious metal generally climbs in price when there is uncertainty in our markets. Investing in a precious metal can be done either by purchasing the physical asset, or by purchasing futures contracts for the particular metal. For example, if an investor thinks the price of gold is going to climb, he or she can buy an option to buy gold in the future at some set price. If the price of gold rises above the set price, then the option to buy (at the lower set price) can be sold to another person in a secondary market. This allows the investor to benefit from the appreciation without ever owning or paying the price of the actual gold.
- RATE OF RETURN: Obviously there is speculation in precious metals. The speculation involves risk and the risk can provide for higher returns, but it can also provide for greater losses. For more information, check *www.monex.com*.

Commodities
- DEFINITION: A basic good used in commerce that is interchangeable with other commodities of the same type. Commodities are most often used as inputs in the production of other goods or services. The quality of a given commodity may differ slightly, but it is essentially uniform across producers. When they are traded on an exchange, commodities must also meet specified minimum standards, also known as a basis grade. The basic idea is that there is little differentiation between a com-

modity coming from one producer and the same commodity from another producer—a barrel of oil is basically the same product, regardless of the producer. However, compare this to electronics, and the quality and features of a given product will be completely different depending on the producer. Some traditional examples of commodities include grains, gold, beef, oil, and natural gas. More recently, the definition has expanded to include financial products such as foreign currencies and indexes. Technological advances have also led to new types of commodities being exchanged in the marketplace: for example, cell phone minutes and bandwidth. The sale and purchase of commodities is usually carried out through futures contracts on exchanges that standardize the quantity and minimum quality of the commodity being traded.

- RATE OF RETURN: You will not see many individual investors contributing to our commodities exchanges. However, you can expose your investment to these markets by investing in a commodity index. A commodity index tracks a basket of commodities to measure their performance. These indexes will often be traded on exchanges, allowing investors to gain easier access to commodities without having to enter the futures market. The value of these indexes fluctuates based on the underlying commodities, and this value can be traded on the exchange in the same way as stock-index futures. There is a wide range of indexes on the market, each of them varying by their components. The Reuters/Jefferies CRB Index, which is traded on the New York Board of Trade, comprises nineteen different types of commodities ranging from aluminum to wheat. They also vary in the way they are weighted; some indexes, for instance, are equally weighted and others have a predetermined, fixed weighting scheme. For more information, check *www.nybot.com*.

12

Investing for Retirement

Previous generations relied on Social Security and pension plans to fund retirement. However, the basic structure of company-sponsored pension plans has changed drastically in the last few decades and the future of Social Security is widely debated. Those who retire from the military often find that their retirement income is not enough to sustain the lifestyle they choose for retirement. Most individuals want to ensure they will never become a financial burden on their children. Therefore, in order for individuals to support their retirements, live financially independent, and prepare for any emergencies that may arise later in life, they must start saving money *now*. This chapter will explore retirement investing options in detail and will provide some considerations for the basic investor.

Retirement Savings Priority

1. Max out servicemember's Roth IRA
2. Max out spouse's 401(k) (only if company matches contributions)
3. Max out spouse's Roth IRA
4. Max out spouse's 401(k) (even if company does not match contributions)
5. Max out servicemember's TSP
6. Mutual funds
7. Stocks and Bonds, CDs, Money Markets

Taxes can drastically erode the value of a lifetime of savings. If you can avoid paying taxes legally, or at least defer paying them, you will be able to increase your wealth faster and increase the likelihood of accomplishing your financial objectives. Fortunately, laws provide taxpayers with several means to defer, and in some cases avoid completely, paying taxes on investments. These include Individual Retirement Arrangements (IRAs); 401(k) and 403(b) plans; and for government employees, including military personnel, the Thrift Savings Plan (TSP).

We will discuss each of these options and provide you with information to maximize your wealth, minimize your taxes, and achieve your goals.

INDIVIDUAL RETIREMENT ARRANGEMENT (IRA)

An Individual Retirement Arrangement (IRA), commonly called an Individual Retirement Account, is a personal savings plan offered to individuals providing them tax advantages as an incentive to set aside money for retirement or, in some plans, for certain education expenses (see chapter 7). In its basic form, establishing and contributing funds to an IRA commits you to an "arrangement" with the federal government. By accepting at least part of the financial responsibility to provide for your family upon retirement with an IRA savings, the government's taxing agent (the Internal Revenue Service [IRS]) gives you a tax break on that savings.

Entering this arrangement is a simple process. Most financial institutions, from your local bank to major mutual fund companies, offer the ability to sign up for an IRA. Enrolling you and your spouse can take less than twenty minutes with the click of a mouse at any one of hundreds of online banking websites. Some of these companies may charge an annual fee to maintain your IRA, but many do not. As with any other economic decision, it pays for you to shop around to find the best deal. You can save time and money by establishing an IRA with the financial institution in which you have already set up checking and savings accounts, making it easy for you to transfer funds into your IRA.

The more difficult part of the process involves three subsequent decisions you must make as an investor in an IRA. First, you must determine how much you can afford to invest, the first step in developing your investment strategy discussed in chapters 10 and 11. After putting together a budget using the procedures outlined in chapter 1, you should have identified how much disposable income you have available to contribute to an IRA and compare that to the limits the IRS has placed on annual contributions (discussed later). If all of your income is consumed by higher priority expenses such as repaying credit card debt, servicing family necessities, and funding your emergency savings account, you obviously cannot put savings into an IRA and realize the tax benefits. However, if funds are available for saving, your first priority should be maximizing the IRA tax advantages for you and your spouse.

> *The first priority for servicemembers who plan to save for their retirement should be to maximize the tax advantages provided by an IRA.*

Second, you must decide which type of investment instrument is most likely to provide the returns necessary for you to meet your financial goals at retirement, based on your personal risk tolerance and the time available until you need or are allowed to withdraw your IRA funds (age 59.5 in most cases). A common misunderstanding is that an IRA is an investment instrument itself. It is not. Instead, think of an IRA as a "bubble" that protects your annual investment contributions, up to the IRS limits, from standard tax treatment. Any account, be it a mutual fund, CD, brokerage account, or standard savings account, can be placed inside the "bubble." In doing so, you agree to an "arrangement" to adhere to the restrictions placed on IRAs (discussed in detail in this chapter) in return for special tax benefits granted by the IRS. Since most servicemembers have more than five years until they reach the government's definition of minimum retirement age of 59.5, IRAs are typically considered a long-term savings goal. You should apply the principles learned in the two previous chapters in selecting the type of IRA investment that best suits you and your goals. There are two other facts concerning your IRA: (1) it can represent a combination of multiple financial instruments (e.g., stock and bond mutual funds) as long as you do not exceed the annual contribution limits, and (2) you can change instruments covered by your IRA as many times as you like (i.e., transfer funds from high-risk assets to low-risk assets as you approach retirement age) as long as you keep all the funds inside the "bubble."

> *An IRA is not itself an investment instrument; it can be a combination of mutual funds, CDs, brokerage accounts, and/or standard savings accounts of your choosing.*

The third decision required of you is to select between two types of IRAs: Roth and Traditional. The main difference centers on whether or not *contributions* (investments made into the plan) are tax-deductible and if the *distributions* (gains made on the contributions) are taxable when withdrawn. The advantages and disadvantages to each are summarized below. While it is feasible for servicemembers to own either or both types of IRAs based on their family's financial situation, in most cases we recommend choosing a Roth IRA.

> *For most servicemembers, a Roth IRA is a*
> *better retirement investment than a traditional*
> *IRA.*

Roth IRAs

Anyone—regardless of age or participation in another pension plan—can set up a Roth IRA, provided he or she has taxable earned income during the year. Current law allows annual contributions of $4,000 in 2007 and $5,000 in 2008 (with incremental adjustments for inflation after 2008) for a Roth IRA. If you turn age fifty by the end of the current year and have not yet started your IRA, you can take advantage of "catch-up" provisions and contribute an additional $1,000 for 2007 and every subsequent year until retirement. However, if your annual taxable income is less than the contribution limit, your contribution can not exceed your income. For instance, if an unmarried Marine gunnery sergeant (E-7), who was deployed during part of 2006 and had taxable income of only $3,000 (because of the tax-free consideration of military pay while serving in a combat zone), then the maximum allowable contribution to his Roth IRA would be $3,000.

Married servicemembers can open a separate Roth IRA for their spouses with the same contribution limits as introduced above, even if their spouses do not earn income. The only restriction is that their combined annual taxable income must be greater than their combined contribution. This means if same the Marine gunnery sergeant got married to an unemployed woman in 2007, he must earn over $8,000 in taxable income to make a maximum contribution of $4,000 in each Roth IRA.

All distributions (earnings) accrued on the contributions made into the Roth IRA "bubble" must remain in the "bubble" for at least a five-year holding period and until age 59.5 or you incur a penalty fee accessed by the IRS. This fee may be waived, however, for early qualified expenses such as the first-time purchase of a home, excessive medical costs, or education. For a complete listing of the withdrawal rules, limitations and qualifications of the Roth IRA, visit the IRS website at *www.irs.gov/publications/p590/index.html*.

For many servicemembers, especially younger ones, being unable to touch their retirement savings until they are nearly sixty years old will deter them from selecting a Roth IRA. However, when you evaluate the advantages of a Roth IRA, it is worth the wait. First, as mentioned, there are opportunities to make penalty-free withdrawals early for specific life events should you need funds before you turn 59.5. Also, you can withdraw your contributions (but not your distributions) at any age as long as they have been held in the Roth IRA for at least five years. Undoubtedly, the greatest advantage is that withdrawals of your contributions and distributions after the age of 59.5 (or earlier for qualified expenses) are tax-free. This means that every dollar you invest in a Roth IRA, and every additional dollar that those investments earn, go straight into your pocket and not Uncle Sam's.

> *Roth IRAs are tax-free when you withdraw your funds (at retirement) but do not reduce your taxes in the years that you contribute to them (today).*

To see how powerful this retirement option is, Figure 12-1 uses an example of a twenty year-old airman first class (E-3) in 2008. She contributes to her Roth IRA the maximum allowed under current law for her entire twenty-year military career and does not contribute any more after military retirement. The example assumes that the $5,000 annual contribution limit does not increase. Her contributions at the end of her military career total $100,000, but if invested in a stock mutual fund and growing tax-free, her IRA investments will have a future value when she retires at age sixty of $1,151,791 if she earns 8% on average ([diamond] in Figure 12-1), $2,119,247 at 10% ([square] in Figure 12-1), and $3,892,218 at 12% ([triangle] Figure 12-1). Remember, this savings is tax-free.

Until recently, servicemembers who deployed to a combat zone and therefore received the majority of their annual income as combat pay were ineligible to make contributions to their Roth IRA. This was because the combat pay they received was tax-free income (i.e., tax-

Figure 12-1
Roth IRA Growth

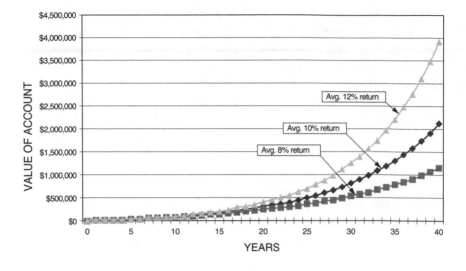

able income would be $0) and Roth IRA regulations stipulated that they could not contribute any amount above their taxable income ($0). In May 2006, Congress passed the "Heroes Earned Retirement Opportunities (HERO) Act," which allows servicemembers earning income in a combat zone to continue to make contributions to their Roth IRA up to the annual limit. For more information on this legislation, search for "HERO Act" at *www.investopedia.com.*

Finally, the IRS does not establish an upper age limit that prevents you from making contributions to, or forces you to withdraw distributions from, your Roth IRA. Such an upper age limit does exist for Traditional IRAs (more on this in the following section).

There are two disadvantages of Roth IRAs worth mentioning: Your annual contributions are not deducted from your annual income when filing your taxes, and your family's taxable income could disqualify you from participation if it exceeds set amounts. While uncommon for most servicemembers, the maximum income limit has been known to affect military families with dual incomes from time-to-time, preventing them from taking advantage of the tax benefits that a Roth IRA provides. Generally speaking, you are not qualified for a Roth IRA if you meet one of the following criteria:

- Combined taxable income is greater than $160,000 if you are married filing jointly, or a qualified widow(er).

- Taxable income is greater than $110,000 if you are single, head of household, or married filing separately and lived apart for the entire year.
- Taxable income is greater than $10,000 if you are married filing separately and lived together at any time during the year.

Again, visit the IRS website if you have questions about the income thresholds or any other Roth IRA qualifying criteria.

Traditional IRAs

An alternative retirement savings plan is the Traditional IRA. While the Roth IRA is recommended for most servicemembers, there may be extraordinary circumstances that disqualify you from participating in a Roth IRA. Only if you find yourself in such a disqualifying situation, and provided you have taxable earned income during the year and have not yet reached age 70.5, a traditional IRA is recommended for your retirement savings. Annual contribution limits and "catch up" amounts, minimum withdrawal age of 59.5, penalties for early withdrawal, and qualified early withdrawals are essentially the same for a traditional IRA as they are for the Roth IRA. You can find this information and more detailed information concerning the rules, limitations, and qualifications of a traditional IRA at the IRS website referenced in the Roth IRA section.

> *Traditional IRAs are taxed when you withdraw your funds (at retirement), but they reduce your taxable income in the years that you contribute to them (today).*

There are two main difference between Roth IRAs and traditional IRAs. First, unlike the Roth IRA, you can never withdraw your contributions early from a traditional IRA. Once the money is placed inside the "bubble" you cannot take it out until age 59.5 or one of the qualified early withdrawal justifications are met. The second is the timing of the tax benefits granted to you for contributing to an IRA. As we discussed, Roth IRA contributions are not deductible from your annual taxes, but your distributions are not taxed when you begin to receive them. Traditional IRAs are treated in the exact opposite manner by the IRS, giving them their most distinct advantage—contributions to traditional IRAs are tax deductible (meaning your annual taxable income will be less, which translates into tax-savings) today. Saving on your taxes today sounds like a financially prudent decision. And when comparing the tax savings you gain by investing in a traditional IRA to that of a mutual fund or savings account without a protective IRA "bubble," it is. However, when comparing the tax savings you gain today with a traditional IRA to the tax savings you gain at retirement with a Roth IRA, the Roth is the clear winner in the overwhelming majority of cases (especially for servicemembers).

Next, the IRA contributions of the same airman first class from above will be used to demonstrate the tax impact on her retirement savings had she chosen a traditional IRA instead of the Roth IRA depicted previously in Figure 12-1. If she contributed to a traditional IRA and withdrew her entire savings at age sixty, she would be forced to pay long-term capital gains taxes (currently 15%). In other words, she would pay $157,769 (at the 8% growth), $302,887 (at the 10% growth), and $568,833 (at the 12% growth) to the IRS respectively. With the Roth IRA, although no tax-deductions can be taken in the years the $100,000 was invested, the airman first class would get to keep the entire capital gains amount. A traditional IRA would have equaled only $15,000 in total tax savings over the course of her twenty-year career (assuming a tax rate of 15%, which represents the average tax rate for Americans).

In addition to the disadvantages already mentioned, Traditional IRAs include mandatory distributions in the year you turn 70.5 and prevent you from making any additional contributions after that year. Another weakness of the Traditional IRA is that some servicemembers and/or their spouses may be ineligible for the tax deductions on their contributions if they are already participating in an employer's retirement plan. Examples of employer retirement plans include the military's Thrift Savings Plan (TSP) and civilian 401(k) plans, both detailed later. These restrictions are explicitly defined on the IRS website at *www.irs.gov/publications/p590/index.html*.

If you started investing in a traditional IRA before reading this book and now realize you should be contributing to a Roth IRA instead, do not worry. You can convert your current traditional IRA to a Roth IRA, although it will cause you to pay the taxes you have deducted to date. More appropriately, you can simply stop contributing to your traditional IRA; then open a second IRA and establish it as a Roth. There is no restriction on the number of traditional and Roth IRAs you can maintain, just a restriction on the total contribution you can make per year ($4,000 in 2007; $5,000 in 2008 and beyond with incremental adjustments for inflation). For example, if you designated four different accounts with four different financial institutions as Roth IRAs, you could spread your $4,000 contribution for 2007 across all four accounts.

Likewise, if you want to consolidate your IRAs with one financial institution, or if you are unhappy with the performance of your existing IRA, you can roll it over into another IRA account; you can do this once a year without incurring taxes or penalties as long as you deposit the entire balance in a new IRA account. In all instances, you need to maintain good records for the life of your IRA to correctly determine your taxes, or lack thereof, when you start withdrawing.

A Roth IRA is a powerful means of building wealth and helps augment your retirement income. The tax-free compounding gains on your annual contributions with withdrawals and reasonable restrictions set by the government make it a very attractive addition to your long-term financial plan. In almost every situation, the benefit of not paying capital gains taxes when the funds are distributed (as with the Roth IRA) overwhelmingly outweighs the benefit of the tax-deductions taken when the funds are purchased (as with the traditional IRA).

COMPANY-SPONSORED QUALIFIED PLANS FOR SPOUSES

A qualified plan is established by an employer to provide retirement benefits for employees and their beneficiaries. These plans can either be *defined-benefit* (like the Army's retirement system in which retirees receive monthly predetermined payments after the member retires) or *defined-contribution* (plans wherein a certain amount or percentage of money is set aside each year for the benefit of the employee).

This section will focus on the defined-contribution plans because most working spouses who are not in the military will often have an opportunity to participate in such an arrangement. Additionally, National Guard and reserve members may have civilian jobs that offer this as part of their compensation. It is important to know the details of these plans because they offer employees a great means to accumulate retirement savings. The two most common forms of company-sponsored plans are the 401(k) and Roth 401(k) plans.

Company Sponsored 401(k) Plans

These are the most common forms of plans offered by companies. 401(k) plans are retirement accounts established by employers to which eligible employees may make salary-deferral contributions (thus reducing their taxable income in the years they participate). However, just like a traditional IRA, distributions are taxed upon withdrawal at age 59.5.

As with either type of IRA, the employee designates the types of financial assets his or her 401(k) contributions are invested. Also, the contributions to this type of plan are subject to limits set by the IRS. As of 2006, the maximum employee annual contribution allowed into a 401(k) plan is $15,000 and will be increased with inflation for 2007 and beyond. A "catch up " provision allows employees over the age of fifty to contribute an additional $5,000.

Many employers make matching contributions to the plan on behalf of eligible employees and may also add a profit-sharing feature to the plan. (Since this is less common, we will not focus on this feature.) The amount that employers are willing to match varies by company; currently employers are limited to contributing up to 6% of the employee's total pre-tax compensation. Therefore, if the employee earns a pretax salary of $100,000, the employer can contribute up to $6,000. The benefits of employer matching contributions should be obvious—they are adding to the employee's retirement savings pool from $15,000 to $21,000. Pay attention to the restrictions employers place on their matching contributions. Frequently, they will tie vesting criteria to their matching funds.

Vesting simply means that the employee gains the rights (takes ownership) of these matching contributions and the employer is authorized to stipulate the conditions upon which vesting occurs. Typical vesting criteria requires the employee to remain with the company for a minimum number of years. Once that minimum time is met, the employee gains the rights (i.e., is *vested*) to the matching contributions the employer made during that time.

Company Sponsored Roth 401(k) Plans

As of 3 January 2006, investors have an additional retirement option in the Roth 401(k). You should contact the employee benefits administrator to confirm whether or not the company where you or your spouse works offers the Roth 401(k), especially since it is still a relatively new investment option. Currently, the Roth 401(k) has the same contribution limits as the normal company 401(k) plans. Therefore, in 2006, an employee has the option to invest the maximum amount his or her employee allows (as a percentage of income) or the maximum the government allows ($15,000, or $20,000 for those over fifty years old), whichever is less.

The difference between these two types of plans is that with the Roth 401(k), employees are taxed on the contributions they make to the plan in the year they were made. A normal 401(k) plan allows you to defer the taxes paid for contributions. However, the distributions from the Roth 401(k) are tax-free (almost exactly identical to the Roth IRA), while the distributions from the regular 401(k) are taxed at your marginal tax rate at the time of distribution.

Comparison and Discussion

The 401(k) plan that is best for your and your family depends on your situation. First of all, not all companies offer them yet, so you should check with your employer. Second, if you are young or in a low tax bracket, the Roth 401(k) plan may be better-suited than the regular 401(k) plan because the benefit you receive of not paying capital gains over a long time horizon will most likely outweigh the costs associated with not being able to deduct pretax dollars. However, if you are in a higher tax bracket at the present time, or you expect to be in a lower or similar tax bracket in retirement, you may want to consider the benefits associated with the tax-deferral of regular 401(k) contributions. The central question you or your financial planner must answer is whether or not to tax the reduction of income taxes now with the regular 401(k) or take the tax-free income later with the Roth 401(k).

As of press time, Roth 401(k) plans are approved all the way through December 31, 2010. Prior to this time, legislatures must extend the law or the Roth 401(k) will expire.

THRIFT SAVINGS PLAN

The Thrift Savings Plan (TSP) is a retirement savings and investment plan made available to civilian and military members of the Department of Defense. Participation in the TSP may limit or completely eliminate your ability to use the tax advantages associated with a Traditional IRA, but it has no effect on your ability to receive the tax benefits of a Roth IRA—just one more reason why a Roth IRA is recommended. Information on the TSP can be found at *www.tsp.gov*.

The purpose of the TSP is to provide another form of retirement income. It offers participants the same type of savings and tax benefits that many private corporations offer their employees under regular 401(k) plans. The TSP allows participants to save a portion of their pay in a special retirement account administered by the Federal Retirement Thrift Investment Board. The money that participants invest in the TSP comes from pretax dollars and reduces their current taxable income; investments and earnings are not taxed until they are withdrawn, which gives it similar tax-deferred characteristics to a Traditional IRA. Military personnel's contributions and earnings belong to them and are therefore portable when they retire or leave the service. Unlike a 401(k), the government does not make matching contributions for military TSP participants.

Once you enroll, the TSP will invest your contributions in the G Fund until you submit a contribution allocation. You can invest any portion of your TSP account in one of five TSP investment funds:

- Government Securities Investment (G) Fund.
- Fixed Income Index Investment (F) Fund.
- Common Stock Index Investment (C) Fund.
- Small Capitalization Stock Index Investment (S) Fund.
- International Stock Index Investment (I) Fund.

Military personnel who invest using the TSP may diversify it across these five funds according to their investment horizon and risk profile (topics discussed in chapter 11). If you do not care to determine the correct mix of these funds over time, there are five Life Cycle Funds (L Funds). These funds were introduced in 2004 and allocate your contributions in a professionally determined investment mix of the individual TSP funds (from above). Each L Fund is based on its own time horizon, allowing each to adjust gradually over time, shifting automatically to a more conservative investment mix as its investment horizon approaches. For example, the L Funds available as of 2007 are L 2040 (for those people who plan to retire or use their money in 2040), L 2030, L 2020, L 2010, and L Income (for those in retirement in need of a steady income with little fluctuation). The main advantage of the L Funds is that it provides a low-cost, worry-free method of investing. The L Funds are made of a mix of individual TSP funds, which result in no additional fees above and beyond those paid for the individual funds. If the TSP is not your only means of saving for retirement (i.e., you contribute to a Roth IRA), these L Funds may not be suitable for you.

Effective January 1, 2006, you can contribute up to 100% of the basic pay you earn each month. Additionally, you may also elect to contribute up to 100% of any incentive pay (e.g., flight pay, hazardous duty pay), special pay (e.g., hardship duty pay), and bonus pay (e.g., enlistment and reenlistment bonuses) that you receive as long as you are contributing from base pay. However, you cannot exceed the Internal Revenue Code's (IRC) elective deferral limit for that year ($15,000 for 2007). For those uniformed members who earn tax-exempt pay while deployed for any part or all of the year, they may contribute up to the IRC's limit ($44,000 for 2007). Finally, the only means to contribute is through monthly deductions. Servicemembers can not make direct contributions.

The following options are available to you when you separate from the uniformed services:

- Receive a single payment that can then be transferred to an IRA or other eligible retirement plan (e.g., a 401(k) plan or a civilian TSP account if you continue to work for the government) without paying a penalty or taxes.
- Request a series of monthly payments based on a dollar amount, a number of months, or your life expectancy. All or a portion of certain monthly payments can be transferred to an IRA or other eligible retirement plan without paying a penalty or taxes.
- Request a TSP annuity (a guaranteed monthly payment for a specific amount). You must have at least $3,500 in your account in order to purchase an annuity. It is important to find out more information before considering this option, as the rules are quite extensive and not covered in detail in this book.
- Keep your money in the TSP until the allowable withdrawal age of 59.5, where it will continue to accrue earnings. You cannot make additional contributions after you leave the service, but you will be able to make interfund transfers. You must begin withdrawing from your account no later than 1 April of the year following the year you turn age 59.5.

Advantages of the TSP:

- The value of the account is not counted in your family financial situation when colleges calculate your Expected Family Contribution (EFC) to determine your child's eligibility for financial aid (see chapter 7).
- The TSP is funded with pretax dollars, thereby reducing your current year's income tax liability.
- The TSP is portable: The funds and growth are yours when you retire or leave the service.

Disadvantages of the TSP:

- There are no matching funds for uniformed military personnel.
- Servicemembers cannot make direct contributions to their accounts.
- Monthly deductions are the only method of contributing.
- Withdrawals are taxed based on long-term capital-gains tax rate (currently 15% for most Americans).

PART IV

RISK MANAGEMENT

13

Life Insurance

Life insurance is one of the most important components of your personal financial plan. Unfortunately, life insurance is often poorly understood, and mistakes by breadwinners—with or without life insurance—invariably cause great misfortune for their survivors. The goal of this chapter is to provide you with a firm understanding of Servicemembers' Group Life Insurance (SGLI), the amount of money your survivors will receive in the event of your death, how much additional life insurance you (and your spouse) need, and what type of policy best fits your situation. To ensure that you can find the life insurance protection you need at a cost your family can afford, you need to answer three key questions before you talk to an insurance agent:

1. Do you need life insurance at all?
2. If so, how much life insurance do you need?
3. What type of policy should you buy?

The primary function of life insurance is to provide protection for you or your survivors from the economic consequences of the death of a member of your household. Three factors complicate the buying process. First, most people hesitate to confront their own death. Second, some life insurance policies have both an insurance component and an investment component, which can make it difficult to remember that the primary goal of life-insurance protection should be replacing family income in the event of a family service provider's death. Finally, there is the somewhat mysterious nature of the life insurance business. The use of statistics and actuarial (life projection) techniques tends to discourage even the most careful shopper. Adding to the confusion are the special terms developed by the life insurance industry to make the subject more appealing and the product more marketable. The terms—premium, permanent insurance, whole life insurance, and term insurance—must be translated so that the typical buyer can understand the full range of options. Consequently, many people are so confused that they decide to simply choose an agent rather than the best product. This can be a very expensive decision.

A life insurance company is a for-profit business that produces an income for its sales force while providing policies to protect your family's economic security. Because insurance agents operate primarily on commissions, they have a natural incentive to sell those policies that produce high commissions. Reputable agents will attempt to match an insurance program to your needs, but you should be aware of the substantial commissions involved and the possibility for high-pressure sales techniques. By doing your homework before talking to an agent, you increase the likelihood of making the best decisions for your family.

THE PRINCIPLE BEHIND INSURANCE

Insurance is based on a very simple concept: The cost of infrequent but catastrophic events can be spread among a large group with a small cost to each member. Individuals share the risk at a fraction of the cost of the catastrophic event. Life insurance is perhaps the best example of insurance that "pays off" for an event that happens most infrequently (once in a lifetime) but with truly catastrophic effects. It is not the insured that life insurance is designed to protect. Life insurance is for the future well-being of the survivors of the policyholder. The policyholder benefits only from the peace of mind that the insurance provides.

> *A clear understanding of the life insurance policy that you buy is critical in order to purchase an insurance plan that is best for you, not your insurance company.*

Life insurance provides protection for your survivors from the economic consequences of your premature death. Insurance will not help with the emotional loss; however, it can remove the fear of economic hardship. Also, the amount of insurance does not demonstrate your love for your family, nor does it delay your departure from this world. Life insurance is not an investment, although some policies have an investment component. Too much insurance can result in high premiums that reduce your monthly budget and therefore your ability to enjoy other good things in life. A clear understanding of what one is buying, and why, is critical to develop a life insurance plan that is best for you, not your insurance company. The first step to determining insurance needs is to understand the insurance and survivor benefits that are already available to servicemembers.

SERVICEMEMBERS'GROUP LIFE INSURANCE
The primary insurance for active duty military is Servicemembers' Group Life Insurance (SGLI). According to the government's website at *www.insurance.va.gov*, SGLI is low-cost life insurance for service-members on active duty, ready reservists, cadets and midshipmen of the four service academies, and members of the Reserve Officer Train-ing Corps. The coverage is available in increments of $50,000 up to a maximum of $400,000. It costs $.07 per $1,000 of coverage, regardless of age. This translates to premium monthly rates of $4.50 for $50,000 of coverage or $29 for the maximum $400,000 of coverage. The most up-to-date premiums are available at *www.insurance.va.gov/sgliSite/ SGLI/sgliPremiums.htm.*

Another life insurance option for military members is Family Ser-vicemembers' Group Life Insurance (FSGLI). This program provides insurance for the spouse and children of a servicemember. The spouse is eligible for a maximum of $100,000 of life insurance, and each dependent child is eligible for $10,000 of life insurance. Premiums depend on family members' ages and can range from $5.50 to $52.00 per month. Premiums are listed on the website at *www.insurance.va .gov/sgliSite/FSGLI/fsgliPremiums.htm.*

When servicemembers leave the military, they have the option of converting their SGLI coverage to a Veterans' Group Life Insurance (VGLI) policy. VGLI is a program of post-separation insurance which allows servicemembers to convert their SGLI coverage to renewable term insurance. VGLI coverage is issued in multiples of $10,000 up to a maximum of $400,000. However, a servicemember's VGLI coverage amount cannot exceed the amount of SGLI that was in force at the time of separation from service. Current premiums for VGLI are at *www.insurance.va.gov/sgliSite/VGLI/VGLI%20ratesAfter.htm.*

Any additional questions concerning SGLI and VGLI may be answered by reading "Servicemembers' and Veterans' Group Life Insurance Handbook," which can be downloaded from the internet at *www.insurance.va.gov/sgliSite/handbook/handbook.htm.* The VA's life insurance website at *www.insurance.va.gov/sgliSite/default.htm* is also an outstanding source of information for military members researching every aspect of their life insurance options.

SGLI most likely will meet the life insurance needs of military members. It is reasonably priced, nontaxable, and provides substantial coverage for servicemembers and their families. Thus, we recommend that military members purchase SGLI life insurance. Once you understand the life insurance available through the military (SGLI), your next step is to learn about the death benefits available to survivors of military members in the event of your untimely death. This knowledge will enable you to make an educated decision concerning additional life insurance needs.

DEATH BENEFITS FOR MILITARY MEMBERS

In addition to SGLI lump-sum payments, military members' survivors also receive benefits through the military, Social Security, and the Department of Veterans Affairs (VA).

Department of Defense Benefits: The military gives a number of lump-sum death benefits to its veterans. The first is the Fallen Hero Compensation (formerly known as the Death Gratuity). This benefit is an immediate cash payment of $12,420. In addition, The Emergency Supplemental Appropriations Act of 2005 increased this payment to $100,000 for "survivors of those whose death is as a result of hostile actions and occurred in a designated combat operation or combat zone or while training for combat or performing hazardous duty." The military also will pay your survivors any accrued leave that you have at the time of your death. This leave payment consists of your base pay, and it is taxable.

Social Security Benefits: Based upon your lifetime credits earned through Social Security (i.e., how much you have paid to Social Security), the Social Security Administration will pay survivor benefits to your surviving spouse and children. First, your survivors under eighteen years of age will receive a one-time sum of $255, and subsequently they will receive a monthly percentage of your benefits. The Social Security Administration has a calculator on their website at *www.ssa.gov/planners/calculators.htm* that you can use to determine your available estimated benefits. This calculator also estimates your maximum possible benefits.

VA Benefits: The VA also has numerous non-taxable survivor benefits for military members, the first of which is Dependency and Indemnity Compensation (DIC). A basic monthly rate of $1033 goes to the surviving spouse. This amount increases based on the number of children or if the spouse is housebound. The VA pays the spouse an additional $250 for the children if they are under age eighteen. This payment is based on a family unit, not per child, and is paid for only two years. Summary DIC benefit tables are listed at *www.vba.va.gov/bln/21/Rates*.

The VA also pays a death pension to survivors of wartime veterans. This monthly benefit is needs based and is paid primarily to non-working spouses. If the spouse's yearly income is less than a specified income level, then the spouse will receive a pension. Details on the income limits are detailed at *www.vba.va.gov/bln/21/Milsvs/Docs/DPeneg.doc*.

The Survivors' and Dependents' Educational Assistance Program (DEA), another VA program, provides up to forty-five months of monthly allowances for a survivor's education including degree and certificate programs, apprenticeship, and on-the-job training as well as correspondence courses for spouses and children of deceased veterans. The monthly allowances are based on the type of schooling and the amount of schooling time. Details for this program are at *www.gibill.va.gov/pamphlets/CH35/CH35_Pamphlet_General.htm*.

The VA also extends home loan benefits to surviving spouses with no down payment required. However, there is a small fee involved. For details regarding these loans, see the VA website, *www.homeloans.va.gov*.

Surviving family members of a veteran must apply for the VA and Social Security survivor benefits and most likely will receive help in the application process from a casualty assistance officer who is familiar with survivor entitlements specified in AR 600-8-1.

Army Sergeant (E-5) Example
In the following example, we provide calculations to estimate survivor benefits for a spouse and two children of a married Army Sergeant (E-5) who dies in a noncombat related accident. This example assumes the spouse does not work, the two children are under sixteen years old, the sergeant is twenty-four years old with six years of active-duty service, military SGLI of $400,000, and thirty days of accrued leave at death. (All calculations are based on 2006 military pay)

DOD BENEFITS (LUMP SUM)	
Fallen Hero Compensation:	$12,420
Accrued Leave (30 days):	$2,274
SGLI:	$400,000
Total DoD Lump Sum Benefit:	$414,694

SOCIAL SECURITY BENEFITS (MONTHLY)

One-Time Lump Sum Benefit:	$255
Spouse Caring for Children under 16 (75% of Estimated $1,049 Social Security Benefits):	$812
Surviving Children ($812 × 2)*:	$1624
Total Social Security Monthly Benefits**:	$1925.50 per month

* Spouses will receive benefits only for children younger than sixteen years. Be aware, however, that surviving spouses will receive benefits for themselves only while they have a child under the age of sixteen who is eligible for Social Security benefits or they (spouse) reach sixty years of age.
** All Social Security benefits were calculated using the benefit calculator at *www.ssa.gov/planners/calculators.htm*. This benefit calculator gave this maximum monthly amount of $1925.50 instead of $2436 because of what is known as a "family maximum." This limit is not set but "is generally between 150 and 180 percent of the deceased's benefit amount. If the sum of the benefits payable to a spouse and the children is greater than this limit, you will receive a benefit amount that is proportionately reduced."

VA BENEFITS (MONTHLY)

DIC—Spouse:	$1033
DIC—Children*:	$250
Death Pension**:	$924
Educational Assistance (Full-Time School)***:	$827
Total VA Monthly Benefits:	$3034

* The children receive this allotment for only two years.
** The Death Pension pays the difference between your income and yearly income limits found on the VA website at *www.vba.va.gov*.
*** A survivor can receive the educational assistance for up a maximum of forty-five months.

These benefits add up to $4,959.50 total monthly benefits and $416,619.50 total lump-sum benefits. Remember that the monthly benefits calculated above are subject to changes based on the ages of your children and your spouse and also upon whether your spouse is working. The websites for Social Security and VA will have the most updated information about rules and amounts of monthly allowances. Suggested websites are listed throughout this chapter and will provide an excellent starting point for further research on your current situation.

Once you have a better understanding of the survivor benefits available to servicemembers from the DoD, Social Security, and VA, the next step is to analyze how much additional life insurance is needed to provide for your loved ones in the event of your untimely death.

NEEDS ANALYSIS

The reason for determining your insurance needs is to estimate your family's actual financial situation in the event that you die. Life insurance is not a measure of devotion to loved ones or a monument to your self-importance. It is insurance in case of premature death, and it should be used to protect dependents against undue financial hardship. If you are not alive to provide for your family, your insurance coverage should be sufficient to enable them to live as you would want them to live.

Financial Obligations: Start your family's needs analysis by determining your financial obligations at death. These financial obligations consist of burial costs, outstanding debts, and income that your family will require for future planned expenses. Burial costs include funeral expenses, burial fees, and headstones fees. Examples of outstanding debts are mortgages, credit card debt, and car loans. Income that your family requires to cover future planned expenses may include children's college expenses, special medical care for predictable problems, and a reserve for emergencies. The DoD's lump-sum Fallen Hero Compensation and other VA funeral benefits should cover the majority of burial costs, while SGLI should be adequate to cover outstanding debts and future planned expenses.

Monthly Income Needs: After you determine your financial obligations at death, you should consider the monthly income that your survivors will need to sustain a preferred lifestyle. If you do not know where to start in estimating these expenses, a good rule of thumb is two-thirds of your present monthly income for those years when children will be at home, and one-half after they have left. Typical monthly expenses to consider include childcare, health insurance, utilities, car and renters' insurance, rent/mortgage, car payments, and entertainment. As previously discussed, your family will receive numerous allowances from Social Security and VA. As the E-5 example illustrated, these allowances are substantial ($4,959.50) and include education allowances for the spouse and children. You should also consider whether your surviving spouse will earn additional income, which will decrease the amount of monthly income you need to provide for your survivors' life insurance needs (although this would also affect the amount of allowances provided by the VA). An analysis of your spouse's earning potential is pivotal to determining the monthly income needed for your family.

Assets: Lastly, your needs analysis should consider the assets you have been able to acquire over time. Examples of assets include money in savings accounts, mutual funds, stocks, CDs, or other investments. It also includes other assets such as life insurance and real estate.

Remember that life insurance is one way to provide an "instant estate" to meet the financial needs of survivors. You can easily estimate the amount of income your accumulated financial assets will provide by multiplying them by the interest rate (less the inflation rate) you think they will be earning. For example, if you have saved $50,000 and had the maximum SGLI of $400,000, your survivors will have $450,000 of assets. If they invest this money conservatively and receive a 4% return after inflation, they will receive an income of $18,000 per year from this money ($450,000 × .04). More information can be found at *www.insurance.va.gov*.

In summary, use this formula to calculate your additional life insurance needs:

$$\begin{matrix} \text{Financial} \\ \text{Obligations} \end{matrix} + \begin{matrix} \text{Net Income Needed} \\ \text{to Support Survivors} \end{matrix} - \text{Assets} = \begin{matrix} \text{Insurance} \\ \text{Needs} \end{matrix}$$

> *Life insurance is **not** a measure of devotion to loved ones or a monument to your self-importance. It is insurance in case of premature death, and it should be used to protect dependents against undue financial hardship.*

Because of the more complicated calculations associated with the time value of money and inflation, we recommend you use a life insurance calculator on the Internet or consult a financial planner. A financial planning service available to military members is The Army and Air Force Mutual Aid Association. This association offers services to complete a needs analysis. There are also useful insurance calculators online to estimate additional life insurance you might require. These calculators give a fairly good assessment of additional life insurance needs. A more comprehensive life insurance calculator that uses this needs analysis formula and incorporates the VA and social security survivor benefits discussed in this chapter is at *www.insurance.va.gov/sgliSite/calculator/introCalc.htm*. Additional life insurance calculators are found at *www.insurance.com/Misc/LifeCalculator.aspx* and USAA's calculator at *www.usaaedfoundation.org/insurance/ins_life_need.asp*.

As you live longer, some of your survivors' needs will disappear. For example, if your children have finished college, there is no longer a need to leave money for their education. Thus, you need to reevaluate your insurance needs periodically as your survivors' situations change. In any case, there is never a requirement to make your family wealthy upon your death; you should buy insurance to provide only the coverage for identifiable needs.

If you determine that you need life insurance in addition to SGLI, you should be familiar with the terminology and types of insurance that companies will attempt to sell you.

LIFE INSURANCE TERMINOLOGY

The life insurance industry uses specific language to describe its products. Understanding this language is important to understanding and selecting the type of life insurance that you should buy. The face amount, the policy period, the premium, and the savings are part of any life insurance policy and can be adjusted to fit the individual needs of each policyholder.

Face Amount. The face amount of the policy is the amount that would be paid to your beneficiary (a person you designate) in the event of your death. The larger the face amount, the higher the benefit to the beneficiary and the higher the cost of the policy premium.

Policy Period. A life insurance policy can be for any length of time—a year or your entire lifetime. The premium is often related to the length of the policy period. Although some policies are for a specific period, a policy can be renewed unless it is explicitly nonrenewable. Reentry policies can be renewed, but renewal requires a new physical examination, and the premiums may be recalculated based on the examination results. Renewable policies guarantee renewal without conditions, and the premium will change only with age, not on the condition of health. Because the insurance company does not have the right to end its obligation to insure the person or to raise premiums during the policy period should health deteriorate, the premiums will be somewhat higher for renewable policies.

In general, nonrenewable policies and policies with shorter renewal periods or that base future premiums on new physical exams have lower annual premiums today. Companies charge lower premiums for these policies because they have a chance to learn more at each renewal point about the factors (health, in particular) that affect the probability of death, and they can refuse insurance or raise premiums for very poor risks. If you are in excellent health, the cheapest possible coverage will be a one-year, nonrenewable term policy. If you want a renewable policy, you will have to pay more.

Premium. A premium is nothing more than a payment, like a car payment or a mortgage payment on a house. The premium pays the insurance company for administering the policy and includes the agent's commission. With certain types of policies, part of the payment goes to a form of "savings." Premiums can stay the same, increase, or decrease over the length of the policy, depending on the policy type.

Savings. Permanent and variable insurance policies (discussed in the next section) include a cash value that can be used as a method of savings. There are some advantages to this type of policy. You can borrow from your account, but you will be charged interest for borrowing; after a specified number of years, your insurance policy can be paid in full and you will no longer need to make premium payments, or you may elect to end the policy and cash out your "savings" portion to spend or invest elsewhere. There are also disadvantages: You typically earn a lower rate of interest on these savings than on alternative financial investments; and, because these policies include both insurance and savings, their premiums are much higher.

TYPES OF LIFE INSURANCE POLICIES

There are three main types of life insurance: *term*, which lasts for just a specific period, with no savings component; *permanent*, in which premiums are paid until the insured's death but also build savings; and *variable*, which has a flexible structure designed to allow greater return on the savings portion of the policy. Within these major categories, there are many variations to meet life insurance needs. As a policyholder gets older, premiums increase. To avoid this problem, the insured may select level-term insurance or permanent insurance.

Whatever the fine points, the underlying principle of distributing the risk over a large group remains the goal of any type of insurance. After reading this information about each of the specialized types of life insurance, think about how the different options fit your personal needs.

Term Insurance. Term insurance protects the policyholder for a specified time period—one year, five years, twenty years, or more. It is pure insurance: the policy "pays off" only if the insured dies within the specified period. In this sense, it provides protection to your survivors only from the economic effects of death. It has no savings feature and thus no "cash value," so there is no borrowing against the policy. Term insurance must be renewed when the "term" is completed. Usually, renewal requires a physical examination, although some companies may relax this requirement.

Since none of the premium is going toward "savings," term premiums are initially far lower than permanent policy premiums. Thus, a young person who has a need for a larger death benefit, perhaps in excess of $200,000, but whose income is low, may be able to afford the coverage by using term insurance.

You should be aware that many agents might try to steer you away from term insurance (or temporary insurance as the agents like to call it) toward permanent insurance. Many agents sell both permanent (insurance plus savings) and term (insurance alone) insurance policies. Premiums for term insurance are based on the expected number of deaths per year for a given age group, and this number can be determined quite accurately using standard data—which makes for good competition among companies as they bid for your business with premiums only slightly above this base cost.

By contrast, the savings component of the permanent insurance policies requires a larger premium; and since the premiums collected greatly exceed the expected pay out for death benefits, the insurance company can make a good income (for the company) investing the "excess premium" in bonds and stocks. As a result, few of the larger companies will "push" term insurance, and they adjust their commission incentives to make this very clear to their sales personnel. When agents sell term insurance, it is often with the goal of converting the policy to permanent insurance as soon as the policyholder can be persuaded to do so. Fortunately, some good companies specialize in term insurance, and a number cater especially to the military community such as SGLI and USAA.

There is an apparent disadvantage to term insurance. As you get older, the premiums increase. At age twenty, you might be able to get a $100,000 term policy for approximately $150 per year, but at age forty-five, that same policy could cost you over $300 per year. The increase in premiums would eventually make term more expensive than the premiums on permanent insurance (bought now) for the same face amount. However, as we will see later, the insurance portion of permanent insurance effectively has the same characteristics. Also, as you grow older, your insurance needs will likely peak and then lessen. Once your children's education is no longer your responsibility, your insurance needs should decrease. You may not need any life insurance when you are older. If you do, however, several different types of term insurance are offered to meet this need.

Level Term. The face value and the premium for level-term insurance remain the same throughout the period of coverage. This type of insurance was designed to lower the high cost of term insurance in the later years of the policy. One method used to calculate the premiums averages the payments so that an equal payment is paid each month, in effect, overpaying the first half of the policy period and underpaying the last half. Even if the term were forty-five years (perhaps until anticipated retirement), the premium would still be less than a permanent policy for the same amount of insurance, because there is no savings component to the policy.

Servicemembers' Group Life Insurance (SGLI) is level-term insurance. Currently, a servicemember may elect to take the maximum $400,000 of coverage for $.065 per $1000 of coverage, regardless of age. This is very inexpensive insurance for older officers and noncommissioned officers. In effect, the large numbers of young servicemembers make possible low premiums for the older servicemembers. For this reason, and because it is convertible after you leave the service, SGLI should be the basic building block of your family's insurance program.

Decreasing Term. Decreasing term insurance has a constant premium over the term of the coverage, but the face value of the policy declines to reflect the higher risk of death as age increases. As an example, a $10 monthly premium might buy a twenty-five-year-old male insurance protection of $100,000; a man in his fifties would get only $15,000 of term insurance for this premium. A decreasing term policy may make a lot of sense if your insurance needs decrease as you get older. For instance, if you had an obligation that was decreasing, such as a home mortgage, then matching decreasing benefits would also make excellent sense. Mortgage insurance, a form of decreasing term, is a fairly common (but often more expensive) way of addressing this particular situation (and is therefore not recommended).

> *The underlying principle of distributing the risk over a large group remains the basis of any type of insurance.*

Renewable, Nonrenewable, and Reentry Term. These term policies have special features that allow you to renew them at the end of the policy period if you meet certain standards. Renewable term eliminates the physical examination requirement: A person who is injured in combat or who has contracted cancer would still be able to renew the term policy. In this regard, term insurance is not really "temporary" at all. This renewal feature will not be available past age seventy when term insurance is no longer available or becomes too expensive. As noted, you may not need insurance coverage in old age when your children are independent and you have sufficient assets to provide a comfortable retirement. Most of the companies that cater to the military sell renewable term.

The second type, nonrenewable, means just that: The policy ends and the policyholder must buy new insurance, qualifying for it with a new physical exam. Reentry term is less expensive than renewable term insurance. You must, however, pass a physical after the end of the term to "reenter" the low-cost policy. The danger is that if you fail the physical examination, you cannot reenter and must pay a higher premium or find a different policy. Finding a new policy can be quite expensive (or even impossible) if you have failed a physical examination. As an example, here is what happens with a thirty-five-year-old nonsmoking male who buys a $250,000 five-year reentry term policy. His annual premium starts out at $400 and gradually rises to $550 over the five-year term. At the reentry point, the now forty-year-old male takes a new physical exam. If he passes, his premium is reduced to $500 and gradually rises from there; but if he fails, his premium is raised to $750. At forty-five years of age, the numbers would be $600 (pass) and $1,100 (not pass).

TABLE 13-1
TERM LIFE INSURANCE

Advantages
- Initial premiums generally are lower than those for permanent insurance, allowing you to buy higher levels of coverage at a younger age when the need for protection often is greatest.
- It will cover expenses that will disappear in time, such as mortgages, children's education, or car loans.

Disadvantages
- Premiums increase or coverage decreases as you grow older.
- Coverage may terminate at the end of the term or become too expensive to continue.

In comparison, once you pass the initial physical examination for a renewable term policy, your premium is the same as that for all others of the same age, regardless of what subsequently happens to your health. Reentry term is best for only a very select group: people who need a substantial amount of insurance for a short period of time. For others, the cost of re-entry goes up when they can least afford it. For individuals seeking insurance, the risk of reentry term probably outweighs the small savings.

Convertible Term. Many term policies offer a feature that allows you to convert the term policy to some form of permanent insurance without having to provide evidence of insurability, usually through a medical examination. While you will pay the higher premium associated with your age at conversion (some policies will allow a retroactive calculation to the original age of buying the policy), you have protected yourself from the loss of insurability. This is a very desirable feature as it protects you and your survivors in the event your insurability changes for the worse at the time that your term policy expires.

Permanent Insurance. The words *permanent, ordinary,* and *whole life* insurance have the same meaning in the insurance industry. These policies combine pure (term) insurance with an automatic savings feature (called "cash value") that provides the companies with funds that they invest to produce most of their profits. The premium on these policies includes two components. One portion goes to the insurance company, and the other goes into a savings account. Insurance salespeople are offered the largest commissions for selling permanent policies, and therefore emphasize them in their sales presentations.

Perhaps "ordinary insurance" really refers to the fact that this is the type of insurance that a company would prefer to sell. Permanent can be explained by the important cash value feature. As years go by, the interest earnings on the savings portion of the premiums will accumulate, slowly at first, but then faster in later years, until there is enough in the account to cover the face value of the policy. This, in effect, gradually replaces the insurance provided by the company with your own savings. The company eventually accumulates enough of a cash value from the policyholder to simply hand it back to the survivors when the policyholder dies. Permanent insurance is really a combination of a decreasing term insurance policy bundled with an enforced savings feature. The company, in paying the face value totally out of cash value, would no longer be providing any pure insurance. These accumulated savings represent a cash value that may be borrowed against (with an interest charge) after some number of years.

An advantage of permanent insurance is that you are insured for your whole life for a constant premium. No matter when you die, if your policy is still in force, the company will pay the face amount to your beneficiary. Although the payments are much higher than term insurance early in life, they are less later because of the accumulated savings portion of the premium. The majority of permanent or whole life policies fall into two categories: straight life and limited-payment life.

Straight Life. Straight life (also called whole or ordinary life) is the most common form of life insurance sold. It provides both protection and savings for the policyholder, who pays premiums throughout his or her life and builds up a cash value in the policy. It has the same premium throughout the life of the policy (which is where the term straight comes from); the premium charged to you at age twenty is the same premium charged at age fifty. The premium amount is determined primarily by your age when you buy the policy; the older you are when you start, the higher the premium. Your physical condition can also play a role.

Whole life policies build a cash value that steadily grows each year you have the policy. Be careful concerning this savings feature. If you close your account, especially in the first few years, you will not have much savings. For example, one company's most popular permanent policy returns an average interest rate of 0.2% on the accumulating savings if you cancel it at the ten-year point. Policy cancellations are not unusual. A Senate subcommittee gathered data on sixty of the leading U.S. insurance companies and found that 25% of permanent policy buyers discontinue their policies within the first year, 46% within ten years, and nearly 60% before twenty years.

The return for a whole life policy does depend on the length of time you keep the policy. Most policies forfeit all cash value if the policy is in effect for less than two years, with the average break-even point at eight years; however, this is where your accumulated savings have earned a zero percent return. Generally, a savings account at your local bank will earn as much interest as, and in some cases even more than, the savings portion of a whole life policy. However, the whole life policy accumulates interest in a tax-deferred fashion; no taxes are paid on the gains in your account until the funds are actually withdrawn.

Another often-stated feature of whole life is the availability of loans against the cash value of the policy. This feature can come in quite handy as a ready source for short-term loans. Although it tends to be less expensive than most signature loans, you must realize that you are really borrowing from your own savings, which is left to accumulate at a lower rate. Policy loans may not have to be paid back; however, borrowing from your policy in this fashion will reduce the death benefits of the policy by the amount you withdraw.

Limited-payment Life. A limited-payment insurance policy provides life insurance protection throughout the policyholder's life similar to whole life. Instead of the same payment throughout, you pay the same (higher) premium for a limited number of years (perhaps for ten, twenty, or thirty years). At that point, the policy is "paid up," meaning that no further premiums are required. In comparison, a whole life policy does not get "paid up" until you reach the age of 100. Insurance protection, in the sense that the beneficiaries get the face amount of the policy upon the policyholder's death, remains throughout the policyholder's life.

Of course, the earlier the policy is paid, the greater the premium must be, so for the short term, these are usually the most expensive of all life insurance policy premiums. For example, a thirty-five-year-old man who purchases a $10,000 twenty-year limited-payment policy might pay $340 per year versus $220 for a whole life policy. Since the payments are so large, the amount of insurance that can be bought with a budgeted amount each month is smaller. Thus, a young couple using limited-payment life may be underinsured, even though they are paying large premiums for insurance. These policies are also the most profitable for insurance companies, since more money comes to them up front.

Variable Insurance. In the 1970s, high interest rates available on alternative savings vehicles made the low rates of return on the savings component in whole life and limited-payment life financially unattractive. Sales of these products declined, and the insurance industry developed a new range of products with higher rates of return and increased flexibility. Some of these plans allow the policyholder to move between term and permanent insurance for a small fee, so that the savings and insurance components of the policies could be adjusted to meet the customer's needs over a period of years. Other new policies simply improve the return on the savings component of the policy. The most common types of these new policies are adjustable life, universal life, and variable life. Most of these policies feature a "single-premium" with one large up-front premium that would not be suitable for most servicemembers.

Adjustable Life. Adjustable life insurance allows policyholders to adjust the terms of the policy as their needs change. Policies may start

---

TABLE 13-2
PERMANENT LIFE INSURANCE

Advantages
- As long as the premiums are paid, protection is guaranteed for life.
- Premium costs can be fixed or flexible to meet personal financial needs.
- The policy accumulates a cash value against which you can borrow. (Loans must be repaid with interest or your beneficiaries will receive a reduced death benefit.) You can borrow against the policy's cash value to pay premiums or use the cash value to provide paid-up insurance.
- The policy's cash value can be surrendered, in total or in part, for cash or converted into an annuity. (An annuity is an insurance product that provides an income for a person's lifetime or a specific period.)
- A provision or rider can be added to a policy that gives you the option to purchase additional insurance without taking a medical exam or having to furnish evidence of insurability.

Disadvantages
- Required premium levels may make it too expensive to buy enough protection.
- It may be more costly than term insurance if you do not keep it long enough.
- Interest returns on the savings portion may be below market returns.

---

as whole life and be converted to term insurance by lowering the premiums or increasing the face value of the policy. Another type of policy initially offers low-cost term coverage with little or no cash value buildup. Later, when the policyholder has more income, the policy can be changed to permanent insurance with higher premiums that include an accumulation of cash value. Dividends may be used to pay premiums or to increase the face value of the policy. The major advantage of this type of policy is flexibility. The interest rate earned is not much better than standard whole life policies. The disadvantage of adjustable life is that the policy owner may not have bought either the best term policy or the best permanent policy, but a compromise between the two.

Universal Life. Universal life is a combination of term insurance with a tax-deferred savings account that is tied to a market interest rate. In many respects, universal life acts like an adjustable life policy in that the face value and premiums can be adjusted to meet changing needs.

The major difference is that the interest rate paid on cash values in universal life is closer to market rates than in whole life policies, so the investment portion grows faster. Universal life usually invests the savings portion of the premium in short- or medium-term bond investments that in the past have offered superior rates of return compared to whole life returns. The return, however, is not guaranteed; what you earn depends on the actual performance of the insurance company's investment portfolios.

It is probably true that the rate of return on a universal life policy's savings component will be higher than the return on a similar whole life policy, simply because the company attempts to tie the return to the performance of its investments. However, it is not clear that the actual return that is earned on a universal policy will be much higher when all the additional fees and restrictions are considered. Beware of sales claims that advertise a rate of return paid on the cash value after all fees and costs have been deducted from your premium payment. The relevant rate of return should be calculated based on what you have paid minus the amount necessary to pay for the pure insurance, an amount that may be approximated by the cost of a decreasing, renewable term policy.

It is important to shop for the best universal life policy, as different companies offer slightly different options. Some companies will only pay 3 percent interest on the first $1,000 in the savings portion of the account. Other companies allow you to vary the amount of your insurance coverage without incurring additional fees. And some companies charge high first-year fees. The return on universal life insurance policies is usually guaranteed for one year but then fluctuates up or down with market conditions over the long term. Many companies will guarantee a high rate for the first year and then a nominal rate after that. Look for maximum flexibility, highest guaranteed minimum rates of return, and lowest fees.

Variable Life. Variable life policies are designed to allow the insured to possibly earn higher rates of return by choosing to put the cash value component of the policy into higher-risk investments: common stocks, bonds, money market instruments, or government securities. There is no guaranteed cash surrender value because the cash value depends on the return actually earned on the investments. Additionally, you will not know exactly what the face amount of your coverage is, although some minimum is normally guaranteed. If the investment portion of your policy is growing, the cash surrender value and face amount of your policy will rise. If your investment does poorly, the face amount of your policy will decline. It is important to recognize that the death benefit your survivors will receive from a variable life policy depends in part on the performance of the investment strategy you elect from the insurance company.

For example, if you choose to have the company invest the savings component of your variable life premium in common stocks, the death benefit paid to your survivors will be higher or lower, depending upon how stock prices change. It is true that in the past long-term bonds and common stocks have paid higher average returns than more conservative investments, but it is also true that the variability of those returns has been greater. Beware of counting on an assumed rate of return on your investment portfolio to deliver the insurance protection your family will have. The rates of return you may see in variable life sales literature are not guaranteed. Base the amount of insurance you buy on your family's needs and be sure what you need is guaranteed to be paid if you die. The potential gains from higher investment returns in variable life policies should be viewed as a means to earn higher expected returns on the cash value by accepting greater investment risk.

PURCHASING A POLICY

Now that you have a basic understanding of the various types of life insurance available, you have the difficult task of deciding what policy is best for you.

Almost all active-duty members elect to take Servicemembers' Group Life Insurance (SGLI). The maximum coverage currently is $400,000 in term insurance for $29 per month. Check your Leave and Earnings Statement to see if you are paying for SGLI and are therefore covered. This low-cost term insurance should be declined only after carefully reviewing your needs for insurance, and then only by those without any dependents. Be aware that SGLI can be converted to a five-year renewable term insurance called Veterans' Group Life Insurance (VGLI) upon separation or retirement from active duty. VGLI is a renewable five-year term policy with a premium that is based upon your age when you leave the service. You can learn more about VGLI at *www.insurance.va.gov/sgliSite/VGLI/VGLI.htm*, which also has links to VGLI premiums.

For term insurance other than SGLI and VGLI, you must generally inquire about rates and collect data yourself. Since the profit margins are low with term insurance, many companies that sell it do not have a sales force. You must decide the amount of insurance you need and then find the best deal for yourself. Group term policies at very attractive rates are frequently advertised in the *Army*, *Air Force*, and *Navy Times*.

Some financial planners say, "Buy term and invest the difference," when giving advice concerning life insurance. Before you rely on this, you must evaluate your own discipline to stick to the plan. If you buy term and do not invest the difference between the term life insurance cost and the higher permanent life insurance cost, there will not be any savings. You will NOT do better than the permanent insurance policy's cash value buildup.

> *Insurance companies with the least expensive policies will probably not have a sales force, so do not expect the best deals to come knocking at your door.*

If you are shopping for permanent insurance, select an agent. The agent will meet with you to discuss your needs and his products. Be aware that agents work on commission and usually are eager to show their products. Your job is to tone down that enthusiasm and buy the right type and amount of insurance to fit your needs, not the agent's. This is not an easy thing to do. Remember, over half of the people who take out permanent policies cancel them within ten years. Your best offense is a good defense: Know something about your options and your insurance needs before the agent makes the sales pitch. Remember also that the insurance companies with the least expensive policies will probably not have a sales force, so do not expect the best deals to come knocking at your door.

It is important that you select a financially secure company; insurance companies are subject to mismanagement, fraud, and poor economic conditions that can bankrupt weaker ones. You can find insurance company ratings in most libraries in *Best's Insurance Reports*, and in magazines such as *Consumer Reports*, *Changing Times*, and *Money*. Each state also monitors the insurance companies licensed to sell policies within its jurisdiction. Insurance commissioners in your state should be able to advise you about complaints or company performance.

In conclusion, it is important that you have a focused and organized plan to protect your loved ones in the event of your untimely death. First, you must understand how to determine if you need additional insurance. This entails understanding how much insurance you already have and what additional survivor benefits are available to your family members. Second, you must know how to conduct a needs analysis to determine the approximate amount of life insurance necessary for your family. Finally, you must understand the types of life insurance available, which enables you to make an educated and informed decision concerning the type of life insurance you should buy to supplement your current coverage. Armed with this knowledge and a focused plan, you should have no problem making an assessment of your life insurance needs and finding an appropriate life insurance plan to meet the needs of your loved ones.

14

Automobile Insurance

Owning and operating a motor vehicle can be a risky adventure. In addition to your personal injuries or damages incurred while driving, the car can inflict injury on other individuals and/or damage property. As the owner or operator of a motor vehicle, you assume the risk and responsibility for compensating anyone injured or replacing damaged property when you are responsible for an accident. Automobile insurance provides a necessary protection against these financial risks. All states require automobile owners to carry some basic minimum insurance coverage.

The goal of an insurance policy is to protect you from the many financial risks associated with owning and operating a car. An insurance policy attempts to cover each type of risk with a specific category of insurance. Each type of coverage has a specific cost, called a premium. The sum of these risk premiums is the total cost of your policy. As a policyholder, by adjusting the level (amount) of risk coverage and the related deductibles (amount you must pay prior to the insurance company paying for a loss), you can adjust your total policy cost. As a general rule, the lower the risk coverage, the lower the premium; however, premiums do not increase in proportion to the increase in coverage. For example, increasing liability coverage from $10,000 to $25,000, a 150% increase, may increase your premium by only 10%. The premium-coverage trade-off is important since your primary concern should be to ensure that your assets are adequately protected against loss. Your second concern should be locating a policy that provides the necessary protection at the lowest cost.

CAR TYPE INFLUENCES PREMIUM
Since your automobile insurance premium is a major budget expenditure, this cost should be considered prior to purchasing a car. Different brands and car models have different claims histories. The claim history

is the typical frequency that the model of car is involved in an accident and the cost required to settle all claims from that accident. Insurance companies use these claims histories and your personal information to calculate your premium. For example, a car with a poor claim history (typically involved in more accidents and repaired at a high cost) can produce a significantly higher cost of coverage than a car with a better claim history. Also, "safe" cars, equipped with dual air bags, antilock brakes, and active theft-deterrent systems, are sure bets for lower premiums compared to cars without these options. Additionally, these lower premiums can, over several years, offset the initial cost of purchasing these options on a new car. Likewise, when considering the purchase of a used car, a better claim history can make the more expensive model actually cheaper than a car with a poor claim history. Your insurance company can calculate your expected premiums if you provide the relevant information (year, make, and model) on the cars that you consider purchasing. Additionally, many insurance company websites will provide the same information.

The following websites will assist you in obtaining both information and premium quotes about your policy: *www.allstate.com*, *www.geico.com*, *www.nationwide.com*, *www.progressive.com*, *www.safeco.com*, *www.statefarm.com*, and *usaa.com*. Note that some of the sites will provide quotes, but others will have a local insurance agent contact you to discuss coverage options and prices.

To review the claim history of a car, you can contact USAA at *www.usaa.com* and receive a copy of *The Car Guide* or *Consumer Reports* at *www.consumerreports.org*.

SELECTING AN INSURANCE COMPANY

You should select your insurance company with the same diligence used to select your car. Policy prices, coverage, and service differ significantly among companies, so comparison shopping is important in order to make an informed decision. Additionally, letting your insurance agent know that you are actively looking at policies from different companies may give you some leverage in pricing your policy.

The company you select should have a reliable, established reputation in the insurance business. Longevity is typically an indicator of sound company management policies. Since military personnel move often, you probably want an insurance company that will provide coverage as you move from state to state and internationally. Though many Americans prefer dealing with the personal service of a local agent, military families may prefer the convenience of a toll-free number or Internet access that provides contact to an insurance professional from virtually anywhere, twenty-four hours a day.

HOW INSURANCE COMPANIES EVALUATE YOUR POTENTIAL RISK

Insurance companies continually analyze the financial risks that you present to their company and the likelihood that you will have a claim the company will have to pay. Since these companies cannot know everything about each and every policyholder, they make simplifying demographic assumptions and "pool" those policyholders with similar characteristics together. Insurance premiums are then based on the "pool" to which you are assigned; the riskier the pool, the higher the premium. By understanding how these pools are assigned, you can materially affect the cost of your insurance premiums.

The common characteristics that determine your pool membership are the type of car you drive and your driving record, as well as age, sex, marital status, frequency and length of commute, annual mileage, zip code, and academic performance. Initially, you are in a specific category, but insurance companies will reassess your categorization as your personal demographics change. For example, when a twenty-five-year-old male marries, he moves to a new category and his premiums decrease. Whatever you do, be honest with your insurance agent when discussing the demographics that affect your pool. You can get into serious trouble if you provide false information just to save a few dollars.

THE INSURANCE POLICY: EXPLANATIONS AND RECOMMENDATIONS

The typical automobile insurance policy consists of five basic types of coverage: liability, medical payments, collision, comprehensive, and uninsured motorist. There are also other optional coverages. The following is an outline of the types of coverages as well as some guidelines to consider. You must balance these guidelines with your personal financial situation and attitude toward assuming risk.

Liability Coverage

Liability coverage pays for injuries and property damage that you (or someone using your car) cause to another as a result of driving negligently. Liability coverage, mandatory in nearly all states, is the most expensive type of coverage and the most necessary. Individuals injured in an automobile accident in which someone else is at fault often seek compensation for personal injury through the courts. You risk losing current and future assets if you fail to carry adequate liability insurance. Therefore, liability coverage is the last place you want to skimp. There are two types of liability coverage: bodily injury and property damage.

Bodily Injury Coverage. Bodily injury (BI) coverage pays for medical expenses and associated litigation fees for losses resulting from injury or death in an accident in which you were at fault. Losses can result from medical bills, lost wages, and pain and suffering. Court awards for pain and suffering can be enough to ruin you financially if you are underinsured. You can expect to be sued in court if you cause an accident that results in personal injury or death.

Bodily Injury Guidelines

1. Carry no less than $100,000/$300,000 (split-limit) or $300,000 (single-limit) coverage.
2. Buy as much bodily injury liability coverage as you can afford. Increasing liability coverage does not raise your premium proportionately. Even if you increase coverage from $50,000 to $300,000 (a 500% increase), your premium might increase by only 25%.
3. Follow guidelines 1 and 2 even if you live in a no-fault state.
4. If you own a home and/or assets worth more than $300,000, consider an umbrella policy that will provide even more protection (see chapter 12).
5. Obtain insurance that covers any car you legally drive, even if it is a rented or borrowed vehicle.

There are two types of bodily injury coverage: single-limit and split-limit (or multiple-limit). Single-limit BI coverage pays a maximum single amount per accident, regardless of the number of individuals injured. For example, if you carry a policy with $300,000 single-limit bodily injury coverage, one injured person could claim up to $300,000 from your insurance company, with the remainder coming out of your pocket. The second type of BI coverage, split-limit, is more common. It pays a maximum amount to each person injured in an accident, subject to a maximum limit per accident. For example, $100,000/ $300,000 split-limit coverage means that the insurance company will pay up to $100,000 to each person injured, but no more than $300,000 per accident. If a single individual suffers damages of $150,000, the insurance policy would cover only $100,000 of the damages, and you would have to cover the remainder. If you injure six people in an accident, the company would be liable for a maximum of $300,000 worth of damages.

Most states mandate minimum limits for liability coverage. The typical amount is $25,000/$50,000, a meager sum in our litigious society. A number of states have no-fault laws, meaning that an injured party receives compensation from his or her own insurance company, regardless of who is at fault. The theory behind no-fault is that the need for litigation after an accident decreases, so insurance premiums should decrease.

Property Damage Coverage. The second type of liability coverage is property damage (PD). PD pays for the necessary repairs when someone else's property (usually a vehicle) is damaged. PD also covers other types of property. The average state minimums are around $10,000— not even enough to cover the cost of a new car.

Property Damage Guidelines

1. Carry property damage coverage of at least $50,000. State minimums may be less, but consider the financial liability you could incur if you damage someone's new Mercedes.
2. Obtain insurance that covers any car you legally drive.

Medical Payments Coverage

Medical payments coverage pays the medical expenses of individuals injured in your car. This coverage is normally optional in states without no-fault laws and coverage amounts range from $1,000 to $100,000 per person.

Most people already have some type of medical and hospital insurance so some may choose to forgo this duplicate coverage. Military families have hospital benefits, but remember that all passengers may not be immediate family members. A small amount of additional coverage may make sense because medical payments coverage often includes a funeral benefit.

Medical Payments Guidelines

---

1. Consider $10,000 in medical payments coverage, even if you have a good health insurance policy for yourself and your family. This will help cover any medical expenses for nonfamily members.
2. If your state requires PIP, purchase $10,000 coverage (or the state minimum, if it exceeds $10,000).
3. If your state requires PIP coverage and your state's no-fault rules allow you to coordinate benefits with your health insurance policy, do so. This coordination may realize sizeable premium savings and means that you would seek reimbursement from your health insurance company before applying to your auto insurer. Military families should ask for coordination of benefits because of their access to the military health-care system.
4. Obtain insurance that covers you if you are injured while using someone else's car.

States with no-fault laws may require you to carry personal injury protection (PIP) coverage. This is a more comprehensive form of medical payments coverage that covers medical bills, lost wages, and some funeral expenses for injuries to you or any passenger, regardless of who is at fault. Some states require a minimum amount of PIP, usually around $10,000, but amounts vary by state.

Collision Coverage

Collision coverage pays for physical damage to your car regardless of who is at fault and accounts for approximately 30% of the total insurance premium on a new car. Collision coverage carries a deductible (an amount you must pay before the coverage becomes effective). By selecting the size of the deductible—ranging from $100 to $1,000— you can affect your premium since the higher the deductible, the lower the premium. For example, increasing your deductible from $100 to $500 or $1,000 could save you from 25 to 40% on your premium. Remember, though, that if you are involved in an accident, you will have to pay this deductible out of pocket in order to repair your car.

Comprehensive collision coverage is related to the "blue book" value of your car. The blue book value (provided by your insurance company, bank, or *www.kbb.com*) on a car is the maximum amount your insurance company will pay you if your car is totaled. For newer cars, comprehensive collision coverage is essential and is usually required if you borrowed money to purchase the car. For cars between four and six years old, the decision to carry collision coverage depends on the financial risk that you are willing to assume in the event that your car is totaled. For cars with a low blue book value, collision coverage is usually a waste of money since the cost of coverage will not be realized if the car is totaled.

Collision Guidelines

1. Carry collision on a car with a substantial blue book value, but choose the highest that deductible you can afford.
2. Drop collision coverage altogether on an older, lower-value car if you can afford to replace it.
3. If you financed your vehicle, check with your financial institution before canceling collision insurance.

Comprehensive Coverage

Comprehensive coverage reimburses you for damage caused by mishaps other than a crash, including vandalism, theft, falling objects, floods, glass breakage, and collisions with animals. It carries a deductible that normally ranges from $50 to $1,000. Additionally, for a relatively small additional premium, you can typically receive full glass-damage coverage with no deductible.

Comprehensive Guidelines

1. Choose the highest deductible you can afford.
2. Adapt your comprehensive coverage to your post location. In cities with higher crime rates, it is a good idea to maintain comprehensive coverage.
3. Cancel coverage on a car with a low resale value.
4. If you financed your vehicle, check with your financial institution prior to canceling your comprehensive insurance.

Uninsured Motorist Coverage

Uninsured motorist (UIM) coverage protects you and your passengers from damages caused by uninsured motorists and hit-and-run drivers. It is especially important in states without no-fault laws. UIM coverage reimburses you for bodily injury or death in accidents where the uninsured motorist is responsible. UIM covers payments for your medical expenses and losses due to permanent disability or death, loss of income, and any other damages entitled by state law. It does not reimburse you for property damages.

UIM/UNM Guidelines

1. Carry UIM in an amount comparable with your bodily injury liability coverage.
2. Carry UIM coverage unless you are in a state with outstanding no-fault laws or you have an excellent medical insurance policy for yourself and your family.
3. Check with your insurance company to determine if your UIM coverage includes UNM coverage; if not, ask for it.
4. Check to see if UNM coverage pays only if your policy exceeds the liability coverage of the underinsured motorist or if it pays for damages in excess (up to your limit) of the underinsured motorist's coverage.
5. Check with your insurance company each time you move to determine the requirements of your new state.

Minimum coverage offered by insurance companies normally coincides with a state's particular laws. Although UIM is a normal part of every insurance policy, you may generally elect to reject it. However, you must do so in writing. UIM premiums are on the rise because increasing numbers of drivers violate state laws and do not carry insurance. Therefore, the probability of having an accident with an uninsured motorist increases, which yields higher premiums.

There is a newer category of coverage called underinsured motorist (UNM) coverage. UNM coverage applies if you have an accident with another driver who is at fault but whose insurance coverage cannot provide sufficient compensation. UNM coverage pays when the other party's coverage stops. You can buy coverage limits similar to those available for liability. Different insurance companies treat UNM coverage differently. For some companies, UNM is an integral part of your policy. Other companies treat UNM as a separate coverage with a separate premium. State law determines what constitutes a UNM loss and under what conditions you will receive payment.

Optional Coverages

Insurance policies can have as many options as the car itself; and just as you can save money by purchasing a car with fewer options, you can do the same with your insurance policy. One way to save money is to avoid buying unnecessary options. There are many options, but we will discuss only the more prominent ones. If you have adequate personal property, health, and life insurance policies, you can reject any options related to these risk categories. If you need more life insurance, buy more life insurance; do not sign up for limited life insurance on your automobile insurance policy.

Rental Reimbursement Coverage. If you have an accident and your car requires repairs, rental reimbursement will offset the cost of temporary transportation until your car is repaired. This coverage pays a certain amount per day, for a specified number of days. Reimbursement is normally a maximum of $30 a day and lasts for two weeks. If you own more than one car or if alternate transportation means are available (company car, local mass transit), rental reimbursement is not necessary.

Towing and Labor Coverage. The insurance company pays the cost of towing your car to a repair shop and pays for any immediate labor involved. If you are a member of an auto club that already provides this service, you should not carry this coverage. Also, read the fine print in order to understand the limits of the towing arrangement and exactly what labor costs are reimbursable.

Leased Automobile Coverage

Leasing an automobile is becoming a popular alternative to buying. Insurance coverage for your leased vehicle is similar to insurance for a vehicle you own, but there are a few significant differences. The first is that insurance requirements by the leasing company are often higher than the state minimums. Thus, if you lease a car, you may be required to carry more insurance than you would otherwise. You need to consider these added costs when evaluating a car leasing option, compared to purchasing the same car.

Another difference is that if your leased vehicle is stolen or totaled, most leasing companies consider this an early contract termination. You will generally owe the lessor more than your insurance company will pay, due to depreciation of the leased vehicle. The difference, or "gap," between what you owe and what your insurance company will pay needs to be covered by gap insurance or total-loss protection. Some leases include gap insurance in the cost of the payments. Others do not and you will need to buy separate coverage or potentially face a large financial loss if something happens to your leased automobile.

DEPLOYMENTS
During long deployments you may be able to save money on car insurance by temporarily suspending certain types of insurance. For example collision and comprehensive coverage are required by lending institutions. Thus, if your vehicle is financed, you can petition the bank/credit union for temporary exemption from these coverages, (especially if the vehicle will be in storage). In addition, many states will let you suspend liability insurance if you agree to turn in the vehicles license plates. This will require coordination with the department of motor vehicles, and the qualifications and restrictions will vary by state. Your insurer should be able to answer any questions you might have about this process.

AUTOMOBILE INSURANCE CHECKLIST
The following checklist provides you with a list of most of the possible coverage categories as well as other areas of importance when shopping for insurance. Use this list to construct a spreadsheet for comparing insurance companies. In addition, some companies (such as Progressive at *www.progressive.com*) may give you their insurance quotes and the quotes of other reputable companies as well.

TABLE 14-1
AUTOMOBILE INSURANCE CHECKLIST

	Co. A	Co. B	Co. C
Liability coverages			
Bodily injury protection			
Property damage liability			
Personal injury protection			
Uninsured motorist			
Underinsured motorist			
Medical payments			
Collision			
$100 deductible			
$250 deductible			
$500 deductible			
$1,000 deductible			
Comprehensive			
$100 deductible			
$250 deductible			
$500 deductible			
$1,000 deductible			
Special coverages			
Towing and labor			
Rental reimbursement			

15

Protecting Your Wealth with Insurance

Saving and investing to achieve your financial goals is not always easy. Neither is keeping what you have already accumulated. Your assets can be lost by accidental damage or theft, or you could be held liable for large monetary damages in a civil lawsuit. Reducing the risk of potential loss with insurance can be expensive. You will need to balance the amount of risk that you are willing to assume against the cost of eliminating it with insurance. This chapter provides general information on these topics:

1. Homeowners and Personal Property Insurance
2. Liability Insurance
3. The Selection of an Insurer

HOMEOWNERS AND PERSONAL PROPERTY INSURANCE
If you own a home, you will need to insure both real property (the structure itself) and personal property (the contents) against loss. Home insurance policies cover both types.

Five important topics will be discussed in this section:

1. Policy Selection.
2. Amount of Coverage.
3. Inflation Effects.
4. Additional Homeowners Insurance Policies.
5. Other Types of Property and Insurance.

Policy Selection
The term *homeowners insurance* is to some extent a misnomer. The standard homeowners policy can cover just about anything you own. It can provide protection against personal liability and property loss, and sometimes it even covers medical bills. There are six basic types of

homeowners insurance described in Table 15-1. These types are usually designated with "HO numbers" based on the forms that insurance companies use.

All homeowners insurance offer two basic coverage or protection plans:

1. *Property Protection (Section I)*—reimburses you for losses or damages to your house and/or its contents.
2. *Liability Protection (Section II)*—covers any legal liabilities as a result of any unintentional bodily injury or property damage that occurs on your property

For the most updated information on homeowners' insurance policies, we recommend that you visit the Insurance Information Institute web site at *www.iii.org/individuals/homei/*.

Amount of Coverage

Dwellings are insured on a *replacement cost basis*. This means the cost of required repairs.

Replacement value and market value are two entirely different concepts. Market value is simply the price a buyer is willing to pay for your home; it includes the value of the land and many intangibles (location, quality of schools, and so on). Replacement value does not include land value; also, it can vary over time, and depend on things such as wage rates for construction workers and the cost of building materials.

You can determine the replacement value of your home based on estimated construction costs in your area; simply multiply the total square footage of your home by the local building costs per square foot. Other ways to determine replacement value are to ask the insurance company to calculate the replacement cost or to hire an independent appraiser.

TABLE 15-1
HOMEOWNERS' INSURANCE

HO 02	HO 03	HO 04	HO 05	HO 06	HO 08
Low Cost Insurance. Covers dwelling against limited number of perils.*	**Most common form.** Provides open perils** coverage on dwelling.	Renters' Policy. No coverage on dwelling.	Provides open peril coverage on both dwelling & contents.	Condominium insurance.	For older homes built with methods & materials not used today.

* *Peril*—A cause of loss such as fire, hail, or flood.
** *Open Peril*—More generous coverage. Covers all perils unless specifically excluded.

You generally do not need to insure 100% of the replacement value of your home because the probability of a total loss of your home is very low. For example, even a severe fire will not destroy your house's foundation. For this reason, your mortgage lender will usually require that you obtain only 80% coverage.

If a home with a replacement value of $150,000 is covered for $120,000 (80%), the insurance company will reimburse the homeowner for losses to a maximum of $120,000. If you insure for less than 80% of the replacement value, the insurance company will not reimburse you up to the percentage you insured. Be sure to understand the nature of your coverage and how the insurance company will reimburse you as the size of your loss varies.

Example: A fire in your garage totally destroys the garage and adjacent kitchen. The cost of repair is $25,000. If you have 80% coverage (of your $150,000 house), the insurance company will reimburse you the full $25,000. If you had only 70% protection, the insurance company will divide your actual 70% coverage by the 80% "required" coverage to determine its level of reimbursement in the event of such a partial loss (e.g., $70 \div 80 = 87.5\%$ of $25,000, or $21,875). Therefore, you would not receive enough to fully cover your loss.

Coverage for *personal property* is usually set at 50% of the home's replacement cost. It also usually covers 10% of the home's cost for damage to an external structure (shed, boathouse). There are, however, limits to specific types of personal property—for example, in many policies silverware is limited to $2,500, computers to $3,000, and jewelry to $1,000.

The MSN Money website is an excellent resource for homeowners' insurance basics. You can find information to help you determine your insurance requirements at *moneycentral.msn.com*.

Inflation Effects

Another thing to keep in mind is that the replacement value you determine for your home when you first take out your policy is valid only at that moment in time. Given the general tendency for construction costs to increase, the replacement value of your home will also increase over time. So, 80% today may be something less than 80% tomorrow. However, if your insurance company offers (for a fee) a replacement cost endorsement option, you can shift—from you to your insurance company—the responsibility for keeping the replacement cost coverage at 80%.

Additional Homeowners Insurance Policies
Some perils are not covered by a standard homeowners policy. Among them are flood, earthquake, sinkhole, landslide and sometimes windstorm coverage—if you live in a high-risk coastal region. Coverage for these perils usually can be purchased through *endorsements* (which are provisions added to an existing insurance policy to modify its coverage) or by purchasing separate policies.

Flood Insurance
Damage caused by floods is not covered by homeowners policies. If you live in a community susceptible to flooding and your community participates in the National Flood Insurance Program (NFIP), you can obtain flood insurance through the Federal Emergency Management Agency (FEMA). You can determine if your community participates in NFIP at *www.fema.gov/fema/csb.shtm* or at *www.floodsmart.gov*.

Earthquake Insurance
Basic homeowners policies do not insure against damage caused by earthquakes. Therefore, we recommend that you consider adding earthquake insurance to your homeowners policy if you live in an earthquake-prone area. In major disasters, the federal government has generally provided some level of assistance to the owners of damaged homes, usually in the form of subsidized loans. As a result, many experts debate the need for this insurance. You will have to balance cost of purchasing private insurance against your family's tolerance for risk and the degree to which you expect the government to respond rapidly and generously in the event of an emergency. You can get more information on earthquake coverage from the California Earthquake Authority (CEA) and the Insurance Information Institute at: *www.insurance.ca.gov/0100-consumers/0100-insurance-guides/0400-residential-series/earthquake-insurance.cfm* or *www.iii.org/media/hottopics/insurance/earthquake/*.

Title Insurance
A *title* is a legal document establishing evidence of ownership and possession of land. There are two types of title insurance: One protects your lender; the other protects you. At settlement, you are required to pay for a policy to protect the lender; however, you are not protected against a defective title unless you purchase a separate policy for yourself. "What could be wrong with the title?" you ask. A lawyer or

lender will tell you any number of horror stories. For example, a previous owner may have had thousands of dollars in unpaid traffic tickets, and the state may have put a lien, or a legal claim against an asset, on his or her property. If the lien against the property is not noted until after the property is transferred, you would be liable for the unpaid tickets. It is better for an insurance company to deal with these rare but costly surprises. Once you have paid the mandatory fee for the lender's title insurance, you will find that the cost of an additional owner's policy (for yourself) may be less than you think and worth the peace of mind. We strongly recommend that you purchase an owner's title insurance policy when buying real estate. Since you can choose your insurer, be sure to shop around so that you do not overpay for coverage. For more information on title insurance see *www.kiplinger.com/ personalfinance/basics/managing/insurance/title.html.*

> *It is recommended that you purchase an owner's title insurance policy when buying real estate.*

Mortgage Life Insurance (or Credit Life Insurance)

This insurance repays the remaining balance on your mortgage in the event of your death or the death of your spouse. The premium is added to your mortgage payment. This is normally a very expensive form of life insurance and can be three to ten times more expensive than term life insurance coverage for the mortgage or loan amount. We recommend that you have adequate life insurance and avoid mortgage life insurance. For more information, see chapter 13 on life insurance.

> *Avoid purchasing mortgage life insurance because it is typically more expensive than standard term life insurance policies.*

Other Types of Property and Insurance
Insuring Your Rental Property

A military family may purchase a home and then decide to rent it out after making a PCS move. Since they still own the home, they are responsible for insuring it. It is very important to check with your insurance company to determine what your homeowners policy coverage protects once you move and for how long that protection is in force. Also, verify whether or not it matters if your home is vacant. The following general guidelines apply if you decide to rent your home to someone else:

- You should normally replace your homeowners policy with a fire policy. This provides coverage for the dwelling itself and damage to personal property in the event of the perils named in the policy. It does not cover theft of personal property and furnishings left in the dwelling.
- To protect against theft, you can obtain a separate policy that covers the contents of your rental property that belong to you.
- The aforementioned fire policy may be extended to provide personal liability protection (any legal liabilities as a result of any nonintentional bodily injury or property damage that occurs on your property) on request. However, if you have a homeowners policy for your current home or a personal liability policy is already in force, liability coverage can be extended from that policy to the rental property.
- Make sure that your tenants understand that they are responsible for arranging for their own renters insurance to cover their personal property.

Personal liability insurance is covered in greater depth later in this chapter.

Renters Insurance
Given the high number of moves servicemembers make during a career, they often rent houses or apartments rather than purchase them. It is important to know that as a renter you have no vested interest in the building itself, but you may wrongly assume that losses sustained from fire, flood, or theft are covered by the landlord's policy. In fact, renters are provided little or no protection from the landlord's policy. Renters Insurance (HO 04) can provide you with coverage for your possessions. Additionally, Renters Insurance can also cover your responsibility to other people injured at your home or elsewhere by you, a family member, or your pet; and it pays legal defense costs if you are taken to court. Policies may also cover additional living expenses (those above your normal monthly rent) in the event that your rental unit is rendered uninhabitable and you are forced to live in a hotel or other temporary lodging facility.

Insurance in Government Quarters

If you live in government quarters, you are "covered" by government insurance. However, such coverage is normally limited to personal property that is damaged in or stolen from your quarters, and the coverage limits are sometimes surprisingly low. The insurance provided by the government is very limited, especially when it comes to personal liability protection. You would be wise to purchase specific insurance policies for personal property and personal liability protection (see below) or purchase a renters policy (HO 04) that covers both categories of risk. Such a policy can provide protection wherever your tour of duty takes you.

> *Servicemembers living in government quarters should purchase personal property and personal liability protection.*

LIABILITY INSURANCE

Liability protection covers legal liabilities as a result of any unintentional bodily injury or property damage that occurs on your property—or elsewhere—by you, a family member, or your pet; also, it pays legal defense costs if you are taken to court.

Most homeowners policies offer $100,000 liability coverage as a minimum, and your automobile insurance policy will usually include liability coverage. Given our litigious society, the amount of coverage in these policies is usually inadequate. The need to protect your home and the physical things you own is readily apparent to you; however, protecting your future income is not so obvious. Because liability judgments can include that some portion of all your future income must be paid to someone you injure, you could lose not only everything you own today, but also a substantial portion of your future earnings. It is, therefore, imperative that you maintain adequate liability coverage.

> *Purchase adequate liability coverage to protect your current and future assets.*

Automobile and homeowners policies provide only limited personal liability insurance. An *umbrella policy* picks up where your existing coverage leaves off and goes to whatever limit you select, normally the

$1 million to $5 million range. Coverage extends well beyond damages assessed for physical injury. An umbrella policy covers judgments for injuries on your property, unintentional libel or slander, catastrophic automobile accidents that exceed your policy limit, sickness or disease, shock, defamation of character, mental anguish, wrongful entry, malicious prosecution, wrongful eviction, and more. Compensation for defense costs and court costs is also included. For additional information on an umbrella policy visit *personalinsure.about.com/cs/ umbrella/a/aa110503a.htm.*

CHOOSING AN INSURANCE COMPANY

All homeowners policies are not the same, nor do all standard policies cost the same. As with all insurance, the first rule is to shop around. Because there are so many options, this is not as easy as it sounds. The following websites offer excellent advice about selecting a company: *www.iii.org/individuals/homei/hbs/pickco/*, *money.cnn.com/pf/101/ lessons/19/page4.html*, and *www.smartmoney.com/insurance/home/.*

There are hundreds of companies that provide homeowners' and related insurance. Two that are very popular among servicemembers are USAA and Armed Forces Insurance, but many other firms can serve your needs. You may find that local agents of nationwide firms have lower rates because they have better knowledge of the local housing market. Always get more than one quotation. You can also get more detailed information from insurance commissioners in your state. These offices can be found through the Insurance Information Institute web site at *www.iii.org.*

Additionally, we recommend that you research the insurance companies for their financial health. You can obtain this information from the major rating agencies at the following websites: A.M. Best Company Inc. at *www.ambest.com*, Fitch Ratings Inc. at *www.fitchratings .com/*, Moody's Investor Services at *www.moodys.com/cust/default.asp*, Standard & Poor's Insurance Ratings Services at *www.standardand-poors.com*, and Weiss Ratings at *www.weissratings.com.*

Additionally the Insurance Information Institute publishes an excellent checklist for homeowners at *www.insurance.info/static/img/ brochures/homeowners_checklist.htm.*

For additional information on homeowners insurance, we recommend the following overview: *www.usaaedfoundation.org/insurance/ hi01.asp.*

PART V

TRANSITIONING FROM THE MILITARY

16

Transition Assistance, VA Benefits, and Social Security

"Of the 25 million veterans currently alive, nearly three of every four served during a war or an official period of hostility. About a quarter of the nation's population— approximately 70 million people—is potentially eligible for VA benefits and services because they are veterans, family members, or survivors of veterans."

—VETERANS ADMINISTRATION

Every servicemember leaves the military, whether by choice, necessity, or misfortune. Most leave the military through voluntary retirement, separation at ETS, or voluntary resignation from active or reserve duty. Some leave the military involuntarily because they have reached mandatory retirement age, have become ineligible for reenlistment, or have been separated under administrative or legal proceedings. Others leave the military for medical or health reasons, including injuries suffered in the line of duty. And a few have paid the ultimate price in answer to our nation's call. Regardless of the reasons for separation, military service qualifies servicemembers, and in many cases, their dependents, for a wide range of benefits and services (see Figure 16-1). This chapter provides a short summary of the many benefit programs that are available to servicemembers and their dependents as they transition from the military to the private sector.

The first section provides informational coverage of the benefits and services available from the Department of Veterans Affairs (VA) while in service and after leaving the military. The VA provides comprehensive assistance for veterans of the Armed Forces. You may be entitled to other benefits not discussed in this chapter, including one-

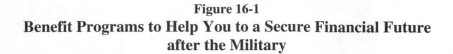

Figure 16-1
**Benefit Programs to Help You to a Secure Financial Future
after the Military**

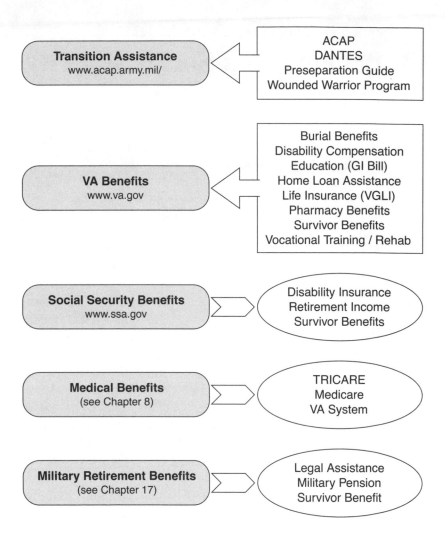

time dental treatment on separation. Make sure that you and your dependents are counseled thoroughly on all of these benefits before you leave the military and take the time to become familiar with the VA's website at *www.va.gov*.

The second section of this chapter summarizes benefits available from the Social Security Administration (SSA) for those transitioning out of the work force due to death, disability, or old-age retirement. Social Security benefits can constitute a significant portion of your retirement income. These benefits can also provide you with a valuable supplement if you became disabled and are no longer able to work. Finally, these benefits can provide your survivors with an important source of income should you die. You do not receive these benefits automatically. It is worth your time to become familiar with the SSA's website at *www.ssa.gov*, especially as you approach retirement.

> *As is the case with veterans benefits, you or your eligible dependents will receive Social Security benefits only if you apply for them.*

Eligibility rules for each of the programs and services discussed in this chapter are rather complex and can vary substantially depending on the length and classification of service. Our purpose is to make the reader aware of these benefit programs, give the reader an indication of the value of these benefit programs, and encourage the reader to account for these benefit programs when conducting personal financial planning. An exhaustive treatment of Social Security benefits and VA benefits is beyond the scope of this book, but this chapter provides an overview of their essential components and their impact on your personal financial plan. For more detailed information, contact your nearest Social Security Administration (SSA) or Department of Veterans Affairs office, or browse the websites listed in this chapter.

BENEFIT PROGRAMS FOR YOUR TRANSITION FROM THE MILITARY
Transition Assistance
The authoritative reference for information about your transition from the military is DoD's *Preseparation Guide*. (A link to other pamphlet, DA Pam 635-4, NAVMC 2916, AFJMAN 36-2128, or NAVPERS 15616, is available on the website of the U.S. Army Publishing Direc-

torate at *www.usapa.army.mil* and at *www.acap.army.mil/transitioner/ presep/index.cfm.*) Each of the services operates a Transition Assistance Program (TAP). Transition Assistance Programs are managed and operated by the Army Career and Alumni Program (ACAP), the Family Support Center, the Fleet and Family Support Center, and the Personnel Services Center in the Army, Air Force, Navy, and Marine Corps, respectively. Servicemembers should visit their respective transition assistance office when they have about one year left in service, but not later than 180 days prior to their separation date.

> **Visit your Transition Assistance Center one year before your expected separation date.**

Transition Assistance Programs help servicemembers make the transition from a military career to a civilian career through the provision of special transition benefits, job assistance workshops, automated employment tools, guidance and referral tools, access to job networks, and many other types of information services including financial planning. Transition counselors help servicemembers develop a transition plan, create a résumé that effectively parlays skills and experience developed while in the military into language easily understood by civilian employers, gain access to civilian and federal job networks, and understand the financial and educational benefits available to those who have served honorably. In many cases, spouses and dependents of servicemembers are also eligible for transition counseling. The services often operate special assistance programs for wounded soldiers. One such program is the Army's Wounded Warrior Program, which supports soldiers who have become seriously injured while serving their country. The program is designed to meet the needs of both disabled soldiers who want to work and employers who actively recruit them. For more information, see *www.aw2soldierconnection.army.mil.*

While still in service, members can participate in off-duty voluntary education programs in pursuit of achieving higher educational attainment or enhancing their human capital skills through the Defense Activity for Non-Traditional Educational Support (DANTES). DANTES programs encourage service-members to pursue their educational ambitions and achieve their education goals. These programs include testing, assessment, certification, tuition assistance, scholarships, higher education, and distance learning. In most cases, servicemembers and eligible dependents can qualify for tuition reimbursement up to $250 per credit hour and $4,500 per fiscal year for education programs taken during off-duty hours. For more information, visit the DANTES website at *www.dantes.doded.mil* or stop by your installation's education center.

> **Servicemembers and spouses are eligible for up to 100% tuition assistance through DANTES.**

VA BENEFITS

Whether still in the service or after leaving the military, most veterans are or will be eligible for one or more benefits provided through the Department of Veterans Affairs (VA). VA benefit programs include burial benefits, disability compensation, education benefits, home loan assistance, life insurance, pharmacy benefits, survivor benefits, and vocational training and rehabilitation programs. The VA also provides medical care that promotes, preserves, and restores the health of eligible veterans. A complete description of benefits is in the VA's annual edition of a booklet titled, *Federal Benefits for Veterans and Dependents*, which can be accessed at *www1.va.gov/opa/vadocs/Fedben.pdf*. These benefits are subject to regular change by Congress, so it is worthwhile to visit your local VA office or regularly check the VA website at *www.va.gov*.

In general, to be eligible for VA medical benefits, a veteran must have a service-connected disability, have an annual income and net worth that falls below the VA's means test threshold, be eligible for Medicaid benefits, or have a particular disorder that is connected to exposure to potentially hazardous circumstances while in service (i.e., Agent Orange, nuclear testing, Gulf War syndrome). Eligibility rules for VA medical care are relatively complex and will not be covered in this book. Veterans who are eligible for VA medical benefits are grouped by priority, and access may be denied or limited for those in lower-priority groups. Also, combat veterans can get free medical care through the VA for any illness possibly associated with service during a period of hostility. For more information about medical care, see chapter 8.

Education Benefits

A well-known VA program is the Montgomery GI Bill. As of 2006, servicemembers can earn up to $1,034 per month (with annual increases to keep up with inflation) for a maximum of thirty-six months for use in eligible education programs after separating from the military. Veterans are eligible if they first enlisted on or after July 1, 1985, had a pay reduction of $1,200, and had continuous active duty service equal to or greater than their initial enlistment period. Persons who are discharged for the convenience of the government must serve twenty months of a two-year enlistment and thirty months of a three-year enlistment to be eligible. For those discharged early, the period of eligibility for the entitlement is for a time period that is the same as the number of months served. Payment rates are based on the length of original enlistment, the type of training or education program undertaken, and whether the veteran is a full- or half-time student. Payment rates are determined by Congress and usually change each year.

> *Through the GI Bill, veterans can get up to $1,034 per month for up to thirty-six months in pursuit of a degree or certificate.*

The GI Bill buy-up program allows eligible active-duty members before discharge to make a one-time additional contribution of $600 to the fund, which will give the veteran up to $150 per month in addition to the Table 16-1 payment rates as a full-time student. Also, some members are eligible for college fund programs, which are usually given as an incentive to members who enlisted in specific job specialties. Veterans have ten years from the date of discharge to use their GI Bill benefits. Veterans can use the benefits in programs that lead to a college degree (Associate, Bachelor, Master, or Doctorate), vocational programs that lead to a degree or certificate, licensing and certification programs, flight training, and other types of training programs such as on-the-job or apprenticeship training.

TABLE 16-1
MONTHLY PAYMENT RATES FOR THE ACTIVE DUTY
MONTGOMERY GI BILL (2006)

	Original Enlistment of Two Years or Less	Original Enlistment of Three Years or More
Full-Time Student	$840	$1,034
Half-Time Student	$420	$517

Source: Department of Veterans Affairs, 2006.

There are also two types of GI Bill programs for reservists. As of 2005, a new program called the Reserve Educational Assistance Program (REAP) was enacted to provide education assistance to members of the Reserves called to active duty in response to a war or national emergency. Furthermore, servicemembers who first entered active duty between January 1, 1977 and June 30, 1985 may have participated in the Veterans Educational Assistance Program (VEAP), the predecessor program of the GI Bill. For more information about these programs and the reserve duty version of the GI Bill, please visit *www.gibill.va.gov.*

For most, the GI Bill payments will not cover the full costs associated with pursuing a degree or training certification. In most cases, the benefits will likely help the veteran cover a portion of tuition costs, book expenses, and administrative fees. A veteran who pursues full-time education or training will need to develop a plan for meeting the everyday living expenses related to housing, transportation, sustenance, and medical care.

Finally, the VA provides education and training opportunities through the Survivors' and Dependents' Educational Assistance Program (DEA) to eligible dependents of veterans who are permanently and totally disabled due to a service-related condition, or who died while on active duty or as a result of a service-related condition. The program offers up to forty-five months of education benefits that can be used for degree and certificate programs, apprenticeships, and on-the-job training. Current payment rates as of 2006 are $827 per month for full-time degree programs and $413 per month for part-time enrollment.

Vocational Rehabilitation

The VA's Vocational Rehabilitation and Employment (VR&E) service delivers services to veterans with service-connected disabilities. The goal of this program is to enable injured soldiers, sailors, airmen, and marines with disabilities to make a seamless transition from military service to a successful rehabilitation and on to suitable civilian employment. The desired outcome is to help the eligible veteran find suitable employment that is consistent with the individual's aptitudes and interests, as well as to achieve independence in daily living.

> *The VA provides vocational rehabilitation and employment services for veterans with service-connected disabilities.*

VA Home Loan Program

A VA-guaranteed home loan is a loan made by private lenders, such as a bank or a savings and loan, to eligible veterans for the purchase or refinancing of a home, condominium, or manufactured home. Based on the individual's personal financial situation, the maximum loan limit for which the VA will provide a guarantee is $417,000. The lender from whom the servicemember or veteran borrows money is protected against loss up to the amount of the guarantee if the borrower fails to repay the loan. Since the VA provides this guarantee to the lender, the servicemember or veteran can qualify for a mortgage with an extremely competitive interest rate without making a down payment. Additionally, the VA home-loan program has several provisions that safeguard veterans from unscrupulous lenders or home builders. For example, the builder of a new home is required to give the purchasing veteran a one-year warranty that the home has been constructed to VA approved plans and specifications. Furthermore, the veteran who gets a VA loan can prepay the entire loan without penalty. Like most home mortgage loans, there are certain fees and closing costs that will apply, and a portion of these fees must be paid at settlement.

> *The VA Home Loan Program allows service-members and veterans to obtain home mortgages at competetive rates with no down payment required.*

In general, those purchasing a home should attempt to find the best value mortgage for which they are eligible (see chapter 5). In many cases, a military servicemember or veteran may be able to find a better mortgage or refinancing option without using the VA home loan program. The primary advantage of a VA loan is that it affords somebody the opportunity to purchase quality housing even if the individual has not had the opportunity to save enough money to make the type of down payment and cover the types of settlement fees normally associated with conventional loans. If the individual can afford a relatively large down payment, then he or she might be able to find a mortgage with a more cost-effective rate than could be found through the VA home loan program.

Veterans, active-duty servicemembers, guard and reserve members, and military spouses are potentially eligible for the VA home loan program. Eligibility is based on an individual's (or a spouse's) service.

Those currently on active duty are eligible after serving continuously for at least ninety days. Those with active wartime service or veterans with peacetime service of at least 181 continuous days of service and a discharge under honorable conditions are eligible. Eligibility rules for guard and reserve members vary but generally require at least six years of service. Eligibility may be extended to unremarried spouses of veterans who died as a result of service or a connected disability. The spouse of a servicemember who becomes missing in action or a prisoner of war qualifies. U.S. citizens who served in an allied armed force in World War II and various other groups that include cadets and midshipmen at the service academies also qualify for the VA home loan program.

Life Insurance

The VA manages and operates several different insurance programs to include SGLI, VGLI, and special programs for disabled veterans. The Service-Disabled Veterans Insurance (S-DVI) program provides term or permanent life insurance with a maximum benefit amount of $10,000 for veterans with a service-connected disability. (Those who become eligible for a waiver of premiums due to total disability can apply for a supplemental S-DVI of up to $20,000.) Application for S-DVI must be made within two years of being granted a service-connected disability rating. (Application for the supplemental must take place within one year of being notified of eligibility for waiver of the basic policy premium.) Disabled veterans should investigate other life insurance options prior to purchasing S-DVI, as commercial policies, especially group plans through employers, may be better buys.

The Veterans' Mortgage Life Insurance (VMLI) is a program that provides mortgage life insurance to severely disabled veterans. To be eligible, a veteran must have received a Specially Adapted Housing Grant from the VA. (The purpose of the grant is to help the veteran build or modify a home to accommodate his or her disabilities.) VMLI is payable to the mortgage holder. If the veteran dies before being able to repay his mortgage, VMLI covers the balance of the mortgage still owed. VMLI allows severely disabled veterans to qualify for mortgage loans for which they would not otherwise qualify due to being high credit risks for lenders.

The most well-known insurance programs run by the VA include the Servicemembers' Group Life Insurance (SGLI) and the Veterans' Group Life Insurance (VGLI) programs. SGLI is a program of low-cost, group, term life insurance for servicemembers on active duty, ready reservists, cadets and midshipmen of the service academies, and members of ROTC. For more information, see chapter 13. As of December 1, 2005, all servicemembers with SGLI were automatically enrolled in TSGLI for "traumatic injury" protection. TSGLI pays a benefit of between $25,000 and $100,000 to servicemembers covered by SGLI who sustain traumatic injuries that result in certain severe losses. The amount that will be paid under TSGLI is related to the type and severity of loss. For example, the total and permanent loss of sight in both eyes qualifies for a $100,000 payment.

> *Separating servicemembers can convert SGLI into VGLI, which allows veterans to maintain life insurance coverage despite their age or health status.*

The SGLI program also provides family coverage for the dependents of servicemembers. Family SGLI (FSGLI) provides up to $100,000 of insurance coverage for spouses (but not to exceed the amount of SGLI that the insured servicemember has in force), and $10,000 for each dependent child. There are no additional premiums for FSGLI coverage of dependent children. For more information about FSGLI, see chapter 13.

Veterans' Group Life Insurance VGLI is a post-service group life insurance program which allows servicemembers to convert their SGLI coverage to renewable term insurance. Servicemembers with full-time SGLI coverage are eligible for VGLI upon release from service. An eligible veteran must submit an application for conversion of SGLI coverage to VGLI coverage within one year and 120 days from the date of discharge. VGLI is available in multiples of $10,000 to a maximum of $400,000. However, VGLI coverage cannot exceed the amount of SGLI that was in force at the time of separation from service. VGLI does not provide disability or other supplementary benefits; it has no cash value nor does it pay dividends. VGLI premium rates are substantially higher than SGLI premiums because VGLI premiums are based on the separating servicemember's age. For example, as of 2006, a forty-year-old servicemember pays $26 per month for $400,000 of SGLI coverage but a forty-year-old veteran pays $76 per month for $400,000 worth of VGLI coverage. A complete listing of current VGLI premium rates is available on the VA's Life Insurance Program webpage at *www.insurance.va.gov*.

The main advantage of VGLI is that if you submit a VGLI application within 120 days following separation from service, you do not have to provide proof of good health. However, if you submit an application after 120 days of discharge, you must provide proof of good health and you might be disapproved if you are not in good health. Furthermore, VGLI might be an attractive option for separating servicemembers, particularly if they have any health issue that might jeopardize their ability to obtain affordable insurance from civilian sources. Lastly, veterans can keep their VGLI coverage for life, as long as they continue to pay premiums.

> *Veterans must apply for VGLI within 120 days from the date of discharge in order to receive insurance coverage without providing proof of good health.*

As with any decision to purchase an insurance policy, care must be taken to carefully evaluate insurance needs. SGLI and Family SGLI provide valuable life insurance coverage at affordable rates. However, insurance plans more affordable than VGLI may be available. Please refer to chapter 13. To file a claim for SGLI, FSGLI, TSGLI, VGLI, S-DVI, or VMLI, contact a VA office or a military personnel assistance center. Phone numbers and addresses are found in the phone book or on the web.

Disability Compensation
Disability compensation is a benefit paid to veterans for injuries or diseases that occur while on active duty, or for preexisting conditions that were made worse by active military service. These benefits are tax free. Veterans may be eligible for this program if they have a service-related disability rated at 10% or higher and were discharged under other-than-dishonorable conditions. The degree of disability represents the average loss in wages resulting from such diseases and injuries, as well as their complications in civilian occupations. As of 2006, the amount of the basic benefit ranges from $112 to $2,393 per month, based on the veteran's disability rating. Veterans may be paid additional amounts, in certain circumstances, if they have severe disabilities, limb amputations, dependents, or a seriously disabled spouse. Except in cases of the most severe injuries, VA benefits are only supplemental income, and most veterans will want to find other employment. Disabled veterans might also be entitled to priority medical care in the VA health system, clothing allowances, grants for specialty housing, federal employment

preference, exchange and commissary privileges, vocational rehabilitation, service-disabled veterans' life insurance, and other forms of state and local veterans benefits.

The Civilian Health and Medical Program of the Department of Veterans Affairs (CHAMPVA) is a comprehensive health insurance program for dependents of disabled veterans and, in certain cases, for surviving dependents of deceased veterans. This program is independent of CHAMPUS and TRICARE. To be eligible for CHAMPVA, you cannot be eligible for TRICARE/CHAMPUS and you must be (1) the spouse or child of a veteran who has been rated permanently and totally disabled for a service-connected disability by a VA regional office, (2) the surviving spouse or child of a veteran who died from a VA-rated service connected disability, (3) the surviving spouse or child of a veteran who was at the time of death rated permanently and totally disabled from a service connected disability, or (4) the surviving spouse or child of a military member who died in the line of duty, not due to misconduct. For more information, visit *www.va.gov/hac/forbeneficiaries/champva* or contact CHAMPVA Eligibility at PO Box 469028, Denver, Colorado 80246-9028, phone 800-733-8387.

> *Veterans with a disability rating of 10% or higher may qualify for disability compensation with a value of up to $2,393 per month.*

Dependency and Indemnity Compensation

Dependency and Indemnity Compensation (DIC) is a monthly benefit paid to eligible survivors of a servicemember who died on active duty, a veteran who died as a result of a service-related injury or disease, or a veteran whose death resulted from a nonservice-connected disability. In general, to be eligible for DIC benefits, the surviving spouse must have been married to the veteran, cohabitated with the veteran until the veteran's death, and cannot be currently remarried. Specific eligibility rules can be quite complex, and those who might be eligible should browse *www.vba.va.gov/survivors/VAbenefits.htm* or contact their local VA office. Surviving children are eligible if they are not included in the surviving spouse's DIC, they are unmarried, and they are under age eighteen (or between the ages of eighteen and twenty-three but attending school). As of 2006, the basic monthly rate of DIC is $1,033 for an eligible surviving spouse. The rate is increased for each dependent child or if the spouse is housebound or in need of aid and attendance.

The VA adds a transitional benefit of $250 per month for two years to the surviving spouse's DIC if there are children under the age of eighteen in the family unit. Survivors might also be eligible for health care through the VA, the VA home loan program, federal employment preference, and educational assistance.

> *Survivors may be entitled to a monthly compensation benefit when a servicemember dies on active duty or when a veteran dies from a service-related injury or disease.*

Other Death Benefits for Survivors

Veterans discharged under conditions other than dishonorable and servicemembers who die while on active duty may be eligible for the following burial benefits: (1) burial in a national, state, or military installation cemetery, (2) a government furnished headstone or marker, (3) a presidential memorial certificate, (4) a burial flag, and (5) reimbursement of a portion of burial expenses. Spouses and dependent children of eligible servicemembers and veterans may also be buried in a national cemetery. The funeral director or the next of kin makes interment arrangements for the eligible veteran or dependent at the time of need by contacting the national cemetery in which burial is desired. The VA provides headstones and grave markers for the graves of veterans anywhere in the world and for eligible dependents who are buried in military post, state-veteran, or national cemeteries. Niche markers are also available for identifying cremated remains in columbaria and memorial markers are provided if the remains are not available for burial.

> *Death benefits for veterans and servicemembers include burial in a national cemetery, headstone or grave marker, presidential memorial certificate, burial flag, military funeral honors, and reimbursement of burial expenses.*

A certificate bearing the president's signature is issued to recognize the service of deceased veterans who were discharged under honorable conditions. Eligible recipients include next of kin or other loved ones. A certificate can be issued to more than one eligible recipient.

VA regional offices can help in applying for certificates. A U.S. flag is provided, at no cost, to drape the casket or accompany the urn of a deceased veteran who served honorably in the U.S. Armed Forces. The flag is furnished to honor the memory of a veteran's military service to his or her country. Generally, the flag is given to the next of kin, as a keepsake, after its use during the funeral service. When there is no next of kin, the VA will furnish the flag to a friend making a request for it.

The VA will pay a burial allowance up to $2,000 if the veteran's death is service-connected. The VA might also pay the cost of transporting the remains of a service-disabled veteran to the nearest national cemetery with available gravesites. The VA will pay a $300 burial and funeral expense allowance for veterans who, at the time of death, were entitled to receive pension or compensation or would have been entitled to compensation but for receipt of military retirement pay. Note that the VA will pay burial costs only if the veteran was receiving benefits from the VA at the time of his or her death or if the veteran dies in a VA hospital. The VA's burial benefits are important items to include in your personal financial planning because these benefits may reduce the need for life insurance, which can help you save money through lower premium payments; or they can allow you to leave a larger inheritance or reduce the financial burden of your death on your survivors.

DoD will, upon request, provide military funeral honors for the burial of military members and eligible veterans. A basic military funeral honors ceremony consists of the folding and presentation of the U.S. flag by two or more uniformed members of the armed services and the playing of Taps. DoD maintains a toll-free number (877-MIL-HONR) for use by funeral directors to request an honors ceremony. Family members should inform their funeral directors if they desire military funeral honors for a veteran. Finally, the VA provides bereavement counseling for survivors.

> *Survivors of those killed on active duty are entitled to a tax-free death gratuity of $12,420, temporary housing assistance, exchange and commissary privileges, continuing medical care, and education benefits.*

When a servicemember dies on active duty, active-duty training, or inactive-duty training, the military service pays a lump-sum death gratuity of $12,400 to the survivors. This death gratuity is 100% tax-free.

Survivors can also stay in military housing or receive Basic Allowance for Housing (BAH) for 180 days following the servicemember's death. Unlimited exchange and commissary store privileges in the United States are available to surviving spouses of members or retired members of the armed forces, recipients of the Medal of Honor, and dependents and orphans of military retirees. For nonretirees, death must be service-connected. Dependents of reservists also may be eligible. The VA provides a certification letter for your use in obtaining commissary and exchange privileges from the armed forces. Eligible family members may receive inpatient and outpatient care, including pharmacy services at uniformed services medical treatment facilities where adequate services and facilities are available. Eligible family members of active-duty members who died while on active dut and who were on active duty for at least thirty days before death, will continue to be treated as active-duty family members for three years after their active-duty sponsor dies. If a widowed beneficiary remarries someone outside the uniformed services, he or she is no longer covered.

Finally, the National Defense Authorization Act for FY2004 made a provision to provide a Survivor Benefit Plan (SBP) annuity for the surviving unremarried spouse or dependent children under eighteen (or twenty-two if the child is a full-time student) of a member who dies while on active duty but is not yet eligible for retirement. Thus, for active duty deaths occurring on or after November 24, 2003, eligibility for the SBP includes the servicemember's spouse, former spouse (if court ordered), or child (when there is no surviving spouse). Previously, active duty members qualified for SBP only if they were retirement eligible with twenty or more years of service or were medically retired prior to death. The current law treats members who die on active duty as 100% disabled in order to calculate their retired pay entitlement. Under the High-3 retirement plan, the retired pay entitlement would be 75% of the average of the basic monthly pay during the servicemember's three highest years of military earnings (normally the last three years of service). The monthly SBP payments would then be 55% of the retired-pay entitlement. See Table 16-2 for a comparison of current death benefits across grades for servicemembers who die while on active duty.

(Note: These calculations do not include all of the in-kind and cash assistance programs for which the survivors might be eligible from the VA, the SSA, or DoD. For example, these calculations do not include any death gratuities, burial benefits, continuation of basic allowance for housing, or SSA survivor benefits; nor do they include continuation of exchange, commissary, and medical facility privileges.)

In general, as a servicemember's rank and pay increase, death benefits from DIC, SBP, and SGLI replace a smaller portion of the servicemember's monthly regular military compensation. This information can be helpful as you conduct personal financial planning and decide how much life insurance to purchase and how much personal saving and investing to do.

Casualty Assistance Officers

There are many benefits and entitlements to assist the survivors of those killed or missing in action. As discussed previously in this chapter, some of these benefits include a death gratuity, housing assistance, dependency and indemnity compensation, commissary and exchange privileges, burial services, financial counseling services, unpaid pay and allowances, and potentially several others. Surviving spouses and dependents may have difficulty navigating their way through the bereavement process and the compensation process simultaneously. Thus, the military typically assigns a Casualty Assistance Officer (CAO) to assist the family members of those killed or missing in action. The CAO, among other responsibilities, helps the family mem-

TABLE 16-2
ESTIMATED MONTHLY DEATH BENEFITS FOR MEMBERS WHO DIE ON ACTIVE DUTY

	E3 2 Dependents	E7 3 Dependents	O3 3 Dependents
Dependency and Indemnity Compensation (DIC) (Taxable Equivalent)	$1,378	$1,749	$1,749
High-3 SBP Benefit	$561	$1,191	$1,593
$400,000 SGLI Annuity*	$1,333	$1,333	$1,333
Total (DIC + SBP + SGLI)	$3,272	$4,273	$4,675
Estimated 2005 Monthly Regular Military Compensation (RMC)**	$2,901	$4,794	$6,221
Fraction of RMC Replaced by Death Benefits (DIC + SBP + SGLI)	113%	89%	75%

Source: Office of Economic and Manpower Analysis, U.S. Military Academy, 2005.

* The SGLI annuity assumes that the surviving spouse invests the entire SGLI payout of $400,000 in an asset that yields a 4% after-tax annual return. The survivor could earn $1,333 per month without consuming any of the principal. An SGLI payment strategy which includes some consumption of the principal would yield a higher monthly payment to the survivors.

** RMC includes base pay, basic allowance for housing, basic allowance for subsistence, and the federal tax advantages associated with the allowances.

bers learn about and apply for all of the benefits to which the survivors are entitled. When a soldier, sailor, airman, or marine is assigned duty as a CAO, the casualty assistance mission takes precedence over all other obligations. The CAO's mission is to provide assistance to the primary next of kin (PNOK) or the person authorized direct disposition (PADD) during the period following a military servicemember being declared missing or deceased. In the event that you are a PNOK or PADD for a servicemember who is declared missing or deceased and you are not assigned a CAO, you should contact the servicemember's unit commander, rear detachment commander, or the closest military personnel service center to ensure that you receive adequate support in accessing your entitled benefits.

> *A casualty assistance officer will guide your beneficiaries through the process of applying for and receiving their survivors' entitlements.*

Remember, to receive any of these benefits, you must apply for them. Make sure that you and your dependents are counseled thoroughly on all of these benefits before you leave the military, and take the time to become familiar with the VA's website at *www.va.gov*.

BENEFIT PROGRAMS FOR YOUR TRANSITION OUT OF THE WORKFORCE (SOCIAL SECURITY)

Social Security is a federal social insurance program for people of all ages. There are several other major programs that come under the general heading of Social Security, including Medicare, Black Lung Benefits, and Supplemental Security Income. Also, the fifty states operate two other categories of "social security" programs: unemployment compensation and public assistance programs. Social Security is a set of programs designed to provide income security for workers and their families. The term Social Security is commonly used today to refer to only one set of these programs: Old Age, Survivors, and Disability Insurance (OASDI). This chapter is primarily concerned with OASDI.

Social Security insures workers and their families against the financial hardships associated with living an extremely long life, becoming disabled, or passing away prematurely. Social Security is not a personal retirement program. It provides income for workers and their dependents during their retirement years; however, it is meant to supplement retirement income but *not* comprise total retirement income. The average retired worker can expect to receive Social Security benefits replacing approximately 25 to 40% of pre-retirement income. To qualify yourself and your dependents for Social Security benefits, you must be a worker and earn a specified amount of work credits. Military service counts towards your work credits. Benefits vary substantially based on a rather complicated set of rules. The purpose of this chapter is to inform you of the benefits that you earn as you work and to give you an approximate idea of the level of these benefits so that you can account for them in your personal financial planning.

> *Social Security provides income security for American workers and their dependents.*

Today's Workers Pay for Today's Beneficiaries
Many Americans do not understand how the Social Security system works. Social Security is not a savings plan. You do not pay your Social Security taxes into an account—with your name on it—from which you draw payments after retirement. Instead, you pay taxes into a general trust fund. The taxes you pay today are primarily used to pay the benefits of today's retirees and disabled persons. Social Security is a social contract. You pay taxes today for the benefit of today's elderly with the understanding that the government will provide benefits for you in your retirement or disability by taxing tomorrow's workers. Thus, you should pay close attention to the political decisions concerning the future of Social Security. The amount of benefits you can expect has implications for the long-term savings plan that you establish as part of your budget (see chapter 1) and your investment strategy (see chapters 10, 11, and 12).

> *Social Security is a "pay-as-you-go" social contract: Taxes collected from current workers pay for the benefits of current beneficiaries while future beneficiaries will be supported by the taxes collected from future workers.*
>
> *You should have some type of savings plan to supplement Social Security in your retirement.*

Active-duty members of the uniformed services have been covered by Social Security on the same basis as civilian workers since 1957.

Participation in the Social Security program is mandatory—you must pay the Social Security tax, which is annotated FICA (Federal Insurance Contributions Act) on your pay statements. For servicemembers, only basic pay is taxable for Social Security purposes, and taxes are withheld by law in the full amount from each active-duty monthly paycheck. If you or your spouse has additional income from self-employment, you must pay a self-employment tax to the IRS. You must also file Schedule SE, "Computation of Social Security Self-Employment Tax," with your tax return if your net annual earnings from self-employment are greater than $400.

As of 2006, the Social Security tax rate is 15.3% of earnings. You pay a Social Security tax of 7.65% of your earnings (1.45% is applied to Medicare and 6.20% is applied to non-Medicare Social Security). Your employer is required to make a matching contribution of 7.65% of your earnings. As a self-employed worker, you must pay the entire Social Security tax rate of 15.3%. The Medicare portion of the tax (2.9%) applies to all of your earnings, while the non-Medicare rate (12.4%) is applied only to your first $94,200 of earnings. The $94,200 limit is automatically increased for inflation each year.

> *To be eligible for Social Security benefits, you must earn work credits and pay FICA taxes. Military service counts as part of your work history.*

Eligibility for Social Security Benefits

Eligibility for each type of benefit (Old Age, Survivors, and Disability Insurance programs) depends on your insurance status, which, in turn, depends on your employment history. Because servicemembers pay Social Security taxes, they become insured workers. Working spouses (who must also pay Social Security taxes) become insured workers in their own right. Nonworking spouses are eligible for Social Security benefits based on the benefits of their working spouses. The rules on how you get insured and how much money you are entitled to receive are a bit complex. In general, what matters is how long and how much you have paid into the Social Security system. Thus, the accuracy of your records at the Social Security Administration (SSA) is crucial. You should request a statement of your earnings from the SSA every year. You can ask for a copy of Your Social Security Statement online, by calling your local Social Security office or by filing a Request for Social Security Statement (Form SSA-7004) through the mail. Within six weeks of your request, the SSA will send you a record of your earnings and an estimate of your projected benefits in today's dollars. Compare the SSA's numbers to your records (W-2 statements or LES) and write back to them to correct any errors immediately. The government is not obligated to correct mistakes in your earnings record that are more than three years old. For more information, visit the official website of the U.S. Social Security Administration at *www.ssa.gov* or call 800-772-1213.

> • *Contact the SSA annually to receive your Social Security statement.*
> • *Verify your earnings history and correct any errors immediately.*
> • *Account for your estimated benefits as part of your personal financial planning.*

Basic Benefits

This section explains the three types of Social Security benefits. The amount of each benefit is based on the primary insurance amount (PIA). This section shows briefly how to calculate the PIA. For further information, get your own estimate of your projected benefits from the SSA. Since the purpose of Social Security is to help maintain a reasonable portion of the standard of living that you achieved during your working lifetime, the benefits you receive from Social Security will depend on the wages you earned (and the taxes you paid). A secondary purpose of Social Security is to provide a minimum standard of living for all elderly persons. Therefore, workers who earned a lower level of wages will retain a larger percentage of those low wages in their benefits. For example, a lifetime minimum-wage worker will get a Social Security benefit of approximately 58% of his working wage, whereas a person who always earned the maximum covered earnings will receive a benefit of about 24% of his working wage. The assumption is that the minimum-wage earner could not save enough to provide other income during retirement, while the well-paid worker could.

Calculating PIA. The primary insurance amount is based on your average indexed monthly earnings (AIME). The AIME adjusts your actual earnings for inflation. The best way to find out what your benefits are is to ask the SSA to calculate your benefit for you. If you submit a Request for Social Security Statement (Form SSA-7004), the Social Security Administration will determine how much you will receive (in today's dollars) when you retire. As noted above, this will also verify that they have an accurate record of your earnings information. You can access an online PIA calculator at *www.ssa.gov/OACT/ANYPIA/ description.html*.

> *SSA benefits for low-income workers replace about 60% of their working wages. For higher-income workers, the replacement ratio can fall to 25% or lower.*

Retirement Benefits. There are three options for retirement under Social Security: (1) retire at the full retirement age associated with the year of your birth and receive full benefits, (2) retire earlier than normal retirement age and receive reduced benefits, or (3) retire later than your normal retirement age but prior to age seventy and receive increased benefits. Full retirement age is determined by the SSA based on the year

TABLE 16-3
FULL RETIREMENT AGE AND REDUCTION IN BENEFITS
FOR EARLY RETIREMENT

Year of Birth	Full Retirement Age	Benefit as a Percent of Full Retiremen PIA if Retirement at Age 62 Rather than at Full Retirement Age
1937 or Earlier	65	80%
1938	65 and 2 Months	79.2%
1939	65 and 4 Months	78.3%
1940	65 and 6 Months	77.5%
1941	65 and 8 Months	76.7%
1942	65 and 10 Months	75.8%
1943–1954	66	75%
1955	66 and 2 Months	74.2%
1956	66 and 4 Months	73.3%
1957	66 and 6 Months	72.5%
1958	66 and 8 Months	71.7%
1959	66 and 10 Months	70.8%
1960 and Later	67	70%

Source: SSA, 2006.

of your birth. Workers who were born during or before 1937 (and will retire before 2002) can normally retire at age sixty-five, whereas those born after 1937 cannot retire with full benefits until a slightly older age. Most current servicemembers (born after 1959) cannot retire with full benefits until they are sixty-seven years old. Early retirement at age sixty-two is still possible under the rules outlined in Table 16-3, but retiring exactly on your sixty-second birthday will mean that your monthly check will be an even smaller percentage of the PIA. For example, workers born after 1959 who retire at age sixty-two will receive only 70% of the PIA.

Just as retiring before you reach full retirement age can reduce your Social Security benefits, you can increase your Social Security benefits by delaying your retirement past your full retirement age. When you retire after your full retirement age, you receive a delayed retirement credit. Each month in which you are at least full retirement age, but not yet age seventy, is an increment month. For example, if you reach full retirement age after 2008, you would receive 100% of your PIA plus 8% for each year that you continue to work past your full retirement age (see Table 16-4). Once you reach age seventy, you no longer accumulate delayed retirement credits.

TABLE 16-4
CHART OF DELAYED RETIREMENT CREDIT RATES

Attain Full Retirement Age	Annual Percentage
Prior to 1982	1%
1982–1989	3%
1990–1991	3.5%
1992–1993	4%
1994–1995	4.5%
1996–1997	5%
1998–1999	5.5%
2000–2001	6%
2002–2003	6.5%
2004–2005	7%
2006–2007	7.5%
2008 or Later	8%

Source: SSA, 2006.

For 2006, the maximum Social Security benefit for a worker who retires at full retirement age is approximately $2,050 per month. The estimated average monthly Social Security benefit payable in January 2006 for all retired workers is approximately $1,000 per month. For an aged couple, both receiving benefits, the average is about $1,650 per month. Benefits are adjusted each year to keep up with inflation.

Survivor Benefits. Another important goal of Social Security is providing for families when an insured worker dies if the family members are too young, old, or disabled to work. Benefits paid to the dependent family members of a deceased worker are called survivor benefits. There are many categories of survivor benefits corresponding to the many circumstances that qualify someone to be a dependent family member of an insured worker. Table 16-5 presents information for four of the most frequently used categories of survivor benefits.

> *Dependents of eligible workers are entitled to survivor benefits if the worker dies and the dependents are too young, too old, or too disabled to work.*

From the table, you can see that each child under age eighteen receives a monthly check for 75% of the insured worker's PIA. However, in the event that the family has many children, the total amount paid to the family is subject to a cap. Notice also that nonworking spouses over age sixty who are not insured themselves are entitled to the benefits of the deceased spouse if that spouse was fully insured before dying. The benefit will range from 71.5 to 100% of the PIA of the deceased worker, depending on the age of the surviving spouse. Divorced surviving spouses are entitled to the benefits of a deceased worker if the marriage lasted at least ten years. Generally a surviving spouse over age sixty does not forfeit this entitlement by remarrying. There are several rules associated with remarrying, so we suggest you contact the SSA directly with your specific situation.

One final survivor benefit is the lump-sum death payment of $255. Surviving spouses living with an insured worker at the time of death are eligible; divorced spouses are not.

Disability Benefits. For the purposes of Social Security, disability means "the inability to engage in any substantial gainful activity by reason of any medically determinable physical or mental impairment

TABLE 16-5
SOCIAL SECURITY SURVIVOR BENEFITS

Benefit Insurance Status	Amount of Payment
Payment to Each Child Under 18	75% of PIA
Payment to Each Child 18 or 19 and a Full-Time High School Student	75% of PIA
Payment to a Widow(er) Caring for any Children Under 16	75% of PIA
Payment to a Widow(er) Over 60	100% of PIA

Source: SSA, 2006.

which can be expected to result in death or which has lasted or can be expected to last for a continuous period of not less than twelve months." If a worker has a serious disability, he or she will receive the full PIA. Disability of a servicemember involves not only the SSA but perhaps also the VA and the military disability compensation system. In this complex area, consult your legal assistance officer, the VA, and the SSA for details about all of the entitlements.

Other Factors Affecting Benefits
If you are receiving Social Security benefits and have a large amount of earnings, then your benefits may be reduced. Workers who retire from the full-time workforce before reaching their full retirement age will have their benefits reduced $1 for every $2 of income over $12,480 per year. Workers who continue to work in the year they reach full retirement age will have their benefits reduced $1 for every $3 of income over $33,240 per year only for those months before they reach the full retirement age. Once a worker reaches full retirement age, his or her Social Security benefit is no longer subject to the earnings test and is not reduced based on his income.

In addition to being offset in the manner described above, Social Security benefits also may be taxed as ordinary income for some retirees. This will apply only if you have other substantial income in addition to your benefits (for example, wages, self-employment, interest, dividends, capital gains, military pension, and other taxable income that you have to report on your tax return). If you file a federal tax return as a single filer and your combined income (the sum of adjusted gross income, nontaxable interest, and one-half of your Social Security benefits, after any offset) is between $25,000 and $34,000, you may have to pay income tax on 50% of your Social Security benefits. If your combined income is greater than $34,000, then up to 85% of your benefits are subject to the income tax. If you file a joint return, you may have to pay taxes on 50% of your benefits if you and your spouse have a combined income that is between $32,000 and $44,000. If your combined income is greater than $44,000, then up to 85% of your Social Security benefits are subject to the income tax. For more information about income taxes, see chapter 4.

> *Your Social Security benefits might be adjusted or taxed if you earn additional income (i.e., interest, dividends, capital gains, military pension, self-employment).*

Each year, Congress determines the Cost of Living Adjustment (COLA) that will be applied to Social Security benefits. The COLA is probably the most valuable provision in Social Security. Once your benefit amount is determined, it is adjusted every year to protect its purchasing power from inflation. For 2006, the COLA enacted by Congress was 4.1%, meaning that all AIME, PIA, and benefit calculations are adjusted upwards by 4.1%, which enables beneficiaries to maintain their purchasing power.

> *Social Security benefits are adjusted annually for inflation.*

As is the case with veterans benefits, you or your eligible dependents will receive Social Security benefits only if you apply for them. You do not receive these benefits automatically. Become familiar with the SSA's website *www.ssa.gov*, especially as you approach retirement.

Other Resources for Your Transition

Military.com is a free information service designed to provide resources to connect and inform servicemembers, veterans, family members, defense workers, military enthusiasts, and those considering military careers. This website is the online presence of Military Advantage, whose mission is to connect the military community to all the advantages earned in service. The website strives to help members make the most of military experience, enhance access to benefits, find transition support, and enjoy military discounts. See *www.military.com.*

Military HOMEFRONT is the official Department of Defense website for reliable, up-to-date Quality of Life information, focusing on Department of Defense benefits and services. See *www.militaryhomefront .dod.mil.*

Military OneSource Online is an official Department of Defense website designed to serve American troops and their families by providing information related to a host of personal, financial, and legal issues, especially those pertaining to Department of Defense benefits and services. See *www.militaryonesource.com.*

One further source of information for Social Security and VA programs is the local office of each administration; check your local telephone directory under "U.S. Government." The SSA and the VA have pamphlets explaining each of their programs, which they will send to you at no charge.

PREPARING FOR YOUR FINANCIAL FUTURE "AFTER THE MILITARY"

- Visit a Transition Assistance Center and make an appointment with a transition counselor one year prior to your separation. Army Career and Alumni Program
  (*www.acap.army.mil*)
  Air Force Family Support Centers
  (*www.afpc.randolph.af.mil/famops/trans.htm*)
  Navy Fleet and Family Support Centers
  (*www.npc.navy.mil/Channels*)
  Marine Corps Personal Services Center
  (*www.usmc-mccs.org/tamp/index.cfm*)
- Become familiar with the wide range of veterans' benefits.
- Regularly check your Social Security statement to ensure the SSA has an accurate record of your employment history.
- Discuss VA and SSA benefits with your spouse and dependents so that they know of their entitlements should you die.
- Account for potential disability benefits from the VA and SSA if you are considering the purchase of private disability insurance.
- When making life insurance decisions, factor in your veterans burial benefits and Social Security survivors benefits.

17

Military Retirement Benefits

This chapter will explain the three Department of Defense retirement systems. It will also discuss several benefits, as well as insurance and health-care alternatives that most servicemembers consider upon retirement. The chapter will conclude with some tax considerations for retirees.

The profession of arms requires considerable energy and stamina. As a result, national policy makers have provided a generous retirement plan for career soldiers, sailors, airmen, and marines. The authority for nondisability retired pay, commonly known as "length-of-service" retired pay, is contained in Title 10, U.S. Code.

There are three ways to retire from the Armed Forces. The first is *length-of-service*. You may retire after twenty years of active service, and in most cases, you must retire after thirty years of active service. The second is due to *age*. Comparatively few people retire due to age. Pay and benefit calculations are exactly the same as for length-of-service retirees. The final way to retire is due to *disability*. If you suffer a serious physical or mental disability, you can be retired from service.

RETIREMENT SYSTEMS

Currently, there are three different Department of Defense retirement systems in place and summarized in Table 17-1. The retirement pay you receive depends upon the length-of-service and the rank achieved before retirement. Congress has changed the retirement system in the past twenty years but has always "grandfathered" current servicemembers into the older system. Consequently, there are three ways to calculate your retirement pay. The method you should use depends on the date you initially entered military service (DIEMS), which is reflected by the "DIEMS" entry in the remarks section of your Leave and Earnings Statement (LES). All updated information on military retirement pay is available online at *www.dod.mil/militarypay/retirement/ad/18_summary.html*.

In all three systems your retirement pay is subject to income tax but not Social Security tax. Regulations also specify that your retirement pay must be paid by direct deposit (electronic transfer) on a monthly basis.

Additionally, the Defense Finance and Accounting Service (DFAS) publishes an excellent overview of the preparation required for military retirement. It can be found online at *www.dod.mil/dfas/retiredpay/preparingforretirement.html*.

1. If you entered service before September 8, 1980, your retirement pay will be based on your final basic pay (System 1).
2. If you entered service between September 8, 1980, and July 31, 1986, your retirement pay is calculated using the average of your highest 36 months, or three years, of basic pay, hence the name, High-3 (System 2).
3. The Career Status Bonus (CSB)/REDUX retirement system (System 3) applies to those who entered Service on or after August 1, 1986, AND who elected to receive a $30,000 Career Status Bonus at their fifteenth year of service. The National Defense Authorization Act (NDAA) of 2000 allows those in this group to choose between the High-3 retirement system and the REDUX retirement system.

The REDUX retirement system and Career Status Bonus is a "package deal." In exchange for the bonus at the fifteenth year, the servicemember agrees to a reduced retirement basis at the end of the twentieth year. However, if the servicemember

TABLE 17-1
DOD RETIREMENT SYSTEMS

	Retirement System	Basis	Multiplier	Bonus
1	Final Pay	Final basic pay	2.5% per year up to 75%	None
2	High-3	Average of highest 36 months of basic pay	2.5% per year up to 75%	None
3	CSB/REDUX	Average of highest 36 months of basic pay	2% per year for the first 20 years; 3.5% for each year beyond 20, up to 75%	$30,000 at fifteenth year of service with commitment to complete 20-year career

stays on active duty until the twenty-eighth year, the bonus does not affect his or her retirement pay.

A servicemember who selects CSB/REDUX and retires at twenty years receives 40% of the average of the highest thirty-six months of basic pay plus the $30,000 bonus after the fifteenth year. A servicemember who selects High-3 will receive 50% of the average of the highest thirty-six months of basic pay and no bonus. If the servicemember lives for many years after retirement, the difference in percentage of basic pay will more than make up for a $30,000 bonus even if that bonus was invested wisely; this makes the High-3 system the wiser choice.

However, if the servicemember does not retire until the thirty-year mark, the CSB/RDUX system becomes the wiser choice. The servicemember will receive 75% of the average of the highest thirty-six months of basic pay (the same as High-3) and will have received a $30,000 bonus after the fifteenth year.

> *Servicemembers need to understand the major differences between the "High-3" and "CSB/REDUX" retirement systems.*

A retirement calculator is available online at *www.dod.mil/militarypay/retirement/calc/index.html*.

Cost-of-Living Increases (COLA)
Retirement pay is indexed to the consumer price index (CPI) to ensure that its purchasing power is not eroded by inflation. For the latest information on Retirement COLA, see *www.dod.mil/dfas/money/retiredpay/costoflivingallowancecola.htm*.

In spite of the government's effort to adjust retirement pay to keep up with inflation, every servicemember must have a personal savings plan to augment his or her retirement pay. Your financial plan and investment strategy, as discussed in part III, should address this need.

Retirement Due to Disability
If you have been found to be physically unfit for further military service and meet certain standards specified by law, you will be granted a disability retirement. Your disability retirement may be temporary or permanent. If temporary, your status will be resolved within a five-year period. The criteria for rating the severity of various disabilities are

available online at *www.access.gpo.gov/nara/cfr/waisidx_04/38cfr4_04.html*.

The amount of your disability retirement pay is determined by one of two methods:

1. The first method is to multiply your base pay or, depending on your retirement system, the average of the highest thirty-six months of active duty pay at the time of retirement, by the percentage of disability that has been assigned. The minimum percentage for temporary-disability retirees will equal 50%. The maximum percentage for any type of retirement is 75%. This computation is sometimes referred to as "Method A."

2. The second method is to multiply only your years of active service at the time of your retirement by 2.5% by your base pay, which is the average of the highest thirty-six months of active duty pay at the time of retirement (depending on your retirement system). This computation is sometimes referred to as "Method B."

DFAS establishes your account using the method that results in the greatest amount of retirement pay. For the most updated information on disability retirement pay and tax implications go to *www.dod.mil/dfas/retiredpay/concurrentretirementanddisabilitypay.html*.

Severance Pay
Each disability retirement will be accompanied by a line-of-duty investigation. If the disability is not due to your intentional misconduct or willful neglect, and if it was not incurred while AWOL, then you are entitled to disability severance pay in the amount of two months' basic pay per year of service to a maximum of twelve years. For example, a captain with five years of service would receive ten (2 months × 5 years of service) months of basic pay, and a master sergeant with eighteen years of service would receive the maximum allowable twenty-four months of basic pay because he has more than twelve years of service.

Severance pay is covered by Department of Defense (DoD) Pay Regulation, Volume 7A, Active Duty & Reserve Pay, chapter 35—Separation Payments. This regulation can be downloaded at *www.dod.mil/comptroller/fmr/07a/*.

Concurrent Receipt
Concurrent Receipt refers to receiving both military retirement benefits and VA disability compensation (covered in chapter 16), and until

2004 was forbidden by law. To receive VA disability compensation, disabled military retirees had to waive all or part of their military pay. As of 2004, this law changed so that qualified disabled military retirees will now get paid both their full military-retirement pay and their VA disability compensation. For the latest updates on this change, visit *www.dod.mil/dfas/retiredpay/concurrentretirementanddisabilitypay .html*.

BENEFITS, INSURANCE, AND HEALTH CARE ALTERNATIVES
Survivor Benefit Program (SBP) vs. Other Life Insurance Products

The purpose of SBP is to provide the military retiree's spouse (or children, in certain situations) with an inflation-adjusted monthly income after the retiree dies. SBP continues to pay a portion of your retirement pay to your surviving spouse after you die. That portion of your retirement pay, referred to as the *monthly annuity*, is 55% of the *base amount*, an amount that you choose until your spouse begins to collect Social Security (see Social Security Entitlements below). The maximum base amount is your gross monthly retirement pay. Thus, SBP protects up to 55% of your retirement pay against the risk of you predeceasing your spouse.

If you are on active duty and are retirement-eligible with a spouse and/or children, they are automatically protected under SBP at no cost to you while still on active duty. For an extensive overview of the SBP, visit the following websites at *www.dod.mil/dfas/retiredpay/survivor benefits.html* and *www.moaa.org*.

Table 17-2 compares advantages and disadvantages of the program.

Cost of SBP

The SBP premiums for spouse coverage are (1) 6.5% of your chosen base amount, or if less, and (2) 2.5% of the first $635.00 of your elected base amount (referred to hereafter as the "threshold amount"), plus 10% of the remaining amount.

The threshold amount was $635.00 as of January 1, 2006. The threshold amount will increase at the same time and by the same percentage as future active-duty basic pay. If you became a member of a uniformed service on or after March 1, 1990, and you are retiring for length of service (not for disability), SBP costs will be calculated only under the formula in (1) above.

TABLE 17-2
SURVIVOR BENEFITS PROGRAM

SBP Advantages	SBP Disadvantages
• Government subsidized plan	• Annuity is taxed to survivor
• Premiums paid with "before-tax" dollars. This lowers your taxable income.	• Premiums not returned if spouse dies first (*SBP is not an investment; it is a risk transfer device*)
• Benefits are adjusted for inflation.	
• Spouse cannot outlive benefit payments.	• Retirement pay reduced due to cost of program
• Age, health, gender and lifestyle not considered. All retired servicemembers can can participate.	• Program costs are adjusted to inflation.
	• No cash value—you cannot cancel program and collect money paid.
• Can only be changed by Congress.	
• Risk-transference device = peace of mind	• No inheritance provision

Additionally, Spouse and Children Coverage—or only Children Coverage—is available. The additional cost for children is based on the ages of the youngest child, the servicemember, and his or her spouse and therefore varies tremendously. Your local personnel officer will be able to provide you with the factors for your specific situation.

Participation in the SBP is voluntary. When you retire, you should discuss your decision to participate with your spouse. The program was designed during an era when most spouses did not work outside the home. Today, families are very different. For some families, the benefit is not worth the cost. Before declining SBP, the retiree must get signature approval from his or her spouse.

Changes in Coverage

Except as permitted under the SBP open enrollment period, participation in SBP cannot be changed or modified once your application becomes effective—with one exception. As an SBP participant, you have a one-year window to terminate SBP coverage between the second and third anniversary following the date you begin to receive retirement pay. None of the premiums you paid will be refunded, and no annuity will be payable upon your death. Your covered spouse or former spouse must consent to the withdrawal. Termination is permanent, and participation may not be resumed under any circumstance.

SBP vs. Term Life Insurance

Some retirees believe that they can replicate SBP with term life insurance. Basically, the decision is between participating in SBP (and accepting the lower retirement pay that goes with it) and turning down SBP in favor of taking full retirement pay and using part of it to buy term life insurance. Term life insurance will typically be cheaper in the short term. In the long term, though, the increasing year-to-year cost of attempting to maintain insurance protection for the cost-of-living increases and the rising cost of buying term life insurance as your age increases will make the cost of term insurance greater than the cost of SBP.

Table 17-3 summarizes the differences between these two options.

Social Security Entitlements

Many military people, secure in their own retirement and benefit programs, give scant attention to Social Security and what it can provide (see chapter 16). However, Social Security has a direct bearing on SBP benefits through what is known as the SBP offset. If you predecease your spouse, the SBP annuity begins; however, once your spouse begins to receive your Social Security benefits, the SBP annuity will be reduced from 55% of the base amount elected to 35%. Elimination of this offset has been proposed in Congress but had not passed as of this book's publishing.

Supplemental Survivor Benefit Plan (SSBP)

Eligible retirees of the uniformed services can enroll in SSBP, which is a program that replaces some or all of the SBP annuity reduction when a surviving spouse or former spouse reaches the age of sixty-two. SSBP is available only to retirees who have elected SBP at the maximum level (base amount equal to full retirement pay). This SSBP annuity is payable in increments of 5, 10, 15, or 20%. When increments are added to the "standard" SBP annuity (35% of base amount at age sixty-two or older), the total annuity to the surviving spouse or

---

TABLE 17-3
SBP VERSUS TERM INSURANCE

SBP	Term Life Insurance
• Premiums are a constant % of retirement pay and therefore adjusted for inflation.	• Premiums rise or benefits decrease as you get older.
• Premiums paid with "before-tax" dollars.	• Premiums paid with "after-tax" dollars.
• No requirement for insurability.	• Must be insurable.
• Benefits adjust with inflation.	• No inflation protection.
• Spouse cannot outlive benefit payments.	• Spouse *can* outlive benefit payments.

former spouse will equal 40, 45, 50, or 55% of monthly gross military retirement pay. SSBP premiums are added to SBP premiums (6.5% of the base amount elected) and depend on the retiree's age at the time he or she elects to add the supplemental annuity to his or her SBP.

Veterans Administration (VA) Benefits

The annuity paid by SBP is reduced by any Dependency and Indemnity Compensation (DIC) payments, automatically paid by the Department of Veterans Affairs if death occurs on active duty or it the servicemember meets other requirements (see chapter 16). To determine a spouse's actual SBP monthly payment, you would have to determine the SBP planned payment (either 55% or 35% of the base amount depending on age of spouse) and then subtract the DIC payment from that amount.

The DIC payment is tax-free, but the spouse's total payments are capped at either 55% or 35% of the base amount elected. If you die on active duty, your spouse will never receive less than the DIC payment; however, the survivor benefits can be much greater than the DIC payment if your retirement pay and, consequently, SBP benefit are sufficiently large.

Should You Select SBP?

So, "Is SBP a good deal?" We would reply, "Yes, but . . ."

A similar system cannot be bought at a lower cost "on the economy." For a male servicemember and spouse of equal age who has no other source of retirement income, the expected benefits will normally outweigh the expected costs as long as the servicemember dies before reaching age eighty-three.

There are other circumstances, however, in which the benefits are not worth the costs. Clearly, if a retiree pays a premium for a number of years and the spouse dies first, there would be no SBP benefit; all SBP payments made until the spouse's death would be a loss. Or if the spouse dies soon after the military retiree (before predicted life expectancy), he or she is not able to receive the SBP payments long enough to recoup the deductions from retirement pay.

Recommendation:
- First, decide if your spouse needs your retirement pay to sustain his or her retirement needs.
- Buy SBP at retirement if the choice is between SBP and term life insurance. You can then reassess your financial situation between the second and third year of retirement.

- Evaluate SBP/SSBP as insurance, not an investment—"winning" at SBP still means that you are dead.
- If you are male, you probably cannot beat SBP with commercial insurance.
- If you are female, analyze your spouse's age against yours and consider the odds that your spouse might outlive you. (Statistics show that women typically outlive men.)
- If you are a dual-military couple, you probably do not need SBP. Explore the "Children Only" option.

SBP alone is not a complete estate plan. Other insurance and investments are important in meeting needs outside the scope of SBP. For example, SBP does not have a lump-sum benefit that some survivors may need to meet immediate expenses upon a member's death.

On the other hand, insurance and investments without SBP may be less than adequate. Even if they could duplicate SBP, investments may be much more risky and rely on a degree of financial expertise many do not have.

It is important that you look at SBP as an integral part of your total estate planning. Decisions about participation should be based on family discussions with the advice of qualified personnel officers, insurance agents, bank trust officers, or organizations qualified in estate planning, such as the Army and Air Force Mutual Aid Association at *www.aafmaa.com/home.asp*.

Veterans' Group Life Insurance (VGLI)

Veterans' Group Life Insurance (VGLI) is a program of postseparation insurance, which provides for the conversion of SGLI to renewable term coverage. While SGLI is a great deal, VGLI is usually more expensive for healthy retirees. It is a form of level-term insurance.

At the end of each term period, the insured has the right to renew coverage for another term period. A member may convert such insurance to an individual policy with any one of the participating companies at any time.

- VGLI is issued in $10,000 increments to a maximum of $400,000, but not for more than the amount of SGLI that the member had in force at the time of separation.
- If you submit a VGLI application within *120 days* following separation from service, you *do not* need to provide proof of good health to qualify.
- If you submit a VGLI application *between 120 days and one year and 120 days after separation from service*, you need to

provide proof of good health and enclose the first month's premium with your application.

Additional information on VGLI can be found in chapter 16 and on the web at *www.insurance.va.gov/sgliSite/default.htm.*

Recommendation: You may be able to find a less expensive policy by shopping around. (For instance, $400,000 of coverage costs $866 per year for someone in the forty to forty-four year age group.) However, the fact that you do not have to provide proof of good health within the first 120 days following separation cannot be matched with a commercial product. If you need this amount of insurance and have preexisting health issues, we recommend that you strongly consider converting to VGLI. Otherwise, review chapter 13 for more information on life insurance.

TRICARE

As a retiree, you can remain enrolled in the TRICARE program at an additional cost. You still have the same three options as on active duty: Prime, Extra, and Standard. The selection of your plan is dependent on your retirement situation. If you have additional health insurance that serves as your primary coverage (for example, if you continue working and your new employer provides medical benefits), Prime will only pay after your primary insurance has made payment. We recommend that you visit the TRICARE website at *www.tricare.osd.mil* to determine the best coverage for you.

TRICARE-for-Life is a program that continues support for Medicare-eligible military retirees, their spouses, and other qualifying dependents. It functions as a supplement to Medicare. There are no enrollment fees and enrollment is automatic. In order to be eligible, retirees must ensure that their DEERS status is current, be enrolled in Medicare Part B, and ensure that their Military Identification Card is current. For more information on this program, visit *www.tricare.osd .mil/tfl/default.cfm.*

You have earned the medical benefits because of your service; take advantage of them. Determine which TRICARE program is appropriate for you depending on your employment circumstances. Be careful not to over- or underinsure you or your family medically.

Pharmacy Benefits

You also retain your Pharmacy Benefits when you retire. There are four ways to have prescriptions filled:

1. *Military Treatment Facility*: Free of charge. Possibility of limited availability of certain medications.

2. *TRICARE Mail Order Pharmacy*: Medications are mailed directly to you. Available on a pre-paid, cost-share basis.
3. *TRICARE Retail Network Pharmacy*: Pharmacy in TRICARE network. Paid on cost-share basis.
4. *Non-network Pharmacies*: Pay full amount and then file a claim with TRICARE.

For additional and updated information see chapter 8 or visit the TRICARE Pharmacy website at *tricare.osd.mil/pharmacy/default.cfm*.

TRICARE Retiree Dental Plan

TRICARE has a Dental Plan for retirees. Both retirees and their dependents are eligible for this program. This plan is operated by Delta Dental and is not government subsidized. There is no standard monthly premium, and costs will vary based on location. The most current information on this program can be found at *www.ddpdelta.org*.

If you are employed elsewhere after retiring, we recommend that you compare any dental plan that your new employer may offer to TRICARE and determine which plan is more appropriate for your needs.

Federal Long-Term Care Insurance

None of us want to bankrupt ourselves or our children in the final years of our lives. Long-term care insurance is becoming a necessity as we are living longer. The Federal Long-Term Care Insurance Program (FLTCIP) provides protection from the potentially high costs of long-term care. It is sponsored by the U.S. Office of Personnel Management (OPM) and is a result of a partnership between OPM and two insurance leaders—John Hancock and MetLife. The goal of the program is to provide affordable group premiums and comprehensive benefits that can help ensure your independence. For more information on this program, visit their website at *www.ltcfeds.com/off*.

Long-term care expenses are not covered by traditional medical insurance plans such as TRICARE and TRICARE-for-Life or by disability income insurance. While Medicare covers some care in nursing homes and at home, it does so only for a limited time, subject to restrictions. Therefore, you should not rely on Medicare to pay for long-term care. The Department of Veterans Affairs provides limited long-term care services with restrictions on who can receive them.

The Motley Fool website has an excellent primer on long-term care insurance. You can access it at *www.fool.com/insurancecenter/longterm/longterm03.htm*.

Long-term care insurance is a fairly new insurance product. Most financial planners recommend that you explore purchasing this product in your fifties or sixties. We recommend that you conduct research on this product and consult a trusted insurance agent. The earlier you purchase the policy, the cheaper the premiums, but if you purchase too early, you make a larger number of premium payments over time; possibly paying a larger amount. The federal program is definitely one to consider if you choose to purchase this type of insurance.

TAX CONSIDERATIONS

When you retire, we recommend that you examine the tax burden in the state in which you plan to live. Many people planning to retire use the lack of a state income tax as a reason for a retirement destination. Several states also have tax benefits for Military Retirement Pay. Information concerning military pay tax benefits can be found at *usmilitary .about.com/od/taxes*.

You also must take into account sales and property taxes. These can more than offset the lack of a state income tax and any tax breaks on retirement pay. The following website supplies information to retirees on state tax burdens *www.retirementliving.com/RLtaxes.html*.

Glossary of Financial Terms

The following financial terms, along with many others not listed below, can be further researched and defined at *www.investopedia.com*.

accumulation plan. An arrangement that enables an investor to purchase mutual fund shares regularly, usually with provisions for the reinvestment of income dividends and the acceptance of capital gains distributions in additional shares. Plans are of two types: voluntary and contractual.

actuary. One versed in the mathematics, bookkeeping, law, and finance of life insurance.

add-on method. A computational method where (1) the finance charge for an installment credit contract as a whole equals the add-on rate times the principal amount of credit at the start of the contract times the number of years in the credit contract; (2) the finance charge is added to the principal; and (3) the credit user receives the principal and pays back the principal plus the finance charge in monthly (or other periodic) installments.

adjustable rate mortgage. (ARM) A mortgage loan for which interest rates are not fixed but vary with market interest rates.

adjusted gross income. (AGI) See taxable income.

adjusted-balance method of computing interest. Interest is charged on the balance outstanding after it has been adjusted for payments and credits.

amenities. The features of a property that are not a part of the space occupied and that create special attraction, such as recreation rooms, saunas, and pools, or natural amenities like a view or ocean frontage.

amortization. The process of retiring debt or writing off an asset. As regards a direct reduction of self-amortizing mortgage, amortization represents the principal repayment portion of an installment payment.

annual percentage rate. (APR) The effective interest rate applicable to a loan.

annual report. The formal financial statement issued yearly by a corporation to its shareowners. The annual report shows assets, liabilities, earnings, how the company stood at the close of the business year, and how it fared in profit during the year.

annuity. A stated sum of money, payable periodically at the end of fixed intervals.

annuity, certain. An annuity payable throughout a fixed (certain) period of time, irrespective of the happening of any contingency, such as the death of annuitant.

annuity, contingent. An annuity contingent upon the happening of an event that may or may not take place.

annuity, deferred. An annuity modified by the condition that the first payment will not be due for a fixed number of years. Thus, an annuity deferred for twenty years is one on which the first payment is made at the end of twenty-one years, provided the annuitant is still alive.

annuity, life. A fixed sum payable periodically as long as a given person's life continues.

annuity, survivorship. An annuity payable throughout the lifetime of one person after the death of another person or persons.

annuity, variable. A form of whole life insurance where the face value and cash value vary according to the investment success of the insurance company.

appraisal. The estimation of market value of property.

assessed value. The value assessed by the taxing authority for purpose of establishing real estate taxes. This value may not be directly related to market value.

assessment. A charge against real estate made by a unit of government to cover a proportionate cost of an improvement, such as a street or sewer.

asset allocation. The distribution of funds among asset classes in a portfolio, for example: 10 percent cash equivalents, 20 percent bonds, 70 percent stocks.

asset class. A group of investments with similar characteristics or features, for example: cash equivalents, which include savings accounts, checking accounts, money market funds, and Treasury bills.

asset. A resource with economic value owned by a country, firm, or individual with the expectation that it will provide future benefit.

assumption clause. A mortgage loan clause that allows the owner of a house to transfer the mortgage to a later buyer.

assumption of mortgage. The taking of title to property by a grantee, wherein the grantee assumes liability for payment of an existing note or bond secured by a mortgage against a property and becomes personally liable for the payment of such mortgage debt.

automatic paid-up insurance. An amount of insurance, which, without further action by the insured and upon failure to pay a premium when due, is continued as paid-up insurance. (The result will be a lesser value than the original protection guaranteed by the policy.)

average-daily-balance method of computing interest. Interest is charged on the average daily balance outstanding. The average balance is calculated by adding the balances outstanding each day and dividing by the number of days in the billing month. Payments made during the billing month reduce the average balance outstanding.

balanced mutual fund. A mutual fund that invests its assets in a wide range of securities with the intention of providing both growth and income.

balance sheet. A listing of what a person or business owns and owes at a certain point in a certain time period. It has three categories: assets, liabilities, and net worth.

bankruptcy. A legal procedure that allows a person or an organization to give up certain assets in return for release from certain financial obligations.

bear. A person who believes stock prices will go down; a "bear market" is a market of declining prices.

beneficiary. The individual or organization that receives the proceeds of a life insurance policy when the insured dies. The primary beneficiary has the first right to proceeds, and contingent beneficiaries receive the proceeds if the primary beneficiary is no longer living.

bid and asked. The bid is the highest price anyone has declared willing to pay for a security at a given time; the asked is the lowest price at which anyone will sell at the same time. In mutual fund shares, bid price means the net asset value per share, less a nominal redemption charge in a few instances. The asked price means the net asset value per share plus any sales charge. It is often called the "offering price."

blue chip stocks. Stocks of highly stable and financially strong firms.

bond mutual fund. A mutual fund whose objective is to provide stable income with minimal risk.

bonds. A bond is essentially an IOU. The person who invests money in a bond is lending a company or government a sum of money for a specified time, with the understanding that the borrower will repay and also pay interest for using it.

book value. The book value of a firm is equal to its total assets minus total liabilities.

broker. An individual or firm that charges a fee for buying and selling securities on behalf of an investor.

budgeting. A system of record keeping involving detailed planning to account for all incomes and expenses.

bull. A person who believes stock prices will rise; a "bull market" is one with rising prices.

business risk. Risk associated with changes in the firm's sales.

buying on margin. The investor borrows a portion of funds from the brokerage house to buy securities.

call loan. A loan that may be terminated, or "called," at any time by the lender or borrower.

cancellation clause. A unilateral clause in a lease or purchase and sale that terminates an agreement.

capital gain. An increase in the value of an investment that gives it a higher value than the purchase price. This gain is not realized until the asset is sold.

capital improvement. Any structure erected as a permanent improvement to real estate, usually extending the useful life and increasing the value of property. (The replacement of a roof would be considered a capital improvement.)

capital loss. The loss incurred when an investment decreases in value. The loss is not realized until the asset is sold.

cash surrender value. The amount available in cash upon voluntary termination of a policy before it becomes payable by death or maturity.

closed-end investment. Company A mutual fund that invests in the shares of other companies. There are a fixed number of shares, and shares are available in the market only if original investors are willing to sell them.

closing. The culmination of a real estate purchase and sale when the title passes and certain financial transactions occur.

closing costs. Costs paid at closing, such as operating cost adjustments, legal and financial expenses, brokerage commissions, and transfer taxes.

closing date. The designated date of a purchase and sale transaction (see closing).

co-insurance. The portion of the total medical insurance bill for which the patient is responsible after the deductible is paid.

co-payment. The flat fee the insurance company requires the patient to pay for a medical service provided.

collateral. Property, or evidence of it, deposited with a creditor to guarantee the payment of a loan.

commission. With respect to insurance policies, a percentage of the premium paid to an agent as remuneration for services; for stocks or real estate, a sum due a broker for services in that capacity.

community property. Property owned in common or held jointly by husband and wife within the statutes of certain states.

compounding. The act of generating earnings from previous earnings.

conditional sales contract. A sales contract in which title to the goods remains with the lender, while the buyer has physical possession of them. The title goes to the buyer when the loan is repaid. This type of contract is often used with items such as appliances and furniture.

condominium ownership. A form of ownership wherein a multi-unit building is divided so that each owner has individual ownership of his unit and joint ownership in the common areas of the buildings and grounds. Condominiums are frequently used for residential housing and sometimes for office space. In addition to the initial purchase price, each owner in a condominium is liable on an annual basis for a predetermined portion of the expenses of maintaining the common areas.

contingency fund. A fund that provides cash to be used if an emergency arises.

contributions. Payments (investments) made into an individual's IRA.

conventional mortgage. A mortgage that is not insured by the FHA or guaranteed by the VA.

conversion. A right to change from a term insurance policy to a whole life policy without a medical examination. This feature is also called a convertability option.

convertible. A bond, debenture, or preferred share that may be exchanged for other stock in a company.

cooperative ownership. A method of indirectly owning a unit in a multi-unit property through a cooperation. A specially created legal corporation owns the building completely. Each shareholder of that corporation owns a predetermined number of shares that entitle him to a long-term lease on a specific apartment. After paying for the purchase of his or her shares, each shareholder is liable for an annual maintenance charge to support the basic services and debt financing in the multi-unit building.

corporate bonds. Debt securities issued by corporations.

cost index. An index developed by the insurance industry allowing the comparison of different policy costs. A surrender cost index is used to determine the value of a policy if the policyholder decides to terminate coverage. A net payment cost index determines the value of the policy assuming it is not surrendered and the cash value remains in the policy.

coupon interest. Refers to the rate of interest on bonds implied by the annual dollar amount of interest paid and the bond's face value.

credit life insurance. Term insurance designed to repay the remaining balance on a loan in case of the borrower's death.

creditor. A person, group, or company that extends credit; one to whom a borrower owes money.

credit union. An institution whose depositors are also its owners. It lends money only to its owners.

cumulative preferred stocks. Preferred stock that requires that any missed dividends that have accrued be paid first—before dividends can be paid on common stock.

current yield. For a bond, its annual interest divided by its current market price.

custodianship account for minors. An account set up for a child in the form of gifts and managed by an adult other than the grantor.

debenture. A bond not secured by liens against specific assets of the firm.

debit card. Like a credit card, except purchases are deducted from your checking account.

debt consolidation loan. A loan that is used to repay outstanding debts. One consolidated loan payment is substituted for many debt payments.

declarations section of an insurance policy. The section that contains the basic identifying details of the policy. It consists of the name of the policy owner, what is insured, the amount of insurance, the cost of the policy, and the time period covered by the insurance.

declination. The rejection of an application for life insurance, usually for reasons of the health or occupation of the applicant.

decreasing term life insurance. Insurance in which the amount of benefits declines over the life of the policy.

deductible. The amount that must be paid out-of-pocket by a policyholder before the insurance company will pay the remaining costs.

deductible clause. A clause in an insurance policy that allows the insured to retain the loss equal to the deductible amount.

deed. A legal document transferring title from owner to buyer, typically recorded with the clerk of the county in which the property is located.

deed restrictions. Limitations placed on the use of the real property through deed covenants such as land coverage, setback requirements, architectural approval, or construction timing.

DEERS. The Defense Enrollment Eligibility Reporting System, a computerized roster of people eligible to receive health benefits under the Uniformed Services Health Benefit Program.

demand deposit. An account in a bank or other financial institution subject to withdrawal by check.

depreciation. The decline in value of property due to normal wear and tear.

disability waver premium. A guarantee that premiums will be paid on your policy should you become disabled.

discount broker. A firm that processes securities transactions for relatively low commissions.

distributions. Gains made by the investments in an IRA.

diversification. A risk management technique that mixes a wide variety of investments within a portfolio. It is designed to minimize the impact of any one security on overall portfolio performance.

dividend. In insurance, the part of the premium returned to a policyholder after the company pays its expenses; dividends are paid only on participating term or whole life policies. For stocks, a dividend is usually paid quarterly, distributing some portion of earnings to shareholders.

dividend payout ratio. Dividends per share of stock divided by earnings per share.

dividend yield. Dividends per share of stock times 100% divided by the market value of a share.

dollar cost averaging. (DCA) Buying a fixed dollar amount of securities at regular intervals. Under this system the investor buys by the dollars' worth rather than by the number of shares. DCA can be an effective way to limit risk while building assets in stock and mutual funds.

double indemnity. An optional life insurance clause that provides payment of twice the face amount of the policy in death benefits if the insured is killed in an accident.

Dow Jones Industrial Average. Daily index of stock prices of thirty large industrial corporations; a popular measure of the stock market's performance.

down payment. The amount of money that the buyer puts up toward the purchase of a house, car, or other asset; does not include closing costs.

earnings. The net income, or profit, of a company or investment after taxes and dividends.

earnings per share. Net income divided by shares of the stock outstanding.

effective rate, annual or monthly. The finance charge as a percentage of the average unpaid balance of the credit contract during its scheduled life. Also called actual rate or annual effective rate.

emerging market. A financial market of a developing country with a short history but potential for growth.

endorsement. A statement attached to an insurance policy, changing the terms of the policy.

endowment life insurance. A life insurance policy that is fully paid (endowed) after either a specified time period or when the insured attains a certain age.

equity. The interest in or value of a property or estate that belongs to an owner, over and above the liens against it; asset value minus liabilities.

escalator clause. A contract or lease clause providing for adjustment of payments in the event of certain specified contingencies such as an increase in real estate taxes or certain operating expenses.

escrow account. Most mortgage lenders require that borrowers make monthly payments equal to one-twelfth of anticipated real estate taxes and insurance into this account. This assures the lender that there are funds from which the taxes and insurance can be paid.

estate. All of a person's assets, including the appropriate portion of any jointly owned property.

estate planning. The systematic accumulation, management, and transfer of a person's estate to achieve family goals.

estate taxes. Taxes levied on the transfer of estates that are larger than a certain specified sum.

evidence of insurability. Evidence of your health that helps the insurer decide if you are an acceptable risk.

exclusions. Certain medical treatments that are not covered by a patient's health insurance.

exclusive agency. An agreement of employment of a broker to the exclusion of all other brokers; if sale is made by any other broker during term of employment, the broker holding exclusive agency is entitled to commissions in addition to the commissions payable to the broker who effected the transaction.

executor. A person or a corporate entity or any other type of organization named or designed in a will to carry out its provisions as to the disposition of the estate of a deceased person.

face value. The dollar value of a security stated by the issuer. Usually associated with a bond, it is the value due to the lender at the maturity date.

Federal Deposit Insurance Corporation (FDIC). A government agency that provides insurance for accounts held at banks; most banks carry FDIC insurance.

Federal Housing Authority (FHA). A government agency that provides mortgage loan insurance to financial institutions.

fiduciary. A person who on behalf of or for the benefit of another individual transacts business or manages financial assets; such relationship implies great confidence and trust.

finance charge. The dollar charge or charges for consumer credit.

finder's fee. In real estate, a payment made for aid in obtaining a mortgage loan or for locating a property or tenant.

foreclosure. The procedure through which property pledged as security for a debt is "repossessed" and sold to secure payment of the debt in event of default in payment or terms. The rights of debtors and creditors in foreclosure vary from state to state.

grace period. Additional time allowed to perform an act or make a payment. before a default occurs. In insurance, a period of time where if the premium is not paid, it is still in effect with or without penalty conditions. Generally an insurance grace period is thirty-one days after the premium due date. Some credit cards have a twenty-five-day grace period to avoid finance charges.

gross. Before any deductions.

growth stock. Stock that is characterized by the prospect of its increase in earnings and in market value rather than by the cash dividends it earns for the stockholder.

guaranteed insurability clause. A provision allowing policyholders to purchase additional insurance without having to pass a physical examination.

High-3. Military retirement system for individuals who entered service between September 8, 1980, and July 21, 1986. This plan pays the average of your highest thirty-six months of basic pay.

home loan. A real estate loan for which the security is a residential property.

homeowners warranty (HOW) program. Builders in this program guarantee that their workmanship, materials, and construction meet established standards.

"house poor." Buying more house than one can afford to buy.

income. Money received in the form of a salary or investments. It is typically subject to income tax.

income bond. A corporate bond that pays interest only if corporate earnings reach a specified level.

income shifting. The process of transferring income from a high-income taxpayer to a lower-income taxpayer or from a high-tax year to a low-tax year.

incontestability. In insurance, a provision that the payment of the claim may not be disputed by the company for any cause whatsoever except for nonpayment of premium. A life insurance policy in force for at least two years cannot be contested.

inflation. The rate at which the general level of prices for good and services is rising, and subsequently, purchasing power is falling.

insurance, paid-up. Insurance on which there remain no further premiums to be paid.

interest. In practice, a payment for the use of money.

interest rate. The percentage of a sum of money charged for its use.

intestacy. The condition resulting from a person's dying without leaving a valid will.

joint account. A checking or savings account in the name of two or more persons. There are two types of joint accounts. One type allows any owner to withdraw funds. The other type requires the permission of all owners before funds can be withdrawn.

joint and survivorship annuity. An annuity that continues payment to a secondary beneficiary if the primary one dies. This annuity guarantees income for life to the surviving beneficiary.

joint ownership. Two or more persons jointly own the property in question. There are three forms of joint ownership: (1) joint tenancy; (2) tenancy in common; (3) tenancy by the entirety.

joint tenancy. A type of ownership wherein property is held by two or more persons together, with the distinct character of survivorship. In other words, during the life of both, they have equal rights to use the property and share in any benefits from it. Upon the death of either, the property automatically passes to the survivor(s).

junk bonds. Bonds that investment advisors consider to be risky investments.

landlord. One who rents property to another.

lapse. The voidance of a policy, in whole or in part, by the nonpayment of a premium or installment on a premium date.

lease. An agreement in which one party gains long-term use of another party's property and the other party receives a form of secured long-term debt.

lease-option. A lease written in conjunction with an option agreement, wherein the payments may be credited toward the purchase price if the option is exercised.

lessee. The party contracting to use the property under a lease.

lessor. The owner who contracts to allow property to be used under a lease.

lien. The right of an individual to retain possession of the goods of another until the debt has been paid.

limited-payment whole life insurance. Life insurance requiring premiums to be paid only for a specific time period but remaining in force after the payment period is over (e.g., twenty-pay life).

limited warranty. A guarantee that is much more restrictive than a full warranty.

liquid assets. Cash and other investments that can be converted into cash quickly, such as money in checking and savings accounts.

liquidity. The cash position measured by the cash on hand and assets quickly convertible into cash.

listed stock. The stock of a company traded on a securities exchange for which a listing application and a registration statement (giving detailed information about the company and its operations) have been filed with the Securities and Exchange Commission (unless otherwise exempted) and the exchange itself.

listing agreement. A written employment contract between a property owner and a real estate broker whereby the agent is authorized to sell or lease certain property within specified terms and conditions.

load. The portion of the offering price of shares of open-end investment (mutual fund) companies that covers sales commissions and all other costs of distribution. The load normally is incurred only on purchase. Some funds also charge a "back-end" load or "redemption charge" when the shares are sold, or an annual "12B-1" charge.

loading. That addition to the net insurance premium that is necessary (1) to cover the policy's proportionate share in the expense of operating the company and (2) to provide a fund deemed sufficient to cover contingencies.

loan value. The amount of money that can be borrowed from the insurance company, using the policy's cash value as collateral.

management fees. A fixed fee that a mutual fund manager charges investors for his services and work with the fund.

marginal tax rate. The amount of tax paid on an additional dollar of income. Relates directly to an individual's tax bracket.

market capitalization. The market value of a company's outstanding shares found by taking the stock price and multiplying it by the number of shares outstanding.

market value. The highest price that a buyer (willing but not compelled to buy) would pay, and the lowest price that a seller (willing but not compelled to sell) would accept.

maturity. The time at which a bond or insurance policy is due and payable. In insurance, the date at which the face value of an endowment policy is paid to the insured if still living.

mortality. The statistical measure of the probability of death at each age group. The same age groups can have different rates based on the amount of group risk. For example, a lower rate is charged for a twenty-five-year-old nonsmoking male than for a twenty-five-year-old male who uses tobacco.

mortality rate (death rate). The ratio of those who die at a stated age to the total number who are exposed to the risk of death at that age per year.

mortgage. A legal document pledging a described property for the performance of promise to repay a loan under certain terms and conditions. The law provides procedures for foreclosure. The notations of "first," "second," and so forth refer to the priority of the liens, with the lower number representing greater security for the mortgage holder. A direct-reduction mortgage involves a constant periodic payment that will eventually repay the entire loan, providing a specified return to the mortgagee.

mortgagee. The party who lends money and takes a mortgage to secure the payment thereof.

mortgagor. The person who borrows money and gives a mortgage on the person's property as security for the payment of the debt.

multiple listing. An arrangement among Real Estate Board of Exchange members whereby each broker presents the broker's listings to the attention of the other members so that if a sale results, the commission is divided between the broker bringing the listing and the broker making the sale.

mutual wills. Separate wills made by two or more persons (usually but not necessarily husband and wife) containing similar provisions in favor of each other or of the same beneficiary.

negative cash flow. Situation when cash inflows are less than cash outflows.

net. Remaining after all deductions.

net asset value of a mutual fund. The value of one share of a mutual fund. It is equal to the fund's total market value, less its liabilities, divided by the number of its shares outstanding.

net cost. In insurance, the total gross premiums paid, less total dividends credited for a given period.

net surrendered cost. The total gross premiums paid, less the total dividends credited for the given period and the surrender or cash value of the policy, plus the surrender charge (if any) for an insurance policy.

net worth. What a person or business would own after paying all liabilities. Assets minus liabilities equals net worth. Net worth is the same as "equity."

no-fault insurance. A form of automobile insurance where the insured collects from his own company regardless of who was at fault.

no-load mutual fund. A mutual fund that does not charge a sales commission on the sale of its stock.

nominal interest rate. The stated or advertised interest rate.

noncontributory pension plan. A pension plan in which the employee does not make any contributions. Military retirement is an example.

nonforfeiture provisions. Provisions whereby, after the payment of a given number of premiums, the contract may not be completely forfeited because of nonpayment of a subsequent premium but is held good for some value in cash, paid-up insurance, or extended term insurance. These values are usually stipulated in a table that is printed in the policy. One of the two latter options is usually effective automatically; any other option is generally available only upon surrender of the policy.

notary public. A public officer who is authorized to take acknowledgments to certain classes of documents, such as deeds, contracts, or mortgages, and before whom affidavits may be sworn.

note. A legal document in which the borrower promises to repay the loan under agreed-upon terms.

NOW account (negotiable order of withdrawal). Equivalent to checking accounts paying interest on the funds on deposit.

odd lot. An amount of stock less than the established 100-share unit of trading: from one to ninety-nine shares for the great majority of issues.

offer. An initial, brief written contract submitted by a potential buyer of real estate for approval by the seller, giving the price and limited other details.

open-end investment company. A company, popularly known as a mutual fund, issuing redeemable shares, that is, shares that normally must be liquidated by the fund on demand of the shareholders. Such companies continuously offer new shares to investors.

open-end mortgage. A mortgage under which the mortgaged property stands as security not only for the original loan but for the future advances the lender may be willing to make. It is similar to a home-equity line of credit.

open listing. A listing given to any number of brokers without liability to compensate any except the one who first secures a buyer ready, willing, and able to meet the terms of the listing, or secures the acceptance by the seller of a satisfactory offer. The sale of the property automatically terminates the listing.

option. A legal agreement that permits the holder—for a consideration—to buy, sell, or otherwise obtain or dispose of a property interest within a specified time and on specified terms described in the agreement.

Out-of-pocket maximum. The maximum amount that a health insurance company will require a patient to pay for medical services in one year. It is the sum of the insurance plan's deductible, co-insurance, and co-payment expenses.

over-the-counter. A market for securities made up of securities dealers who may not be members of a securities exchange. Thousands of companies have insufficient shares outstanding, stockholders, or earnings to warrant listing on a stock exchange. Securities of these companies are traded in the over-the-counter market between dealers and customers. The over-the-counter market is the chief market for U.S. government bonds, municipal bonds, and bank and insurance stock. NASDAQ is an organized, computerized OTC market handling a large number of stocks.

"paid-up." limited payment whole life insurance Life insurance for which payments are made until the policy holder achieves a target age, after which the policy becomes "paid up."

par value. See face value.

participating preferred stock. A preferred stock that shares with common stock in exceptionally large corporate earnings, thus getting a rate higher than the stated maximum rate.

personal property. Property that is not attached to land, such as furniture, appliances, clothing, and other personal belongings.

points. A loan fee charged by lenders. Each point equals 1% of the amount of the loan. Points are payable up front and add to the effective cost of a loan.

policy. The life insurance contract between the life insurance company and the owner of the policy. The policy outlines the terms and conditions for both the company and the policyholder.

policy, installment. A contract under which the sum insured is payable in a given number of equal annual installments.

policy, joint life. A policy under which the company agrees to pay the amount of insurance at the death of the first of two or more designated persons.

policy, limited payment. A policy that stipulates that only a limited number of premiums are to be paid.

policy loan. A loan made to the policyholder by the insurance company based upon the cash value in a whole life or other permanent insurance policy.

policy, nonparticipating. A policy that is not entitled to receive dividends. Such a policy is usually written at a lower rate of premium than a corresponding participating policy.

policy, participating. A policy that participates (receives dividends) in the surplus as determined and apportioned by the company.

policy year. The year beginning with the due date of an annual premium.

portfolio. The aggregate investment holdings of an individual or institution. A portfolio may contain individual securities (stocks and bonds), mutual funds, collectibles, or other forms of investment wealth.

power of attorney. A written instrument duly signed and executed by an owner of property that authorizes an agent to act on behalf of the owner to the extent indicated in the instrument.

premium. A stated sum charged by a company in return for insurance. It may be payable in a single sum or in a limited number of payments, or periodically throughout the duration of the policy.

prepayment clause. A clause in a consumer loan contract that provides for a refund to a debtor who chooses to repay an installment account early. Or a clause in a mortgage that gives a mortgagor the privilege of paying the mortgage indebtedness before it becomes due.

property. Real property consists of land and, generally, whatever is erected or growing upon or affixed to it, including rights issuing out of, annexed to, and exercisable within or about the same. (See personal property.)

prospectus. The official circular that describes the shares of a company and offers them for sale. It contains definitive details concerning the company issuing the shares, the determination of the price at which the shares are offered to the public, and other financial data as required by the Securities and Exchange Commission's rules.

purchase and sales agreement. A legal contract between buyer and seller of real estate that details the terms of the transaction.

rating. The basis for an additional charge to the standard premium because the person to be insured is a greater than normal risk. A rating can be the result of a dangerous occupation, poor health, or other factors.

real rate. An interest rate expressed in inflation-adjusted terms used to define the growth or decline in purchasing power; usually expressed as a percentage. It is computed by taking the difference between the nominal interest rate and the inflation rate.

real estate investment trust (REIT). Similar to a closed-end investment company. A REIT, however, specializes in buying real estate properties.

real estate syndicate. A partnership formed for participation in a real estate venture. Partners may be limited or unlimited in their liability.

real property. Land, buildings, and other kinds of property that legally are classified as real, as opposed to personal property.

realtor. A coined word that may be used only by an active member of a local real estate board affiliated with the National Association of Real Estate Boards.

reduced paid-up insurance. A form of insurance available as a nonforfeiture option. It provides for continuation of the original insurance plan, but for a reduced amount, and no further premiums.

return. The gain or loss of a security in a particular period. It consists of the income and the capital gains of an investment, usually expresses as a percentage.

reinstatement. The restoration of a lapsed policy after the policyholder pays all unpaid premiums and charges.

renewable term insurance. Term insurance that can be renewed at the end of the term, at the option of the policyholder and without evidence of insurability, for a limited number of successive terms. The rates increase at each renewal as the age of the insured increases.

rent. The payment for use of someone else's property; the compensation paid for the use of real estate.

reserve (policy reserves). The amount that an insurance company allocates specifically for the fulfillment of its policy obligations. Reserves are so calculated that, together with future premiums and interest earnings, they will enable the company to pay all future claims.

retained earnings. On an income statement, changes in retained earnings come from net income minus dividends paid for the year. On the balance sheet, this is cumulated from year to year.

retirement. To give up one's work or business, especially because of age.

revenue bonds. Municipal bonds backed by special sources of income.

reverse annuity mortgage. Contract under which a homeowner can receive monthly income by borrowing against the equity in a home.

revocable trust. A trust that is controlled by the grantor and can be revoked by him or her.

revolving credit. A continuing credit arrangement between seller and buyer in which the buyer (1) agrees to make monthly payments equal to a stipulated percentage of the amount owed at the start of the month plus interest and (2) is permitted to make additional credit purchases as long as the total debt owed does not exceed an agreed-upon limit.

rider. Any additional agreement to an insurance policy usually adding a benefit at an additional cost. A rider becomes part of the insurance policy.

rights or warrants. When a company wants to raise more funds by issuing additional stock, it may give its stockholders the opportunity, ahead of others, to buy the new stock. The piece of paper evidencing this privilege is called a right or warrant. Because the additional stock is usually offered to stockholders below the market price, rights ordinarily have a market value of their own and are actively traded. Failure to exercise or sell rights may result in actual loss to the holder.

risk. The chance that an investment's actual return will be different than expected.

sale-leaseback. A transaction in which the vendor simultaneously executes a lease and retains occupancy of the property concurrently sold.

sales charge. The amount charged in connection with the distribution to the public of mutual fund shares. It is added to the net asset value per share in the determination of the offering price and is paid to the dealer and underwriter. Also called a "load."

sales contract. A contract by which the buyer and seller agree to terms of sale.

savings. Amount of income not spent.

savings account. An interest-bearing liability of a bank, redeemable in money on demand or after due notice, not transferable by check.

savings and loan associations. Financial institutions that have historically specialized in offering savings accounts and in providing mortgage funds.

savings banks. Located in New England and eastern states, these banks provide services very similar to services provided by commercial banks.

secondary financing. A loan secured by a mortgage or trust deed that is secured by a lien subordinate to that of another instrument.

secondary markets. Buying and selling of securities that takes place between investors.

second mortgage. A mortgage next in priority to a first mortgage.

secured installment loans. Loans that are backed by collateral. Examples are loans for cars, home improvements, boats, furniture, appliances, and other durable goods.

securities. Things given, deposited, or pledged to assure the fulfillment of an obligation. In this narrow sense a mortgage is a security, but the term is now generally used in a broader sense to include stock as well as bonds, notes, and other evidences of indebtedness.

Securities Exchange Commission (SEC). A federal agency that oversees securities trading.

Securities Investor Protection Corporation (SIPC). A federal agency that insures investors' accounts at brokerage houses.

securities markets. Places or networks where stocks, bonds, and other financial instruments are traded.

selling short. Selling borrowed securities with the expectation of buying them back later at a lower price.

Series EE bond. A nonnegotiable U.S. savings bond. Interest on these bonds is received only upon redemption.

Series HH bond. A nonnegotiable U.S. savings bond that pays periodic interest, can be redeemed after six months, and has a maturity period of ten years. Series HH bonds have been discontinued and can no longer be purchased, although bond holders can retain them until the last maturity date in 2014.

service contract. An agreement purchased by an appliance owner to keep the appliance in working order.

share. See stock.

simple-interest method. A computation method where the finance charge for a given month of an installment contract equals the monthly rate times the loan balance at the end of each month.

single-premium deferred annuity. An insurance product with a large up-front payment to provide for retirement income and tax savings for high-bracket taxpayers.

speculator. One willing to assume a relatively large risk in the hope of gain. His principal concern is to increase his capital rather than his dividend income. Safety of principal is a secondary factor. (See investor)

Standard & Poor's 500 (S&P 500). An index of five hundred large stocks, a broad measure of the stock market's performance.

standard deviation. As an investment term, standard deviation is used as a proxy for risk. It represents the possible divergence from the expected rate of return and can be used to establish a range of expected returns for an investment or portfolio.

stock. A type of security that signifies ownership in a corporation and represents a claim on part of the corporation's assets and earnings. Stock is also known as shares or equity.

stock dividend. A dividend payable in stock rather than cash.

stock mutual fund. A mutual fund whose objective is to provide the highest possible returns by investing in a number of different companies' stocks. These funds can be characterized by industry, company size, company objectives, or investment objectives.

subletting. A leasing by a tenant to another, who holds under the tenant.

suicide clause. A provision in a life insurance contract that cancels the proceeds from a policy should the insured commit suicide within two years of taking out a life insurance policy. A suicide clause is illegal in some states.

surrender (cash) value. The amount the insurer will pay the policyholder if the life insurance policy is canceled. Term insurance policies have no surrender value.

survey. The process by which a parcel of land is measured and its area ascertained; also the blueprint showing the measurements, boundaries, and area.

tax bracket. The rate at which an individual is taxed based on income level.

tax-deductible. Exempt from inclusion in one's taxable income.

tax deferred. Refers to the investment earnings such as interest, dividends or capital gains that accumulate free from taxation until the investor withdraws and takes possession of them.

tax-exempt. Not subject to taxation.

taxable income. The amount of net income used in calculating income tax. It is gross income minus all adjustments, exemptions, and deductions.

tenancy in common. The means of holding property by two or more persons, each of whom has an undivided interest. In event of the owner's death, the undivided interest passes to the owner's estate and heirs rather than to the surviving tenants in common.

tenancy by the entirety. A tenancy created by husband and wife, who together hold the title to the whole, with right of survivorship upon the death of either spouse. It is essentially joint tenancy, but it is used only for husbands and wives and only in some jurisdictions.

tenant. One who is given possession of real estate for a fixed period or at will.

term policy. An insurance policy that provides that the amount of the policy shall be payable only in event of death within a specified term.

testamentary trust. A trust that is created by placing an appropriately worded clause in the testator's will. The clause places the trust principal under the trustee's control on the testator's death.

testator. A person who has made and left a valid will at death.

thrift savings plan. A tax-deferred 401(k)-like investment vehicle that is available to military personnel.

time deposit account. A savings account in which the account owner receives interest but cannot withdraw funds prior to maturity without a penalty.

time-share homes. The buyer buys the use of the house for a short time period. The time varies from one week to six months.

title. The right to ownership of a property.

title abstract. A history of the ownership of the property.

title insurance. A policy of insurance that indemnifies the holder for loss sustained by reason of defects in the title.

title search. An examination of the public records to determine the ownership and encumbrances affecting real property.

traveler's checks. Checks that are readily accepted as payment because the person must buy them in order to use them. They are safer to carry than cash as they can be replaced if stolen.

TRICARE. A regionally managed health-care program for active duty servicemembers, retired members, and their families. The military has created fourteen civilian health-care networks based upon geographical regions to supplement the care provided by military treatment facilities.

TRICARE Extra. An option similar to TRICARE Standard except that if an insured uses providers who are TRICARE Extra approved, then the insured will receive a discount to the costs he or she would otherwise have to pay under TRICARE Standard. This option should be used by those who do not live in a TRICARE Prime network but wish to reduce their medical expenses.

TRICARE Prime. The managed-care network option. Treatment is received in either the Military Treatment Facility Network or the Civilian Health-Care Network. In return for giving up a personal choice of doctor, the cost of receiving medical treatment is reduced. Because of the high costs of setting up the networks, this option is currently available only in regions that have large military populations.

TRICARE Standard. This is the traditional fee-for-service option. The insured can choose any health-care provider, but his or her costs will be greater than if TRICARE had been used. If TRICARE Prime is not available where an insured is stationed, then he or she must enroll in this option.

trust. A fiduciary relationship in which one person (the trustee) is the holder of the legal title to property (the trust property) subject to an obligation to keep or use the property for the benefit of another person.

trustee. A person who manages a trust.

trustor. A person who establishes a trust.

underwrite. The insurance company's decision on whether an individual qualifics for life insurance based on reviews of his or her occupation, health, age, and so on. Underwrite also means the sale of original securities in the primary market.

variable annuity. An annuity in which the dollar amount of benefits depends on the investment performance of the insurance company's fund managers.

variable rate mortgage. A mortgage loan for which interest rates are not fixed. The rate applicable to the mortgage goes up or down as interest rates in general go up or down.

vesting. The gaining of rights by a worker to the pension contributions made by an employer on the worker's behalf.

volatility. A statistical measure of the tendency of a market or security to rise or fall within a period of time.

waiver-of-premium clause. A provision committing the life insurance company to make premium payments for a policyholder who suffers an injury or illness causing a disability.

warranty. The consumer's assurance that the product will work as it is supposed to. They are guarantees issued by manufacturers or suppliers of goods and services that explain their obligation and, generally, the user's or buyer's responsibilities also.

warranty deed. The safest deed for the buyer, since it guarantees that title is free of any legal claims. There are two kinds of warranty deeds: general warranty deeds and special warranty deeds. A general warranty deed contains a promise by the grantor to "defend the property against every person or persons whomsoever." In other words, it is a promise of protection against the whole world. A special warranty deed contains the more limited promise "to defend the property against every person or persons whomsoever lawfully claiming the same or any part thereof by, from, through, or under him." In other words, it is a promise to protect against the grantor, his heirs, or his assigns.

whole life insurance. Life insurance that remains in force as long as the insured continues to pay the insurance premiums. The premiums remain level and fixed as long as the policy remains in force, and the excess premiums collected in the early years of the policy's life accumulate interest as "cash value."

will. A legally enforceable declaration of a person's wishes in writing regarding matters to be attended to after his or her death, but inoperative until his death. A will usually relates to the testator's property, is revocable or amendable up to the time of his death, and is applicable to the situation that exists at the time of his death.

"window sticker" price. Lists the manufacturer's suggested list price for a car and the itemized prices of the options.

yield. The dividends or interest paid expressed as a percentage of the current price or, if you own the security, of the price you originally paid.

About the Contributors

This book has been written by a number of officers and civilian faculty members who either are or have been assigned to the Department of Social Sciences at the United States Military Academy (USMA). With graduate degrees from many of the nation's leading universities, we provide instruction in economics and finance at West Point. As important as a graduate school education is, our most relevant financial advice for the readers of this book stems from our previous roles as company-level commanders.

Colonel Margaret H. Belknap is the Economics Program Chair at West Point. She is an Academy Professor and a Desert Storm combat veteran. Colonel Belknap is a USMA graduate and has earned four advanced degrees including a Ph.D. from the University of Pennsylvania.

Major Jonathan Byrom is an armor officer who previously commanded a cavalry troop in the 11th Armored Cavalry Regiment at Fort Irwin, California, and deployed in support of Operation Enduring Freedom in 2003. He currently teaches economics at West Point and earned a BS from USMA and an MBA from the Naval Postgraduate School.

Major Joe Clark is a military comptroller assigned as the budget officer for Coalition Forces Land Component Command (CFLCC) in support of Operation Iraqi Freedom and Operation Enduring Freedom. He previously taught economics, accounting, and corporate finance at West Point. He earned a BS from USMA, an MBA from the University of Southern California, and is a Certified Financial Planner.

Major Spencer Clouatre is an aviation officer who previously commanded an aviation lift company in the 18th Airborne Corps at Fort Bragg, North Carolina, and currently teaches finance at West Point. He earned a BS from USMA and an MBA from Owen Graduate School of Management at Vanderbilt University.

Major John P. Cogbill is an infantry officer who previously commanded an airborne infantry company in the 172nd Separate Infantry Brigade at Fort Richardson, Alaska, and deployed with the 75th Ranger Regiment in support of Operation Iraqi Freedom in 2006. He currently teaches economics at West Point and earned a BS from USMA and an MPA from Harvard's Kennedy School of Government.

Major Kris Colwell is a military intelligence officer who previously commanded a direct support military intelligence company in the 25th Infantry Division at Schofield Barracks, Hawaii, and currently teaches financial accounting at West Point. She earned a BS from USMA and an MBA from Hawaii Pacific University.

Professor Dean Dudley is an associate professor of economics at West Point, and has taught nearly every economics course offered at the Academy. He previously taught at Indiana University. He earned a BA from Eastern Washington University and a Ph.D. from Indiana University.

Professor Rozlyn Engel joined the economics faculty at West Point in 2003 and currently teaches principles of economics, intermediate microeconomics, and international economics. She has earned four degrees including a Ph.D. in economics from Columbia University.

Lieutenant Colonel Dan Evans is an infantry officer and operations research analyst who previously commanded an infantry company in the 1st Armored Division and has served as an analyst on numerous Army staffs. He currently teaches banking and financial markets at West Point and earned a BS from USMA and an MBA from the Mason School of Business at the College of William and Mary.

Major Michael Kuzara is an engineer officer who previously commanded engineer companies in the 1st Engineer Brigade at Fort Leonard Wood, Missouri, and Fort Belvoir, Virginia. He currently teaches microeconomics at West Point and earned a BS from USMA and a Ph.D. (ABD) in economics from American University.

Major Michael Marty is a field artillery officer who previously commanded an artillery battery in the 1st Cavalry Division at Fort Hood, Texas, that deployed in support of Operation Enduring Freedom in 2001. He currently teaches corporate finance at West Point and earned a BBA from the University of Notre Dame and an MBA from Harvard Business School.

Ms. Margaret Moten currently teaches corporate finance at the West Point. She earned a BBA from Texas A&M University and an MBA from the University of South Carolina. She has extensive experience in the financial services industry, as a banker, consultant, and risk manager.

Lieutenant Colonel Gary Pieringer is a field artillery and a civil affairs officer who teaches personal finance at West Point. A member of the Army Reserve, he is CEO of a medical products manufacturing company. He earned a BS from USMA and an MBA from Harvard Business School.

Captain Chris Springer is a field artillery officer who previously commanded an artillery battery in the 17th Field Artillery Brigade at Fort Sill, Oklahoma, that deployed in support of Operation Iraqi Freedom in 2003. He currently teaches international economics at West Point and earned a BS from USMA and an MBA from the Olin School of Business at Washington University.

Major Roger Stanley is a strategic intelligence, formerly adjutant general, officer who previously served as the operations officer of a personnel services battalion at Fort Lewis, Washington, and currently teaches international political economy at West Point. He earned a BS from Illinois Tech and two masters degrees from Stanford University.

Major Thaddeus Underwood is a signal corps officer who previously commanded a satellite control company in Army Space Command at Fort Meade, Maryland, and currently teaches macroeconomics at West Point. He earned a BS from USMA and an MBA from Columbia Business School.

Major James Walker is a military police officer who previously commanded a military police company with the 3rd Infantry Division at Fort Stewart, Georgia, that deployed in support of Operation Enduring Freedom in 2002. He is an instructor of money and banking at West Point and earned a BA from Purdue University and an MBA from the Fuqua School of Business at Duke University.

Major Michael Yankovich is an Operations Research and Systems Analyst on the Army staff. He commanded a combat engineer company with the 5th Engineer Battalion at Fort Leonard Wood, Missouri, and has served as an assistant professor of economics at West Point. He earned a BS from USMA and an MPP from Duke's Sanford Institute of Public Policy.

PREVIOUS EDITIONS AND THEIR EDITORS

1st Edition
Lieutenant Colonel Hobart B. Pillsbury, Jr.
Lieutenant Colonel Robert H. Baldwin, Jr.

2nd Edition
Professor Michael E. Edleson
Colonel Hobart B. Pillsbury, Jr.

3rd Edition
Dr. J. Kevin Berner
Lieutenant Colonel Thomas Daula

4th Edition
Lieutenant Colonel Michael J. Meese
Lieutenant Colonel Bart Keiser

5th Edition
Major David Trybula
Lieutenant Colonel Richard

Index

STACKPOLE
BOOKS

Military Professional Reference Library

Armed Forces Guide to Personal Financial Planning
Army Officer's Guide
Army Dictionary and Desk Reference
Career Progression Guide
Combat Service Support Guide
Combat Leader's Field Guide
Enlisted Soldier's Guide
Guide to Effective Military Writing
Job Search: Marketing Your Military Experience
Military Operations Other Than War
Military Money Guide
NCO Guide
Reservist's Money Guide
Servicemember's Legal Guide
Soldier's Guide to a College Degree
Today's Military Wife
Veteran's Guide to Benefits
Virtual Combat: A Guide to Distributed Interactive Simulation

Professional Reading Library

Fighting for the Future: Will America Triumph?
by Ralph Peters

Guardians of the Republic: A History of the NCO
by Ernest F. Fisher

Roots of Strategy Books 1, 2, 3, and 4

Street Without Joy
by Bernard Fall

The 1865 Customs of Service
for Non-commissioned Officers and Soldiers
by August V. Kautz

Stackpole Books are available at your Exchange Bookstore or
Military Clothing Sales Store, or from Stackpole at
www.stackpolebooks.com *or* **1-800-732-3669**